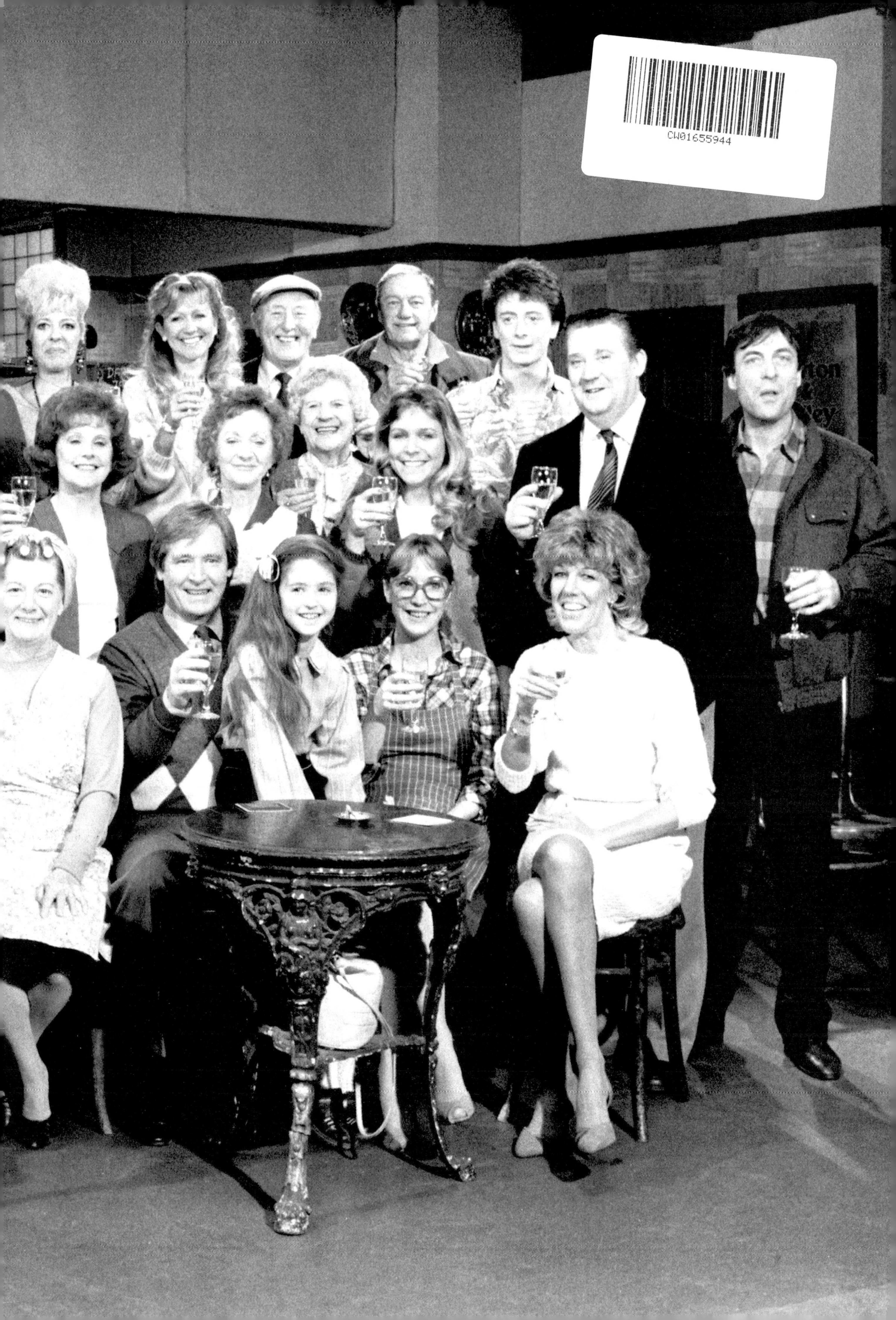

Contents

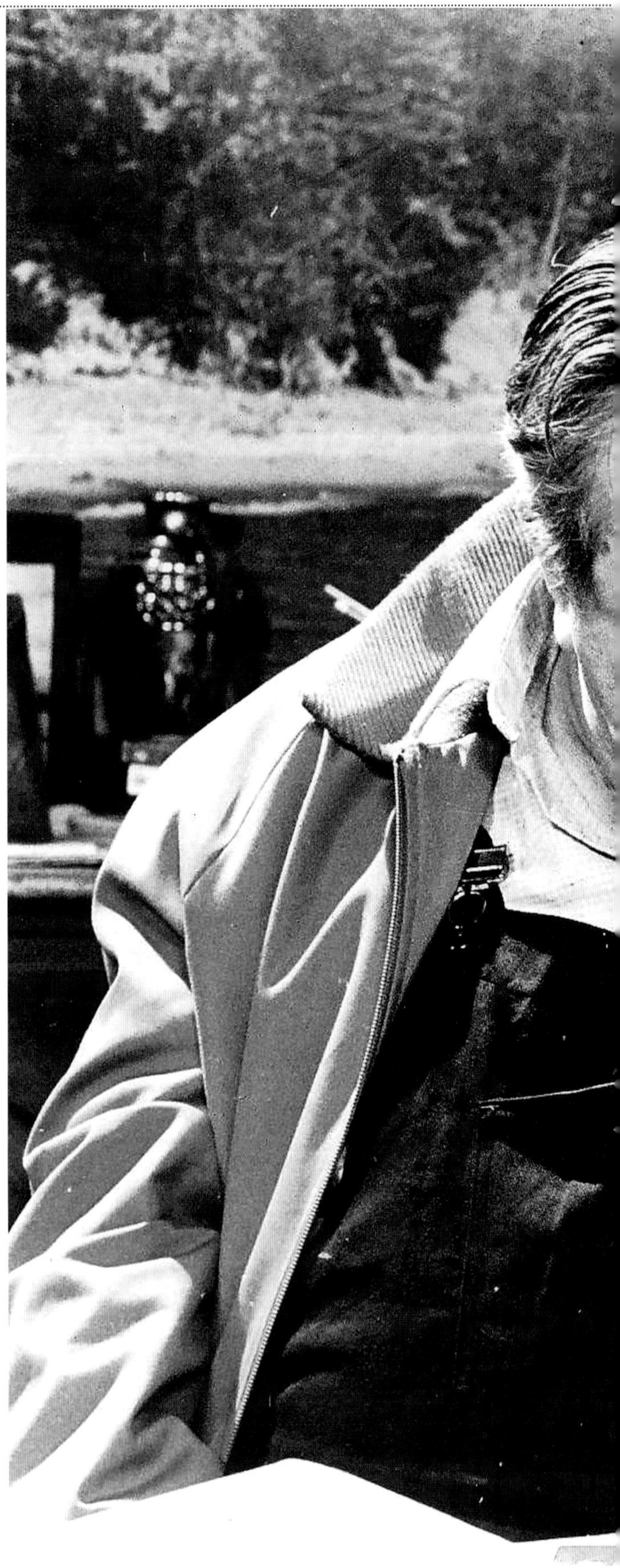

A Mirror publication
Marketing Manager: Fergus McKenna
Mirrorpix: David Scripps and Mel Knight
020 7293 3858

Produced by Trinity Mirror Media,
PO BOX 48, Liverpool L69 3EB
0151 227 2000

Executive Editor: Ken Rogers
Senior Editor: Steve Hanrahan
Senior Art Editor: Rick Cooke
Senior Editor: Paul Dove
Compiled and written by: Vicky Andrews, Alan Jewell
Sub Editor: James Cleary
Design: Colin Harrison, Zoe Bevan

Part of the Mirror Collection

Images: Mirrorpix, PA Photos, Trinity Mirror
Printed by William Gibbons

ISBN: 9 781907 324062

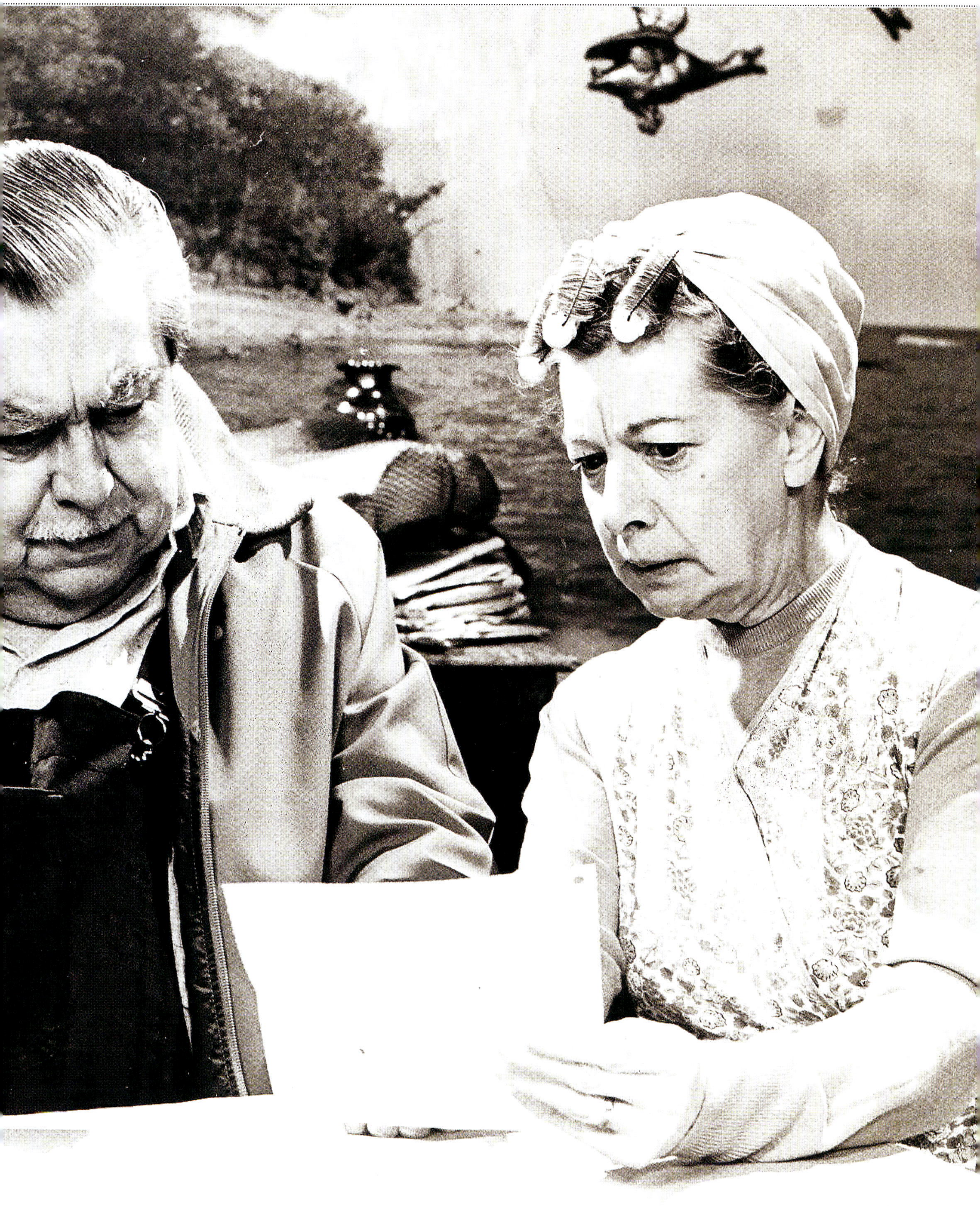

A classic Corrie scene from 1984 – Hilda (Jean Alexander) and Stan Ogden (Bernard Youens)

Coronation Street – fabulous at fifty

By Peter Grant, TV pundit and lifelong Corrie fan

A POIGNANT soundtrack to so many working class lives. Weatherfield, established in 1960, is a unique place.

And, yet, you would have thought Dickens had visited the place. It is known throughout the country and also throughout the world. Forever – a little piece of England.

But places need people and Weatherfield has produced hundreds upon hundreds of 'residents' over the past five decades. And we all know them. Or think we do. Just as surely as the next generation of Corrie characters will become famous to us over the next 50 years.

Weatherfield, the location, is a colourful character in itself. A community that reflects people of all ages and all walks of life. People come and go in Weatherfield – but they leave their mark and their memories linger on.

It is these characters who have frequented that extraordinary – yet ordinary – cobbled Northern suburb that makes it what it is ... yesterday, today and tomorrow. Characters as real as every family in the UK. We all know someone like a character who has been in Corrie. We may not admit to it, but we are like them. We've grown up with them; fell in and out of love just like them and listened and argued just like them. Corrie people are OUR people.

They are rooted and so well defined in where they were born and where they think they are going until fate and the scriptwriters step in. Some have real values – others don't. But all human life is there. Many characters went away, but some came back, unable to forget their roots. Most stayed. There is everything you need in Weatherfield. They have somehow become a 'virtual reality' close-knit family to us.

There are those who we all need in our everyday life. The cornershop; the local school; the council; the taxi firm; café; mechanic and the neighbourhood paper. The wide boys; the flirty girls; the old and wise owls; the rowing partners; the gossip merchants: the money men and the ever-changing barmaids. The sexy women; the hunky blokes and all those – of all ages – who have affairs and think no-one is watching. But we all were. Millions did. Millions still do.

And the pub – oh, that famous pub – the Rovers Return. Frequented through the ages by 'characters.' From the sage-like, hair-netted Ena Sharples; the strained, but ever-loving, partnership of Hilda and Stan Ogden. The 'royal-like' demeanour of first landlady Annie Walker and her no-nonsense hubby Jack. Customers as grumpy as Albert Tatlock and as magnificent as Elsie Tanner and as quiet, but socially disruptive as Minnie Caldwell and then ... there was her cat. Another classic creation, long gone – but not forgotten.

There have been heroes and villains by the ratings-full. Alan Bradley and Richard Hillman are just two, but femme fatales are never, ever far behind. There's been love-gone-wrong; love-gone-right and love caught tragically in the middle. Just ask Ken Barlow.

Over the 50 glorious years viewers have shared the highs and lows of Ken and Deirdre; Curly and Raquel; Bet Lynch and her many followers; Alma; the Baldwins; the Battersbys – and the Websters. It's all an A to Z of emotions.

So much has happened in those plain old terraced houses with so many stories to tell. Characters are people we remember and in 50 years there is not one person in this tribute magazine that we don't all know or who have not come across in our daily lives. Coronation Street will always be character-led.

In writing about TV for thirty years, Coronation Street is still top of the tree for all critics – and me – because it adapts to ever-changing moods, social trends and styles without becoming any different in the process. Producers come and go. Writers shift emphasis. And storylines – well, they tell stories. The great actors – all of them – flesh out the Corrie characters that we celebrate here.

There is laughter, of course, amid the everyday gloom of nine-to-five living.

But what other soap opera could, at its peak with the departure of that immortal character Hilda Ogden, catch 26 million people?

Television changes ... the way we watch television changes – but we still tap into our bit of Corrie that won't change. Why? Because this is where we came in. Corrie is about characters.

That is why it is the longest-running drama in British television history.

End of story. Not the end of Corrie.

Cue the famous music ...

CORONATION ST.

50-YEAR TIMELINE

1960 First episode airs

1961 First birth (Paul Cheveski)

1962 Ken Barlow marries Valerie Tatlock

1963 Sheila Birtles' suicide attempt considered too harrowing and re-shot

1964 Martha Longhurst dies in the Rovers Return

1965 Number 7 collapses

1966 Bet Lynch first appears

1967 Train crashes off the viaduct

1968 The murder of Steve Tanner

1969 First colour episode airs

1970 1000th episode transmitted

1971 Valerie Barlow electrocuted

1972 Deirdre Hunt first appears

1973 Rita starts work at The Kabin

1974 First foreign location filming takes place in Majorca

1975 Warehouse fire

1976 Hilda Ogden gets her 'duck muriel'

1977 Tracy Langton born

1978 Ernest Bishop shot in wages snatch

1979 Lorry crashes into the Rovers

1980 Nicky Tilsley born

1981 Ken marries Deirdre

1982 Queen Elizabeth II opens the new outdoor Street set

1983 Deirdre and Mike Baldwin's affair grips the nation

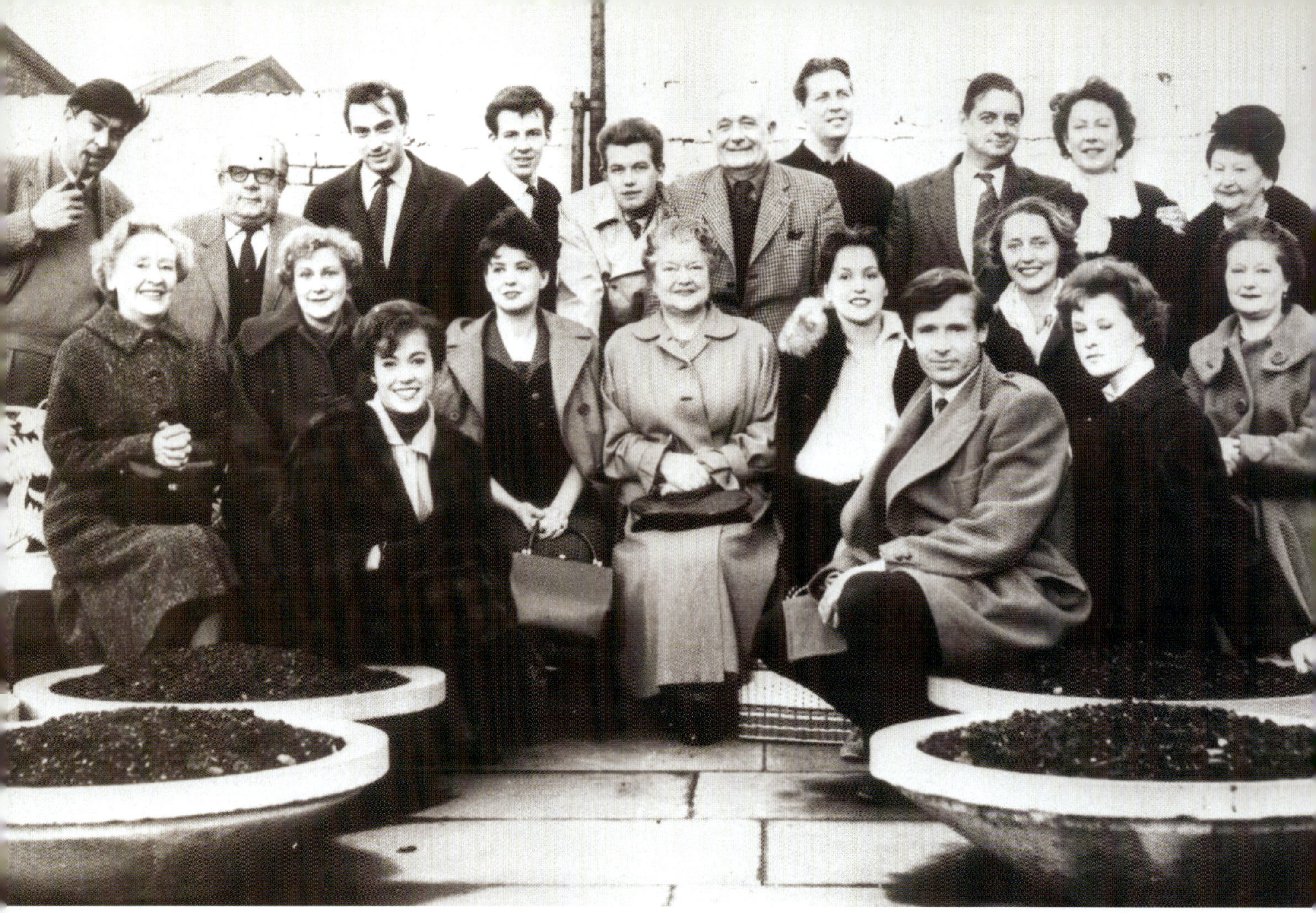

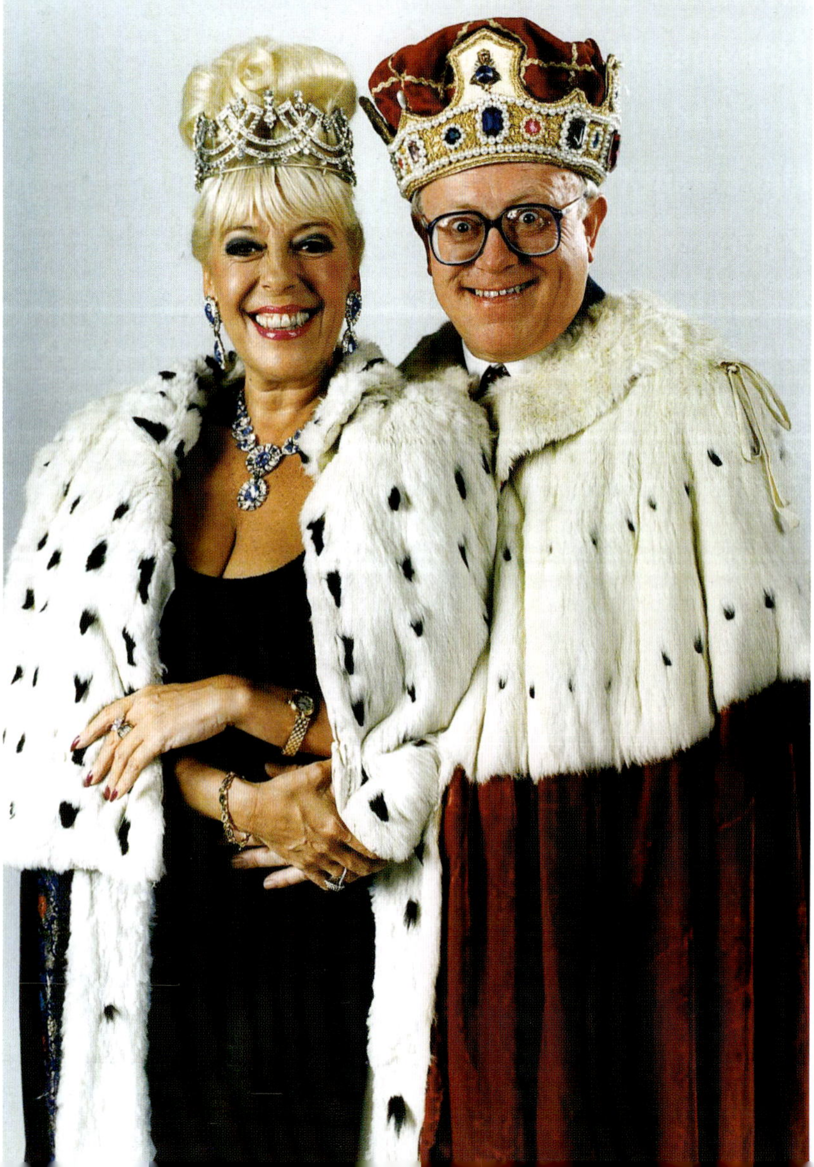

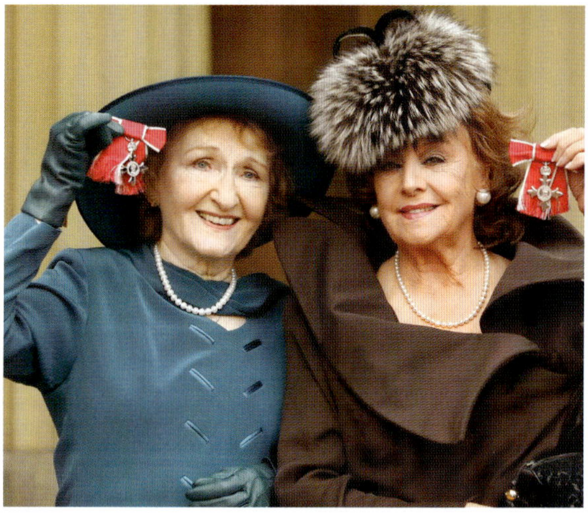

Top, the cast from the first episode in 1960. Above, Street stalwarts Eileen Derbyshire (Emily) and Barbara Knox (Rita) receive MBEs in November 2010. Left, soap royalty Julie Goodyear (Bet) and Ken Morley (Reg). Below, the Mirror's TV listings from December 9, 1960 – the day Coronation Street was first broadcast

TELEPAGE TODAY'S TV

STAR PROGRAMMES IN CAPITAL LETTERS

LONDON ITV

Associated-Rediffusion, Ltd.

2.43—Schools: Books to Enjoy.
3.20—Schools: The Farming Year.
4.45—Small Time: Plans for a party.
5.0—Fact and Fiction: Books.
5.25—Huckleberry Hound: Cartoons.
5.55—News, Weather.
6.10—Right to Reply: Introduced by William Clark.
6.30—The Five Pound Note: Douglas Fairbanks presentation.
7.0—CORONATION STREET: New twice-weekly serial.
7.30—EMERGENCY — WARD 10: Hospital serial.
8.0—THIS WEEK: News magazine.
8.30—TAKE YOUR PICK: Michael Miles's quiz show.
8.55—BOOTSIE AND SNUDGE:

B.B.C.—TV

10.5—People of Many Lands: For Schools.
11.5—Spotlight: For Schools.
11.35—Discovering Science: Keeping Warm.
1.0—Newyddion; Byd Y Ffermwyr.
2.0—Lunchtime News.
2.5—Music Makers: Full Orchestra.
2.30—Watch With Mother: The Woodentops.
5.0—Prudence Kitten: With Molly Blake.
5.10—The Range Rider: Saga of Silver Town.
5.35—Sketch Club: Adrian Hill sets a subject.
6.0—News, Weather, News Magazine.
6.20—Gardening Club: Working on Sticky Clay Soil.
6.50—TONIGHT: Look around with Cliff Michelmore.

Continued...

1984 Elsie Tanner leaves the Street

1985 Alf Roberts marries Audrey Potter

1986 Fire at the Rovers Return

1987 More than 26 million viewers tune in for Hilda's final appearance

1988 Mavis Riley and Derek Wilton marry

1989 Alan Bradley killed by a Blackpool tram

1990 Rosie Webster and David Platt born

1991 Raquel Wolstenhulme first appears

1992 Mike Baldwin and Alma Sedgewick marry

1993 Reg Holdsworth and Maureen Naylor's waterbed disaster

1994 Norris Cole first appears

1995 Raquel marries Curly Watts in the 35th anniversary episode

1996 Jim McDonald hits wife Liz

1997 The Battersby family arrive

1998 Deirdre sent to prison

1999 Ashley Peacock marries Maxine Heavey

2000 Live episode for the 40th anniversary

2001 Steve McDonald marries Karen Phillips

2002 Gail Platt marries Richard Hillman

2003 Richard confesses to murder and tries to drown his family

2004 Maya Sharma sets fire to the Corner Shop

2005 Katy Harris murders her father Tommy

2006 Mike Baldwin dies from Alzheimer's disease

2007 Tracy Barlow kills Charlie Stubbs and is imprisoned

2008 Tony Gordon arranges Liam Connor's death

2009 Steve marries Becky Granger

2010 Gail wrongfully imprisoned for murdering husband Joe McIntyre

The beating heart of the Street

MUCH has happened in The Rovers over the years but the pub itself has seen little change – except, perhaps, for the prices.

A pint of Newton and Ridley mild cost one shilling and one old penny in 1960. A packet of twenty cigarettes was 4s 1d.

Annie Walker and her husband Jack took over the pub in 1939. When the TV saga began it saw their son Billy fresh back from Aden, demobbed from the army in time for his sister Joan's wedding to Gordon Davies.

Policeman's wife Betty Turpin arrived as barmaid in 1969. A year later Jack died suddenly. The brewery told Annie she could stay on. In 1970 Bet Lynch appeared as relief barmaid. Annie made her ne'er-do-well son manager in 1973 but he gambled with the takings and the pub went £200 into the red. In 1976, Annie decided on a live-in barman after two men hid in the Gents and terrorised her. Fred Gee moved in as potman.

Thirty years on and reformed Corrie rogue Steve McDonald ran up his biggest bar bill when he bought the Rovers Return. The ex-jailbird showed how far he had left his wild days behind in 2006 as he joined the illustrious list of people to have owned the famed pub – Alec and Bet Gilroy, Jack and Vera Duckworth, Natalie Horrocks, Duggie Ferguson and Fred Elliott.

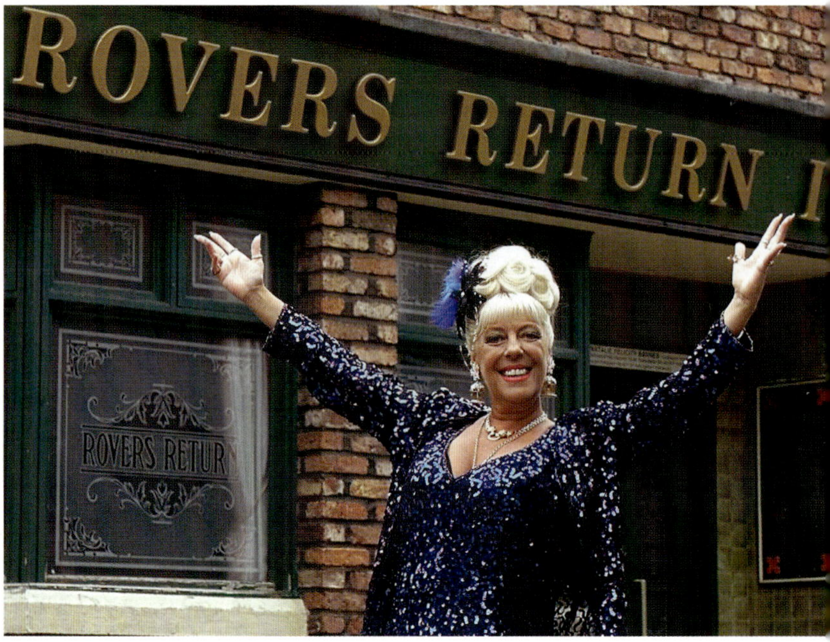

Above: Bet (Lynch, then Gilroy) was landlady between 1985 and 1995.
Below: The regular cast from Corrie in 1987 gather for a photograph

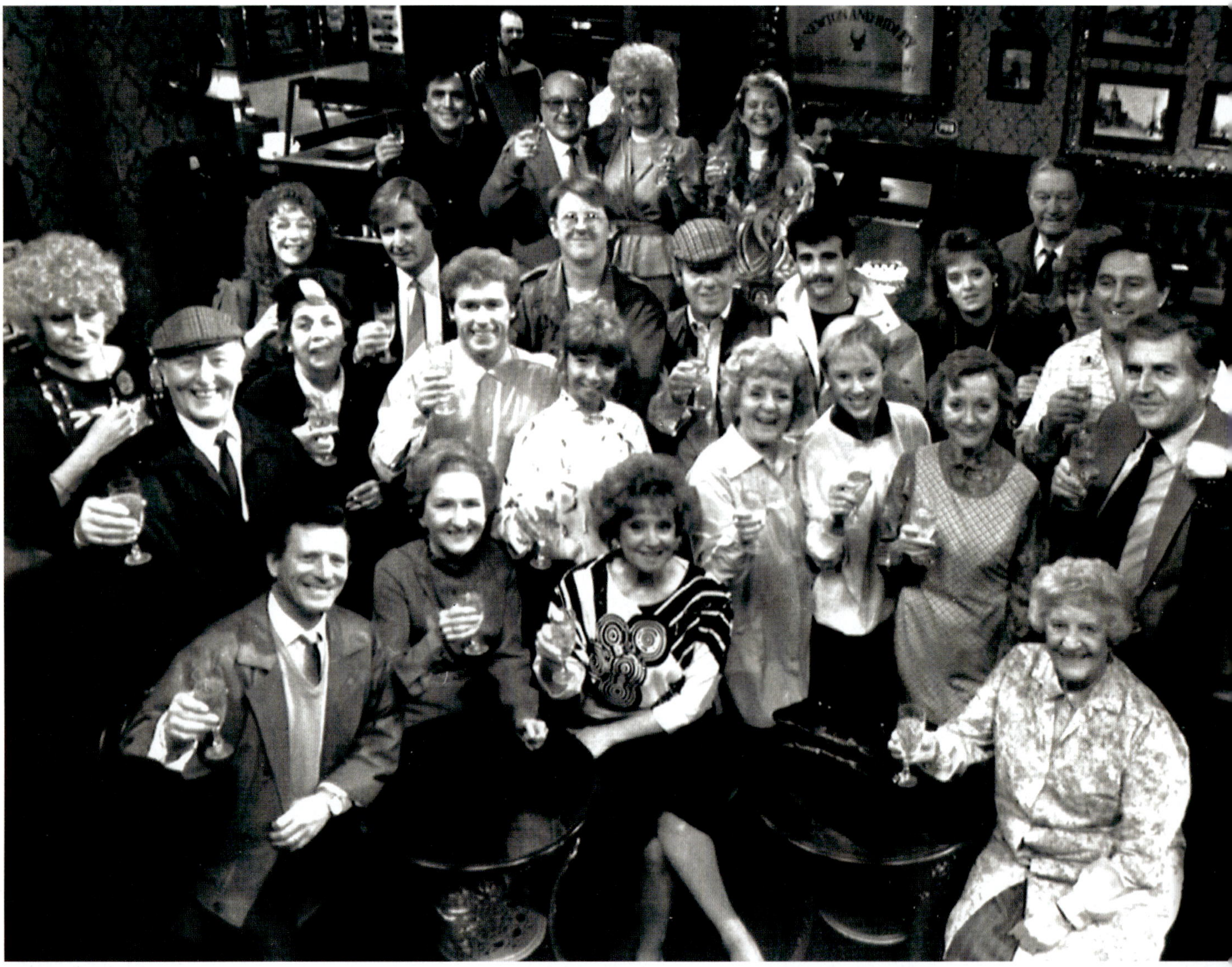

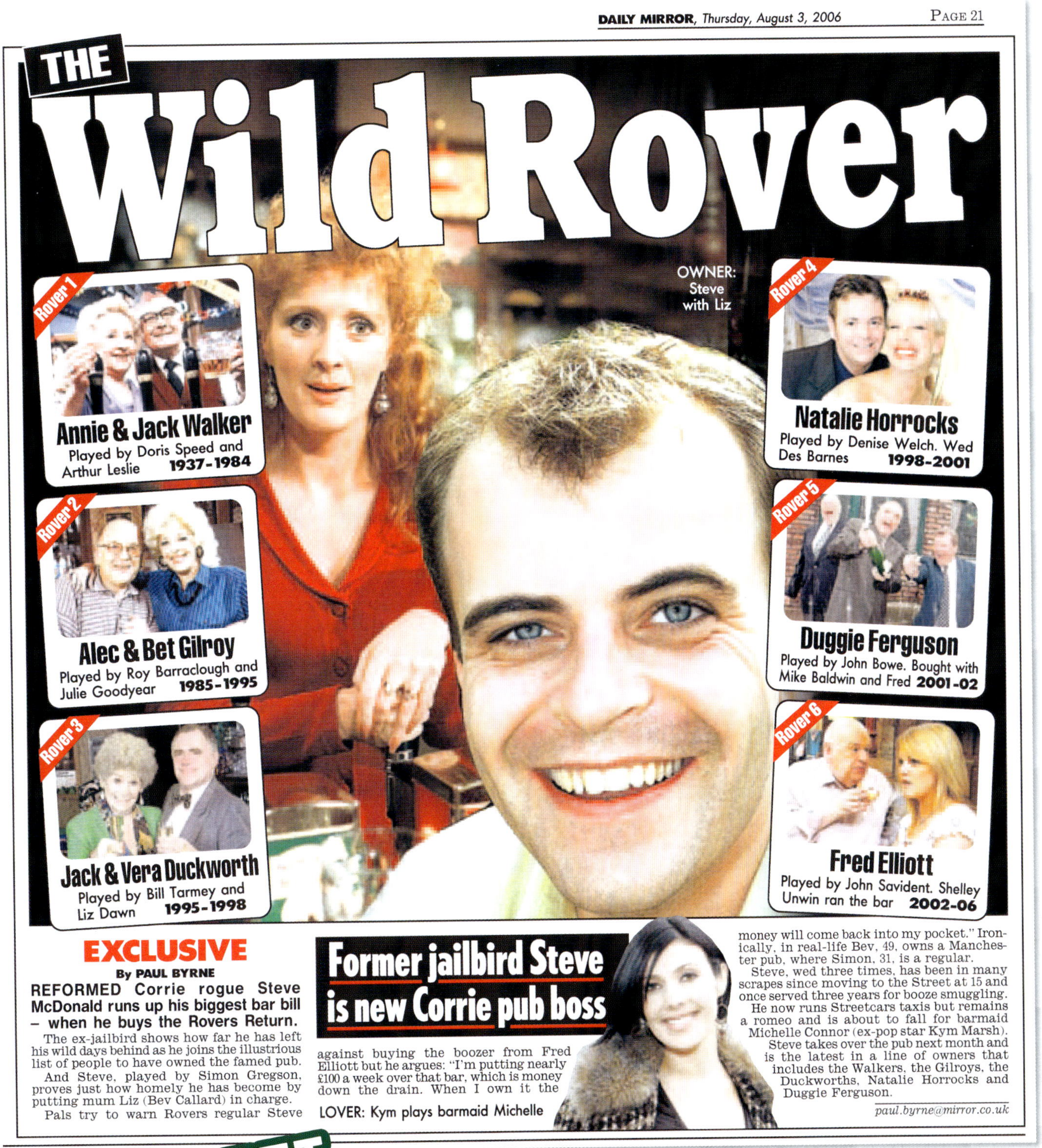

DAILY MIRROR, Thursday, August 3, 2006 PAGE 21

THE Wild Rover

OWNER: Steve with Liz

Rover 1 – **Annie & Jack Walker**
Played by Doris Speed and Arthur Leslie 1937-1984

Rover 2 – **Alec & Bet Gilroy**
Played by Roy Barraclough and Julie Goodyear 1985-1995

Rover 3 – **Jack & Vera Duckworth**
Played by Bill Tarmey and Liz Dawn 1995-1998

Rover 4 – **Natalie Horrocks**
Played by Denise Welch. Wed Des Barnes 1998-2001

Rover 5 – **Duggie Ferguson**
Played by John Bowe. Bought with Mike Baldwin and Fred 2001-02

Rover 6 – **Fred Elliott**
Played by John Savident. Shelley Unwin ran the bar 2002-06

Former jailbird Steve is new Corrie pub boss

EXCLUSIVE
By PAUL BYRNE

REFORMED Corrie rogue Steve McDonald runs up his biggest bar bill – when he buys the Rovers Return.

The ex-jailbird shows how far he has left his wild days behind as he joins the illustrious list of people to have owned the famed pub.

And Steve, played by Simon Gregson, proves just how homely he has become by putting mum Liz (Bev Callard) in charge.

Pals try to warn Rovers regular Steve against buying the boozer from Fred Elliott but he argues: "I'm putting nearly £100 a week over that bar, which is money down the drain. When I own it the money will come back into my pocket." Ironically, in real-life Bev, 49, owns a Manchester pub, where Simon, 31, is a regular.

Steve, wed three times, has been in many scrapes since moving to the Street at 15 and once served three years for booze smuggling.

He now runs Streetcars taxis but remains a romeo and is about to fall for barmaid Michelle Connor (ex-pop star Kym Marsh).

Steve takes over the pub next month and is the latest in a line of owners that includes the Walkers, the Gilroys, the Duckworths, Natalie Horrocks and Duggie Ferguson.

LOVER: Kym plays barmaid Michelle

paul.byrne@mirror.co.uk

STREET LIFE

Since the soap started in 1961, The Rovers has served over 2 million pints of beer, 200,000 hot pots and 120,000 bags of crisps

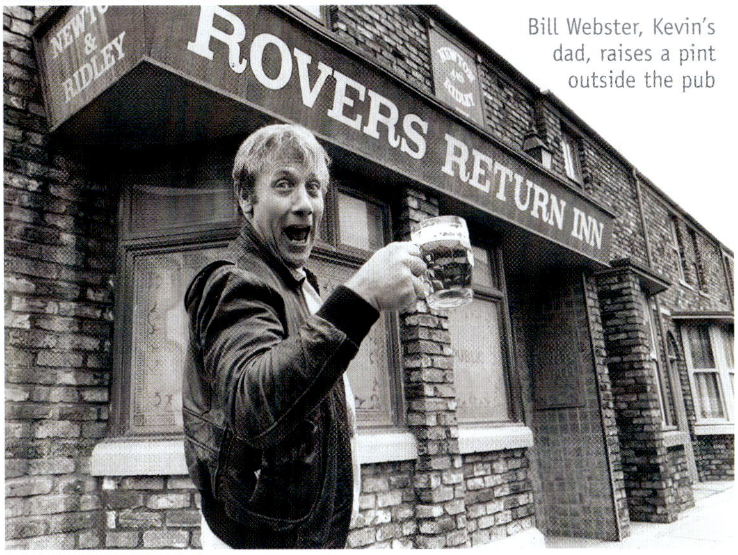

Bill Webster, Kevin's dad, raises a pint outside the pub

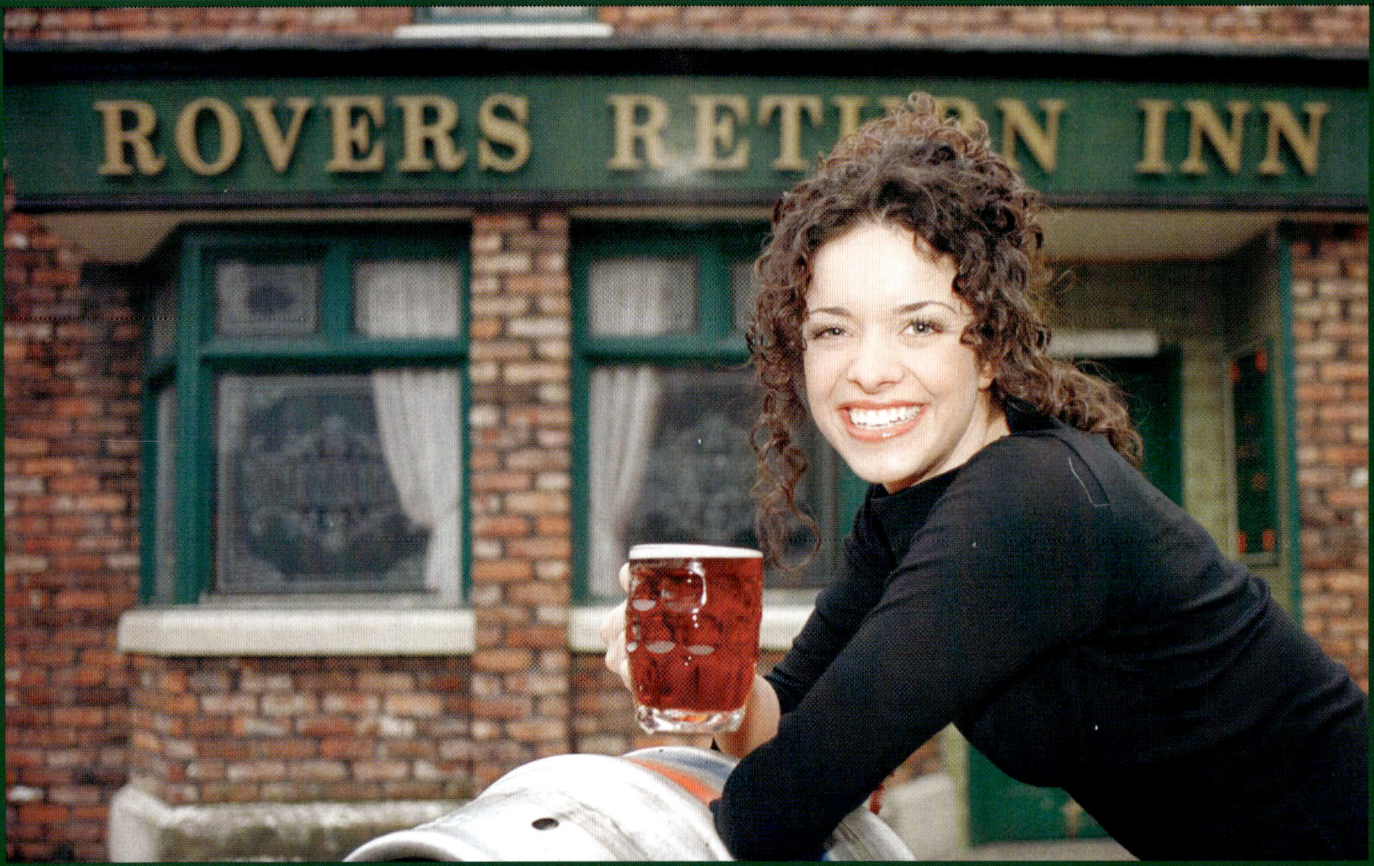

Above: Geena Gregory

PULLING POWER!

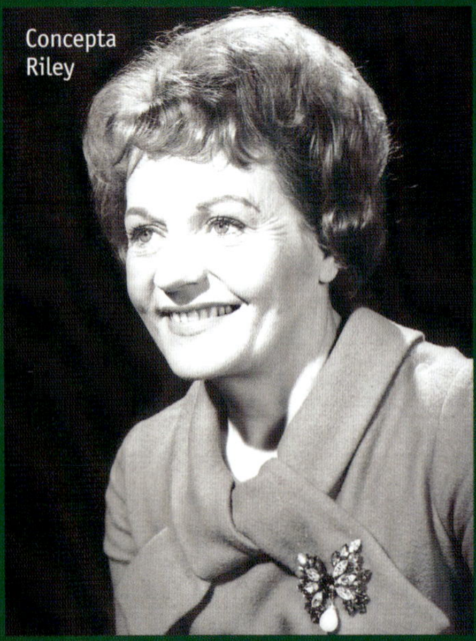

Concepta Riley

CONCEPTA RILEY played by Doreen Keogh from 1960 – 1963
First barmaid ever to work behind the bar at the Rovers Return

NONA WILLIS played by Barbara Ferris in 1961
Brought a touch of early glamour to the bar

DOREEN LOSTOCK played by Angela Crow in 1961
Dizzy Doreen rented the corner shop before leaving to join the Women's Royal Army Corps

IRMA OGDEN played by Sandra Gough from 1964 – 1965
Stan and Hilda's daughter became a Barlow by marrying Ken's brother David

EMILY NUGENT played by Eileen Derbyshire from 1968 – 1970
Helped out behind the bar when she lodged at the Rovers

LUCILLE HEWITT played by Jennifer Moss from late 1960s – 1974
The Walkers' surrogate daughter did shifts at the pumps

BETTY TURPIN/WILLIAMS played by Betty Driver from 1969 – present
The longest-serving member of Rovers staff, celebrating 41 years

BET LYNCH/GILROY played by Julie Goodyear from 1970 – 1995
From humble beginnings, flirty Bet eventually become landlady in 1985

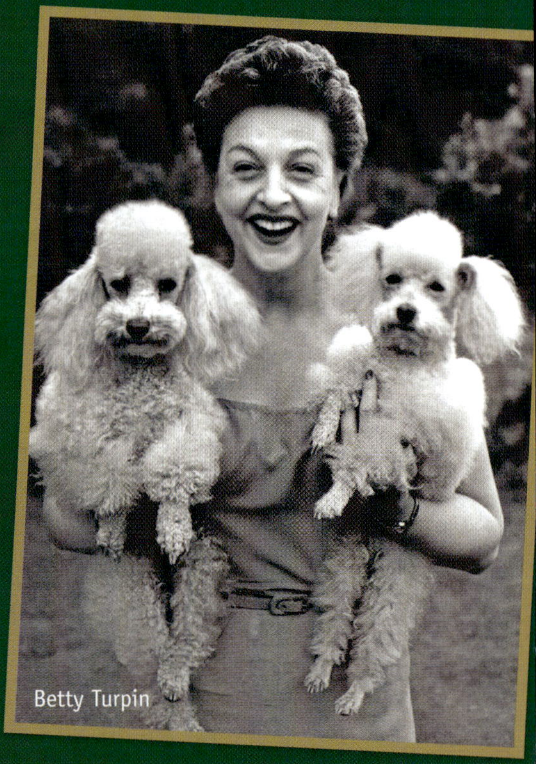

Betty Turpin

BLANCHE HUNT played by Maggie Jones in 1974
Looked after the Rovers for Annie when she went on holiday

GAIL POTTER played by Helen Worth in 1976
Gail only lasted a couple of days before Annie lured Bet and Betty back

DAWN PERKS played by Jeanette Wild in 1977
Made an enemy of Bet when she was courted by Mike Baldwin

ARLENE JONES played by Geraldine Moffatt in 1980
Only lasted a week before deciding the pub was grotty

CAROLE FAIRBANKS played by Greta Schmidt in 1981
Employed by a relief manager and sacked by Annie when she returned

DIANE HAWKINS played by Lottie Ward in 1981
Sacked by Annie at the same time as Carole

SUZIE BIRCHALL played by Cheryl Murray in 1983
Elsie Tanner threw her out when she tried to seduce Gail's husband Brian

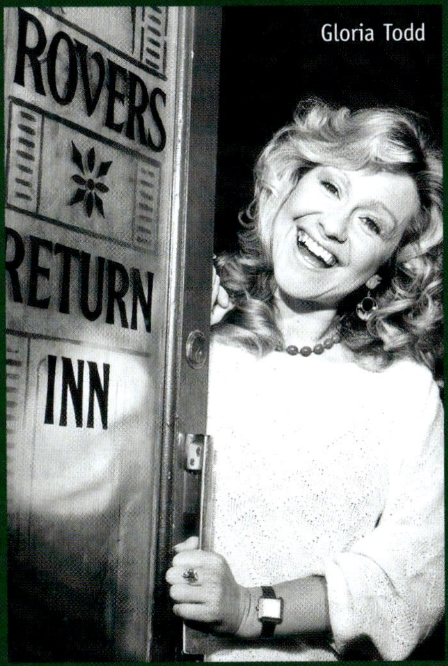

Gloria Todd

GLORIA TODD played by Sue Jenkins from 1985 – 1988
Rovers barmaid and Bet Lynch's bridesmaid

SALLY SEDDON played by Sally Dynevor in 1986
Before marrying Kevin, Sally briefly pulled pints in the Rovers

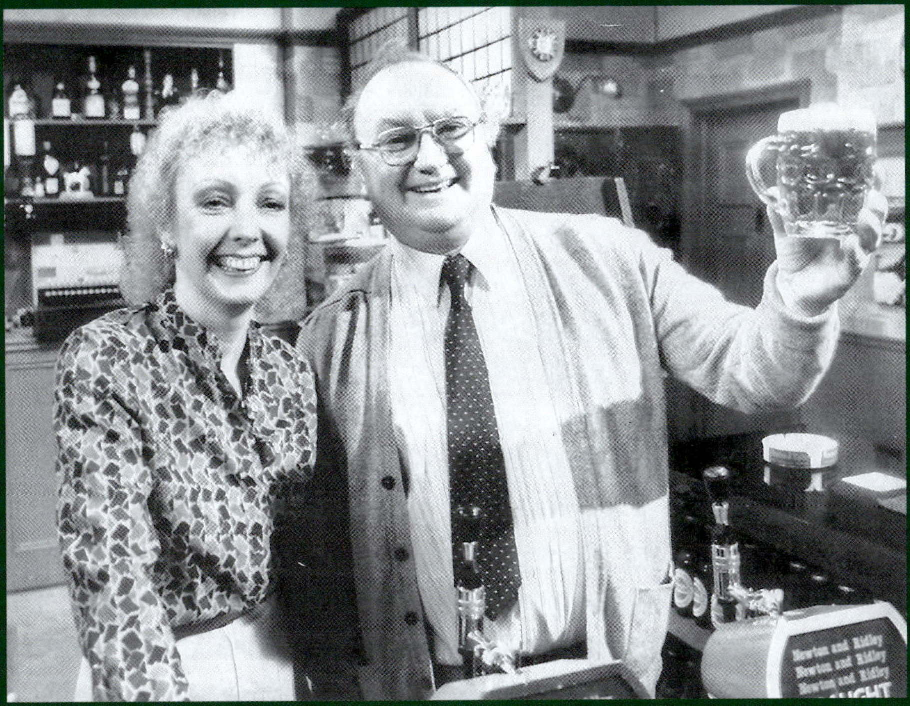

KATH GOODWIN (above) played by Lori Wells in 1984
Attracted the attention of Rovers' stalwart Fred Gee

MAUREEN BARNETT played by Maureen Morris in 1985
Employed as relief barmaid by Betty when Bet disappeared for a week

ALISON DOUGHERTY played by Elizabeth Ritson in 1986
Made a brief appearance behind the bar before being poached

MARGO RICHARDSON played by Vicky Ogden in 1987
Sacked by a jealous Bet after Alec had employed her

TINA FOWLER played by Michelle Holmes from 1989 – 1990
Left the street after an affair with brewery boss Nick Ridley

There have been 51 barmaids in Coronation Street's 50-year history

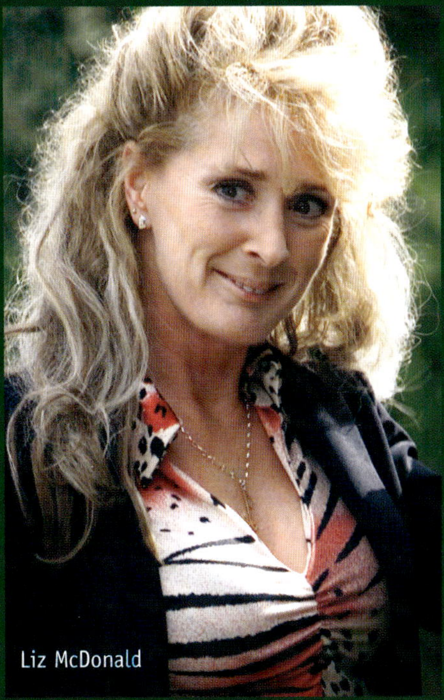
Liz McDonald

LIZ MCDONALD played by Beverley Callard from 1990 – present
Numerous stints at the Rovers before becoming landlady in 2006

ANGIE FREEMAN played by Deborah McAndrew from 1991 – 1992
Resigned after throwing a pint over Des Barnes

STREET LIFE
Betty is the longest serving member of the Rovers' staff, celebrating 41 years

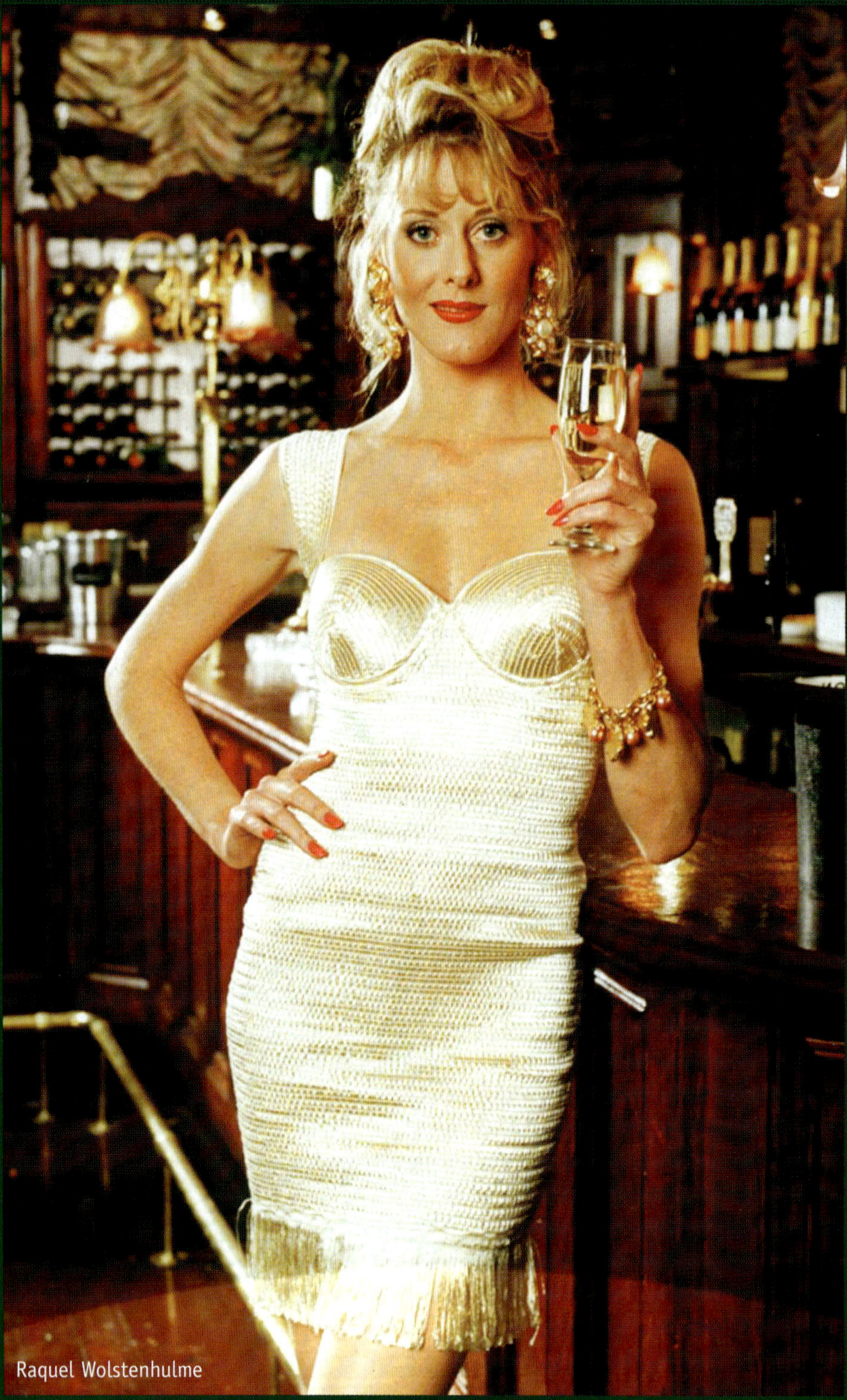

Raquel Wolstenhulme

SAMANTHA FAILSWORTH played by Tina Hobley from 1996 – 1998
Left after causing mayhem in the street with her malicious lies

TRICIA ARMSTRONG played by Tracy Brabin from 1996 – 1997
Lodged with the Duckworths, gave birth to their grandson Jamie

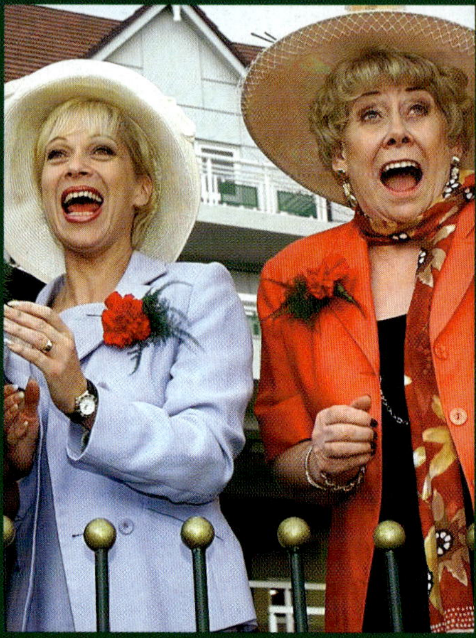

NATALIE BARNES played by Denise Welch from 1997 – 2000
Followed a long line of strong-willed landladies between 1999 and 2000

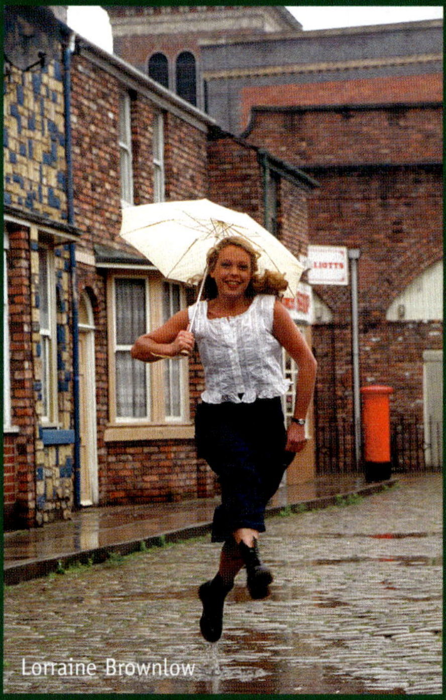

Lorraine Brownlow

LORRAINE BROWNLOW played by Holly Newman from 1998 – 1999
Natalie Barnes' niece

RAQUEL WOLSTENHULME played by Sarah Lancashire from 1992 – 1996
Made up for her lack of intelligence by attracting plenty of male customers

TANYA POOLEY played by Eva Pope from 1993 – 1994
Did a year behind the bar before running off with Bet's boyfriend Charlie

JENNY BRADLEY played by Sally Ann Matthews in 1993
Briefly worked at the Rovers to help fund her college course

CAROL STARKEY played by Kathryn Apanowich in 1995
Only appeared in one episode, quit saying the customers were depressing

LORRAINE RAMSDEN played by Vicky Stevens in 1995
A brief stint in the Rovers, she was sacked after a week

VERA JOYCE SMEDLEY played by Anita Carey from 1996 – 1997
Rovers cleaner who helped out behind the bar

JUDY MALLETT played by Gaynor Faye from 1996 – 1999
Popular Rovers stalwart until her untimely death in 1999

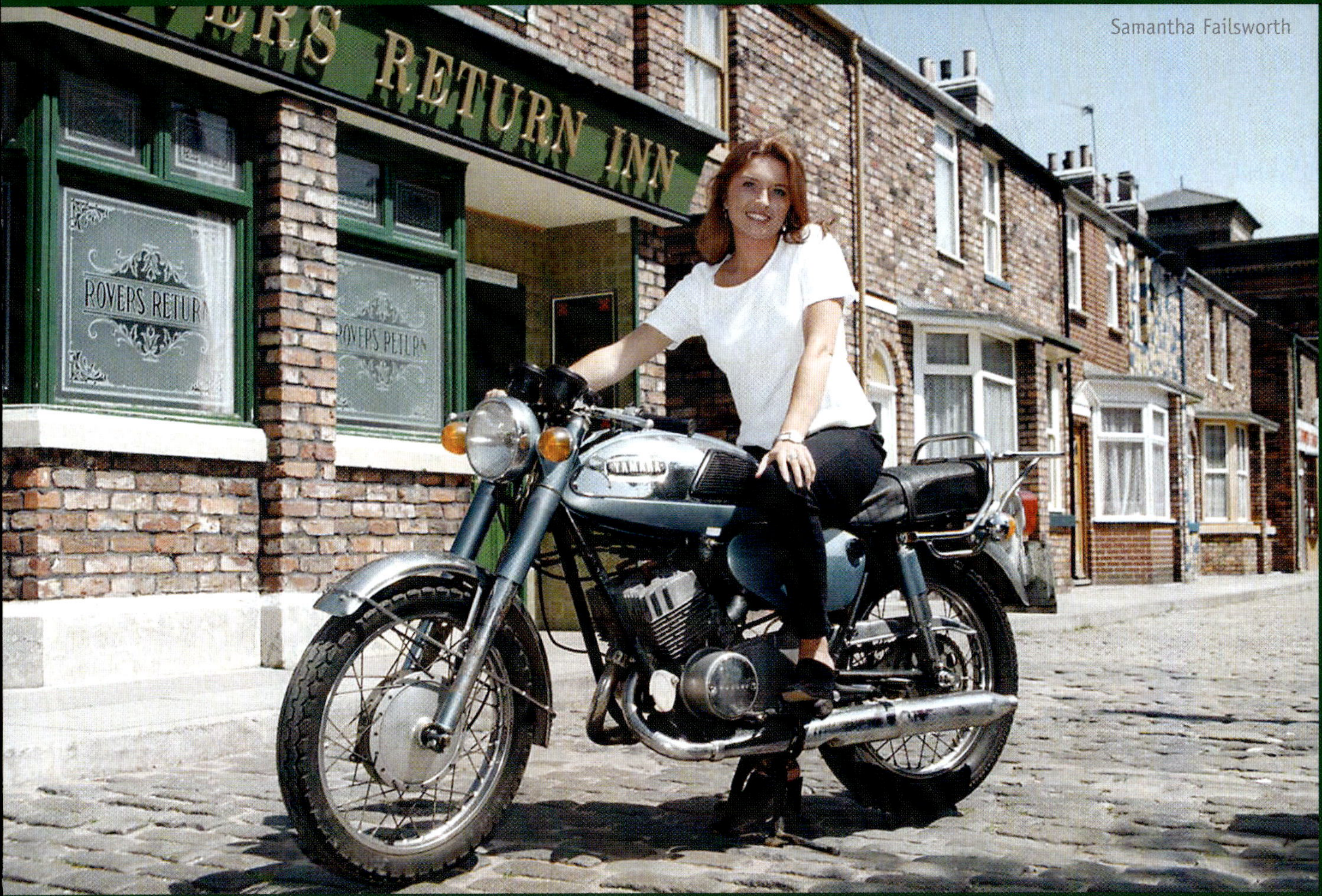

Samantha Failsworth

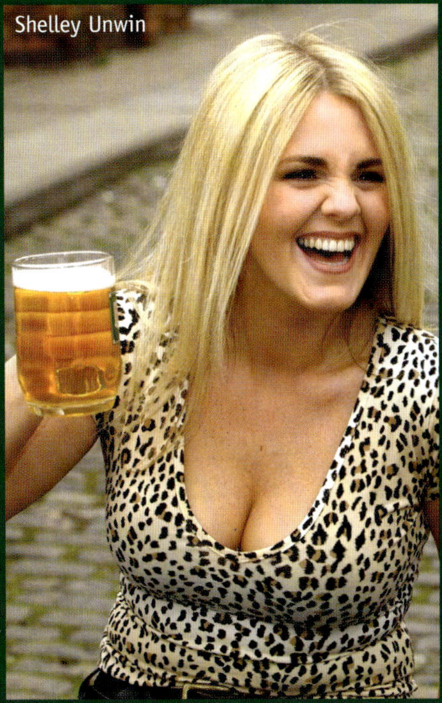
Shelley Unwin

LEANNE BATTERSBY played by Jane Danson from 1999 – 2000 and 2008
One time hellraiser who returned to the bar in 2008 before Liz got rid

AMY GOSKIRKE played by Jayne Ashbourne in 2000
Lied she was expecting Dev's baby and left when her lies were exposed

GEENA GREGORY played by Jennifer James from 2000 – 2002
Popular barmaid who had relationships with Dev and Joe Carter

TOYAH BATTERSBY played by Georgia Taylor from 2000 – 2001
Worked part-time behind the bar while studying at college

SHELLEY UNWIN played by Sally Lindsay from 2001 – 2006
An old friend of co-owner Duggie Ferguson, became manageress

EDNA MILLER played by Joan Kempson in 2001
Misery guts cleaner who only managed a single shift behind the bar

EVE SYKES/ELLIOTT played by Melanie Kilburn from 2001 – 2002
Barmaid who married Fred and became landlady in 2002

MARIA SUTHERLAND played by Samia Smith from 2002 – 2003
Shelley took her on when she came back from Canada

TRACY BARLOW played by Kate Ford in 2003
Lasted a day before Shelley sacked her for laziness

BEV UNWIN played by Susie Blake from 2003 – 2006
Lived in the Rovers with daughter Shelley

VIOLET WILSON played by Jenny Platt from 2004 – 2008
Employed by Fred, gave birth to son Dylan in the Rovers

MICHELLE CONNOR played by Kym Marsh from 2006 – present
Hired by Fred behind Liz's back, dated Steve before Becky

LAUREN WILSON played by Lucy Evans from 2007 – 2008
Violet's sister who worked behind the bar when back from Ibiza

KELLY CRABTREE played by Tupele Dorgu in 2008
Factory girl who only had one shift behind the bar

BECKY GRANGER/MCDONALD played by Katherine Kelly 2008 – present
Had an affair with Michelle's boyfriend Steve, they're now married

POPPY MORALES played by Sophiya Haque from 2008 – 2009
Friend of Liz's who was sacked for upsetting Betty

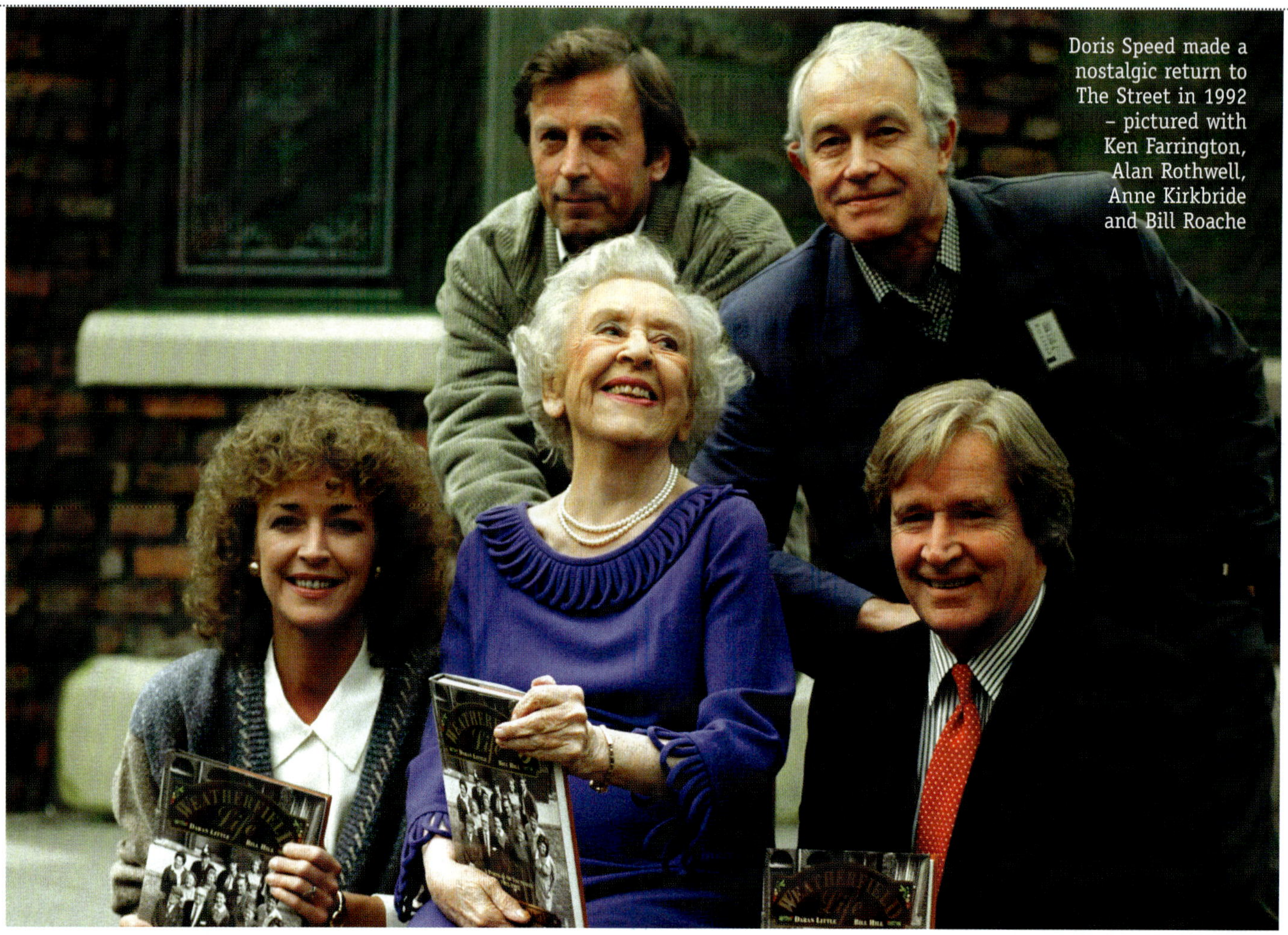

Doris Speed made a nostalgic return to The Street in 1992 – pictured with Ken Farrington, Alan Rothwell, Anne Kirkbride and Bill Roache

A national treasure

ANNIE WALKER was the Rovers' first landlady and the most formidable. A woman with ideas above her station, she was married to laid-back, easy-going Jack and could never quite deal with the pub's "common" working-class clientele.

Annie, played by the late great Doris Speed, spent most of her life behind the bar judging those who failed to meet her standards of refinement. She frequently fell flat on her face, especially with her equally pretentious Lady Victualler friends. She once invited them round, only to be told her living room carpet was the same as the one in the bingo hall.

Doris played the role of Annie Walker for 1,746 episodes from 1960 until 1983. Doris got more fan mail than any other Corrie actor, and was awarded an OBE in 1977. She fainted when the Mirror revealed in 1983 she was 83, not 62 as she claimed. She died aged 95 in 1994.

STREET LIFE

Doris Speed joined the original cast of Coronation Street in 1960 aged 61, but told everyone she was 46

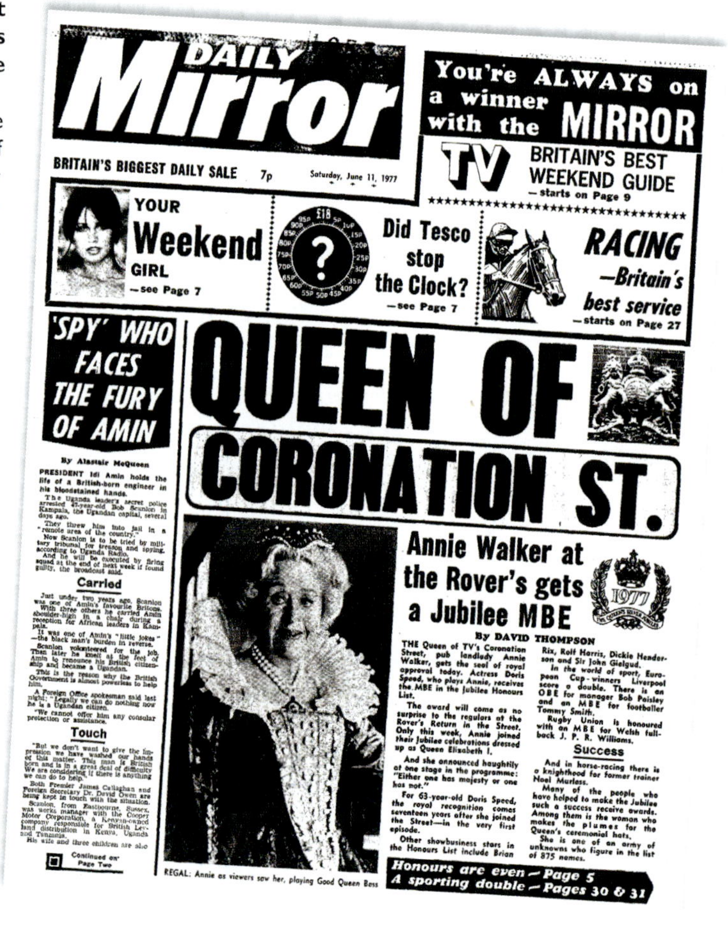

DAILY Mirror

BRITAIN'S BIGGEST DAILY SALE 7p Saturday, June 11, 1977

You're ALWAYS on a winner with the MIRROR

TV BRITAIN'S BEST WEEKEND GUIDE — starts on Page 9

YOUR Weekend GIRL —see Page 7

Did Tesco stop the Clock? —see Page 7

RACING —Britain's best service —starts on Page 27

'SPY' WHO FACES THE FURY OF AMIN

By Alastair McQueen

PRESIDENT Idi Amin holds the life of a British-born engineer in his bloodstained hands.

The Uganda leader's secret police arrested 47-year-old Bob Scanlon in Kampala, the Ugandan capital, several days ago.

They threw him into jail in a "remote area of the country."

Now Scanlon is to be tried by military tribunal for treason and spying, according to Uganda Radio.

And he will be executed by firing squad at the end of next week if found guilty, the broadcast said.

Carried

Just under two years ago, Scanlon was one of Amin's favourite Britons.

With three others he carried Amin shoulder-high in a chair during a reception for African leaders in Kampala.

It was one of Amin's "little jokes"—the black man's burden in reverse.

Scanlon volunteered for the job. Then later he knelt at the feet of Amin to renounce his British citizenship and became a Ugandan.

This is the reason why the British Government is almost powerless to help him.

A Foreign Office spokesman said last night: "Legally we can do nothing now he is a Ugandan citizen.

"We cannot offer him any consular protection or assistance.

Touch

"But we don't want to give the impression we have washed our hands of this matter. This man is British born and is in a great deal of difficulty. We are considering if there is anything we can do to help."

Both Premier James Callaghan and Foreign Secretary Dr. David Owen are being kept in touch with the situation.

Scanlon, from Eastbourne, Sussex, was works manager with the Cooper Motor Corporation, a Kenyan-owned company responsible for British Leyland distribution in Kenya, Uganda and Tanzania.

His wife and three children are also

Continued on Page Two

QUEEN OF CORONATION ST.

REGAL: Annie as viewers saw her, playing Good Queen Bess

Annie Walker at the Rover's gets a Jubilee MBE

By DAVID THOMPSON

THE Queen of TV's Coronation Street, pub landlady Annie Walker, gets the seal of royal approval today. Actress Doris Speed, who plays Annie, receives the MBE in the Jubilee Honours List.

The award will come as no surprise to the regulars at the Rover's Return in the Street. Only this week, Annie joined their Jubilee celebrations dressed up as Queen Elizabeth I.

And she announced haughtily at one stage in the programme: "Either one has majesty or one has not."

For 63-year-old Doris Speed, the royal recognition comes seventeen years after she joined the Street—in the very first episode.

Other showbusiness stars in the Honours List include Brian Rix, Rolf Harris, Dickie Henderson and Sir John Gielgud.

In the world of sport, European Cup-winners Liverpool score a double. There is an OBE for manager Bob Paisley and an MBE for footballer Tommy Smith.

Rugby Union is honoured with an MBE for Welsh full-back J. P. R. Williams.

Success

And in horse-racing there is a knighthood for former trainer Noel Murless.

Many of the people who have helped to make the Jubilee such a success receive awards. Among them is the woman who makes the plumes for the Queen's ceremonial hats.

She is one of an army of unknowns who figure in the list of 875 names.

Honours are even—Page 5
A sporting double—Pages 30 & 31

Friday, November 18, 1994

Farewell to a real Street-heart

ANNIE put on her Sunday best clothes and sat in her favourite armchair. Then she waited calmly to die, it was revealed last night.

Actress Doris Speed, who played the Rovers Return landlady for 23 years, was 95 when she passed away on Wednesday afternoon.

Usually spinster Doris dressed up only if she was expecting a special guest at the nursing home where she lived. But this time, as she put on her smartest frock and applied her make-up, the only visitor on the way was death.

Doris read from a book, To Sir With Love. She lit a cigarette to go with her cup of tea.

After drinking the tea, she put down her cup and left the cigarette burning in an ashtray. She went to sleep . . . and never woke up again.

Doris died from a heart attack.

"It was very peaceful and graceful," said Malcolm Kershaw, owner of Highbank nursing home in Bury, Manchester.

"We shall miss her an awful lot. She was part of the family, a lovely lady. All the girls here are very upset. She has been here for 10 years."

Tonight Coronation Street fans will celebrate the life of Annie Walker – and mourn Doris Speed.

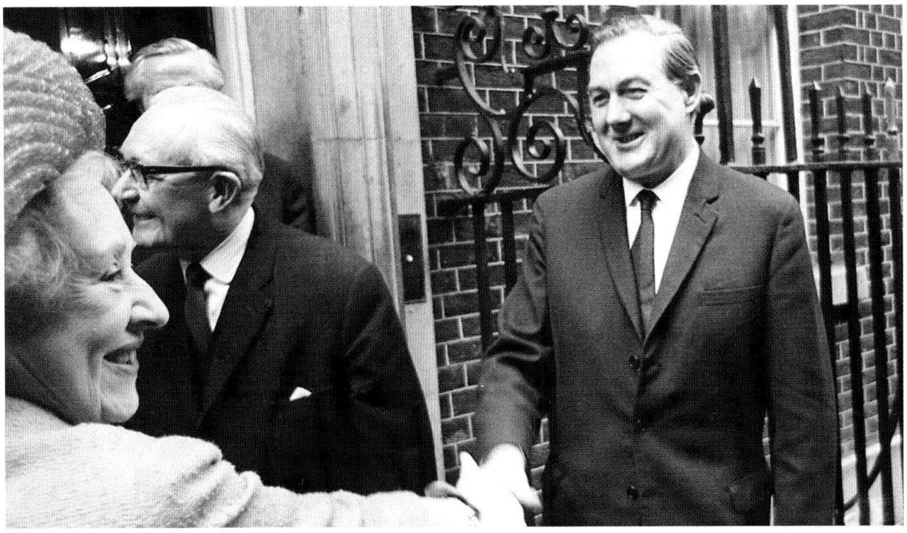

Granada TV are to screen a half-hour tribute Doris Speed Remembered, at 7pm, before the soap's latest episode.

Doris appeared in 1,746 episodes of The Street. And her fame as Annie Walker was also ironic as she firmly believed the show would only last its first scripted 16 episodes.

Above: Doris Speed meets future Prime Minister James Callaghan in 1966
Below: A giant 21st birthday key for the cast in 1981, featuring in the front row Pat Phoenix, Jack Howarth, Doris Speed and William Roache

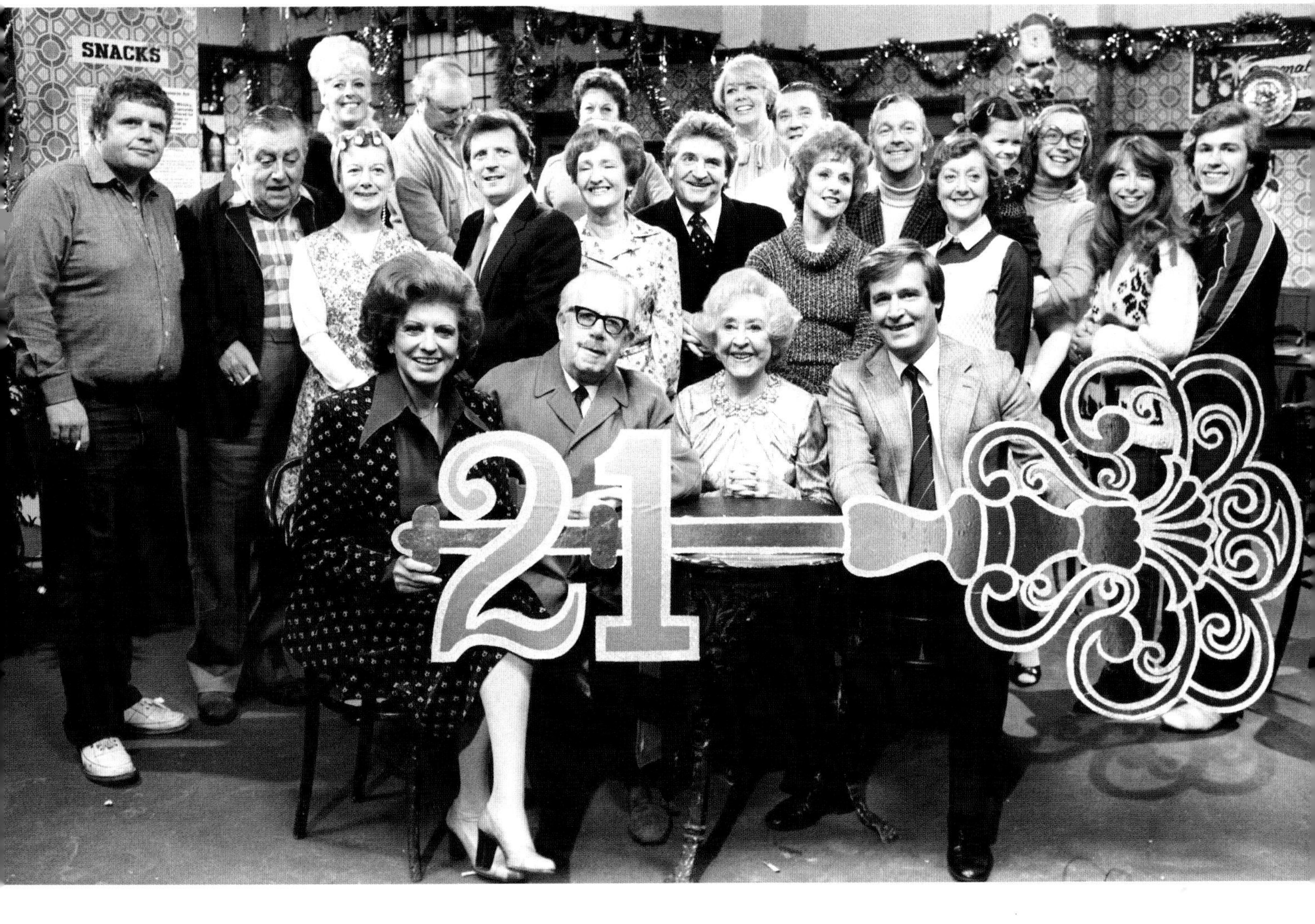

Wedding Album

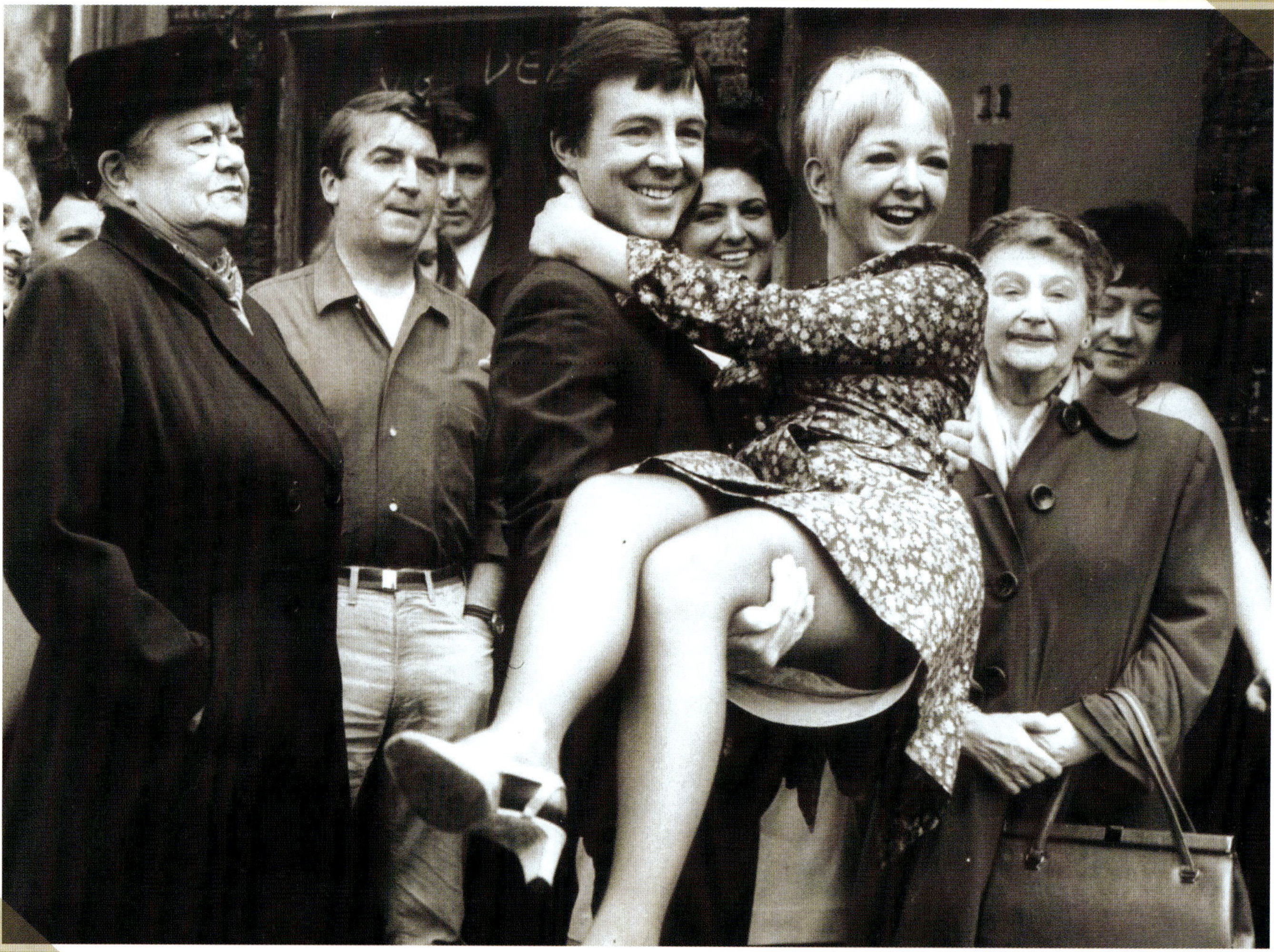

Above: Dennis Tanner marries Jenny Sutton, May 1968

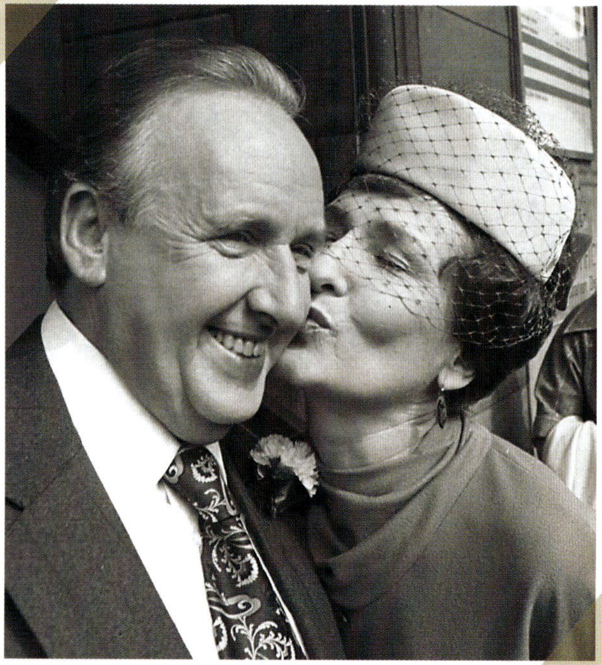

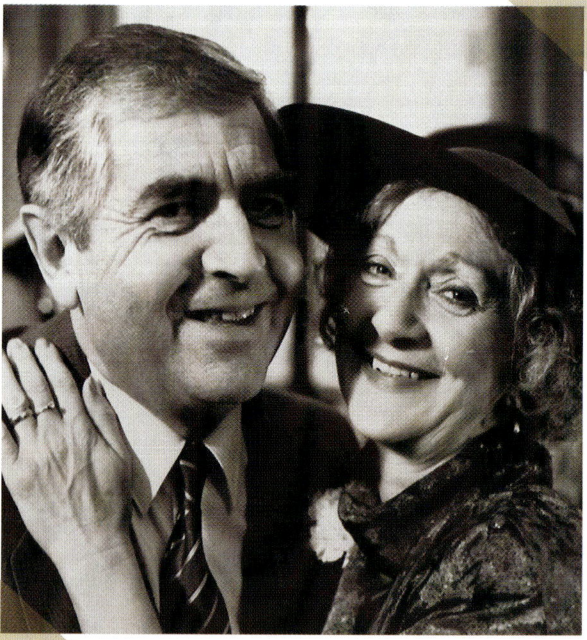

Above: Derek Wilton and Mavis Riley, November 1988
Left: Emily Bishop and Arnold Swain, September 1980

Date and venue

A full list of all the Coronation Street weddings (and a few that didn't quite happen)

Date	Couple	Venue
8.3.61	**Joan Walker/Gordon Davies**	St. Thomas' CE
1.10.61	**Concepta Riley/Harry Hewitt**	St. Theresa's RC
20.6.62	**Christine Hardman/Colin Appleby**	Registry Office/unseen
4.8.62	**Valerie Tatlock/Ken Barlow**	St. Mary's CE
19.10.63	**Myra Dickinson/Jerry Booth**	St. Paul's CE
22.07.64	**Emily Nugent/Leonard Swindley***	Glad Tidings Mission
18.12.65	**Irma Ogden/David Barlow**	Registry Office
4.9.67	**Elsie Tanner/Steve Tanner**	St. Stephen's
29.5.68	**Jenny Sutton/Dennis Tanner**	Registry Office
15.7.68	**Audrey Bright/Dickie Fleming**	Gretna Green/unseen
22.7.70	**Elsie Tanner/Alan Howard**	Registry Office
3.4.72	**Emily Nugent/Ernest Bishop**	Maws Chapel
29.10.73	**Janet Reid/Ken Barlow**	Registry Office/unseen
10.7.74	**Maggie Clegg/Ron Cooke**	St. Mary's CE
7.7.75	**Deirdre Hunt/Ray Langton**	Registry Office
20.4.77	**Rita Littlewood/Len Fairclough**	St. Mary's CE
20.3.78	**Renee Bradshaw/Alf Roberts**	Registry Office
28.11.79	**Gail Potter/Brian Tilsley**	St. Boniface RC
10.9.80	**Emily Bishop/Arnold Swain**	Registry Office
13.5.81	**Eunice Nuttall/Fred Gee**	Registry Office
27.7.81	**Deirdre Langton/Ken Barlow**	All Saints' CE
20.1.82	**Caroline Wilson/Gordon Clegg**	Unseen
31.10.83	**Marion Willis/Eddie Yeats**	All Saints' CE
26.9.84	**Mavis Riley/Derek Wilton***	Unseen
9.1.85	**Elaine Prior/Bill Webster**	Registry Office
23.12.85	**Audrey Potter/Alf Roberts**	Registry Office
14.5.86	**Susan Barlow/Mike Baldwin**	St. Mary's CE
8.10.86	**Sally Seddon/Kevin Webster**	Registry Office
5.8.87	**Rita Fairclough/Alan Bradley***	Registry Office
9.9.87	**Bet Lynch/Alec Gilroy**	St. Mary's CE
24.2.88	**Gail Tilsley/Brian Tilsley**	Registry Office
13.6.88	**Ivy Tilsley/Don Brennan**	St. Luke's RC
9.11.88	**Mavis Riley/Derek Wilton**	Registry Office
14.2.90	**Steph Jones/Des Barnes**	Registry Office/unseen
8.8.90	**Jessica Midgeley/Peter Barlow**	Portsmouth
5.7.91	**Jackie Ingram/Mike Baldwin**	Registry Office
27.9.91	**Gail Tilsley/Martin Platt**	Registry Office
27.5.92	**Lisa Horton/Terry Duckworth**	St. Mary's CE
5.6.92	**Rita Fairclough/Ted Sullivan**	Registry Office
19.6.92	**Alma Sedgewick/Mike Baldwin**	Registry Office
29.9.93	**Olive Clark/Edwin Turner**	St. Saviours
26.1.94	**Maureen Naylor/Reg Holdsworth**	St. Christopher's
25.11.94	**Deirdre Barlow/Samir Rachid**	Registry Office
5.7.95	**Vicky Arden/Steve McDonald***	Registry Office
9.8.95	**Vicky Arden/Steve McDonald**	St. Lucia/unseen
20.10.95	**Betty Turpin/Billy Williams**	St. Mary's CE
8.12.95	**Raquel Wolstenhulme/Curly Watts**	Registry Office
29.12.95	**Angela Hawthorne/Norris Cole**	Unseen
13.11.96	**Tracy Barlow/Robert Preston**	Registry Office
22.9.97	**Maureen Holdsworth/Fred Elliott**	Registry Office
7.11.97	**Fiona Middleton/Alan McKenna***	St. Luke's RC
30.1.98	**Leanne Battersby/Nick Tilsley**	Gretna Green
23.10.98	**Natalie Horrocks/Des Barnes**	Registry Office
7.3.99	**Sharon Gaskell/Ian Bentley***	St. Mary's CE
21.4.99	**Hayley Patterson/Roy Cropper***	Roy's Rolls
24.9.99	**Maxine Heavey/Ashley Peacock**	St. Christopher's
1.11.99	**Sharon Gaskell/Ian Bentley**	Registry Office
23.1.00	**Alison Wakefield/Kevin Webster**	Registry Office
10.09.00	**Linda Sykes/Mike Baldwin**	De Lisle House
30.11.00	**Liz McDonald/Jim McDonald**	Prison
24.12.00	**Emma Taylor/Curly Watts**	St. Mary's CE
30.5.01	**Karen Phillips/Steve McDonald**	Registry Office
5.9.01	**Eve Sykes/Fred Elliott**	Paisley Bridge Hotel
27.7.02	**Gail Platt/Richard Hillman**	Aston Manor & Park
9.12.02	**Sally Webster/Kevin Webster**	Registry Office
24.3.03	**Lucy Richards/Peter Barlow**	Registry Office
19.7.03	**Shelley Unwin/Peter Barlow**	St. Christopher's
17.11.03	**Tracy Barlow/Roy Cropper**	Registry Office
29.12.03	**Sunita Parekh/Ciaran McCarthy***	Registry Office
18.2.04	**Karen McDonald/Steve McDonald**	Walcot Manor
25.10.04	**Sunita Parekh/Dev Alahan**	Hindu Temple
25.12.04	**Claire Casey/Ashley Peacock**	St. Christopher's
8.4.05	**Deirdre Rachid/Ken Barlow**	Registry Office
19.9.05	**Shelley Unwin/Charlie Stubbs***	St. Christopher's
31.10.05	**Cilla Brown/Les Battersby***	St. Jude's
26.11.05	**Cilla Brown/Les Battersby**	Registry Office/unseen
14.8.06	**Sarah Platt/Jason Grimshaw***	Registry Office
9.10.06	**Bev Unwin/Fred Elliott***	St. Christopher's
31.10.07	**Sarah Platt/Jason Grimshaw**	St. Christopher's
31.12.07	**Liz McDonald/Vernon Tomlin**	Registry Office
11.2.08	**Maria Sutherland/Liam Connor**	Douglas Hall Hotel
3.12.08	**Carla Connor/Tony Gordon**	Hotel
12.1.09	**Molly Compton/Tyrone Dobbs**	St. Mark's
13.3.09	**Becky Granger/Steve McDonald***	Registry Office
14.8.09	**Becky Granger/Steve McDonald**	Registry Office
30.9.09	**Fiz Brown/John Stape**	Prison
8.1.10	**Gail Platt/Joe McIntyre**	Registry Office
30.8.10	**Hayley Cropper/Roy Cropper**	Shawbrooke Hotel

* Denotes the wedding never went ahead

There have been 88 weddings in total over 50 years

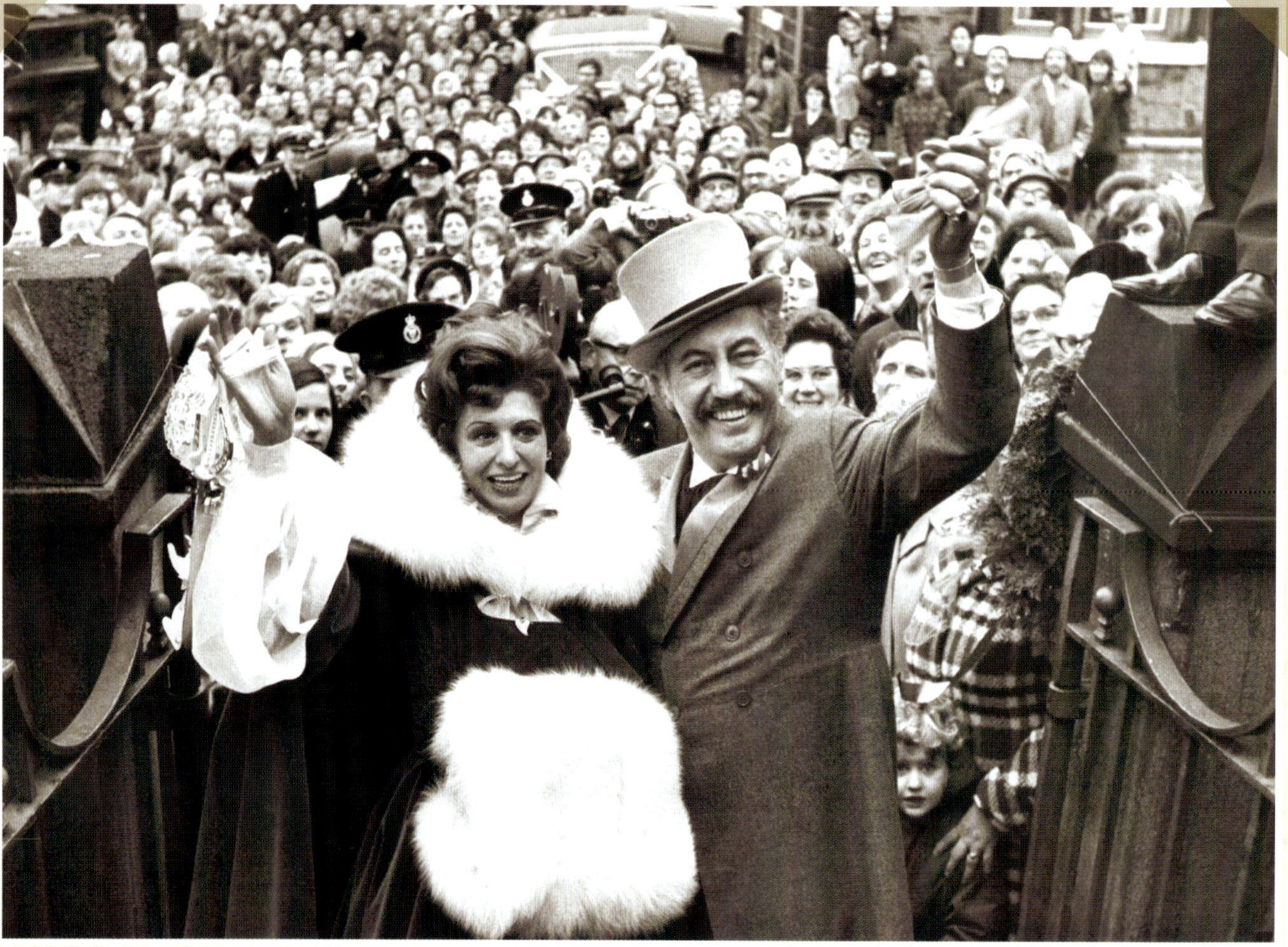

Above: Elsie Tanner married Alan Howard in 1970. The actors who played the characters, Pat Phoenix and Alan Browning, were themselves married two years later and there was a huge turnout of Corrie fans, as can be seen in this photograph

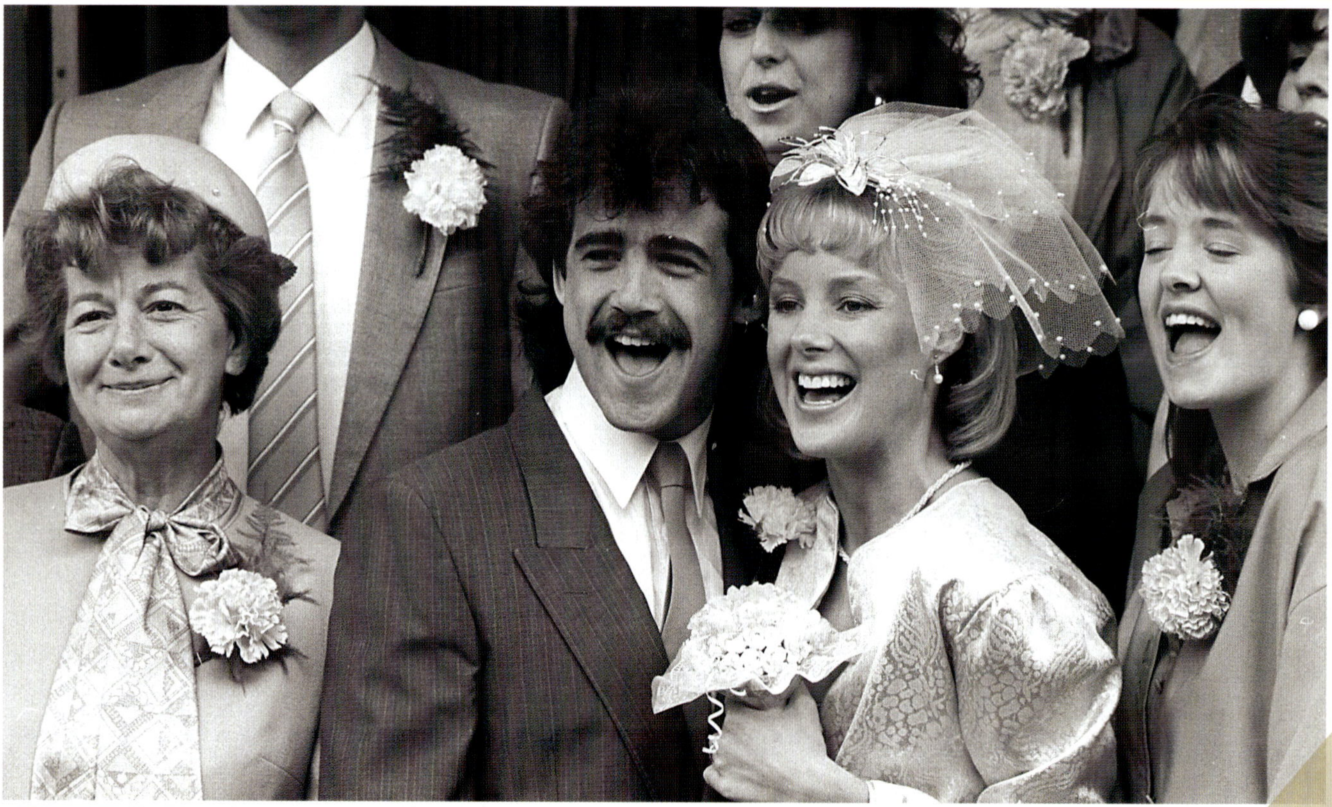

Above: Kevin Webster and Sally Seddon (first time around), October 1986

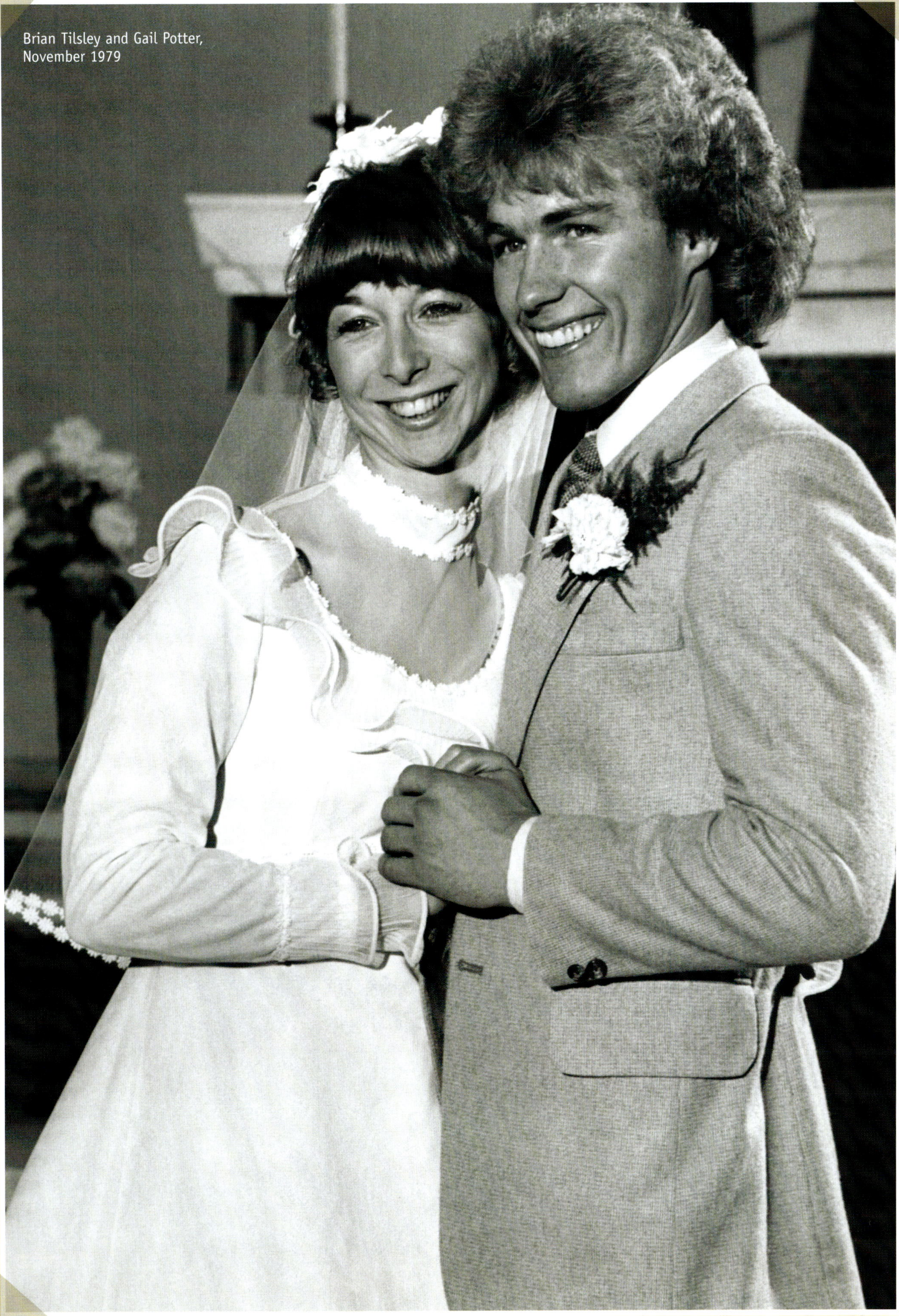

Brian Tilsley and Gail Potter,
November 1979

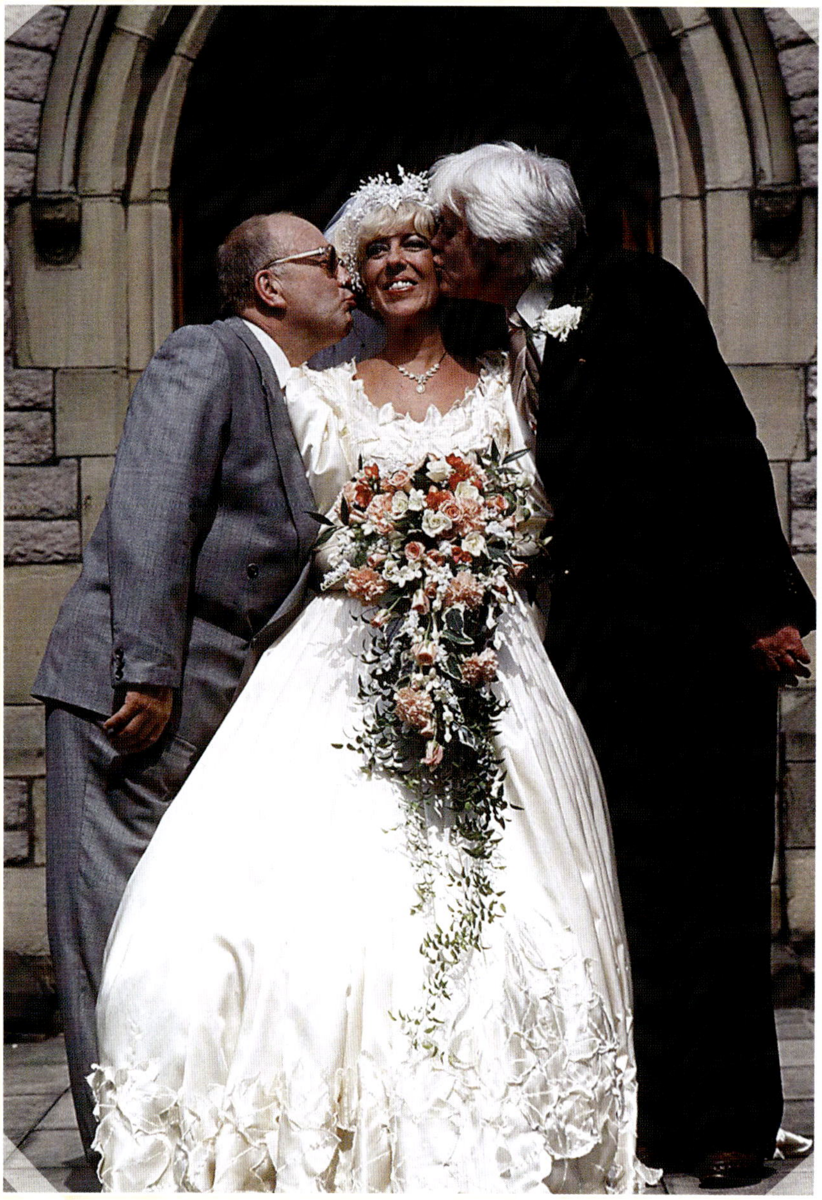

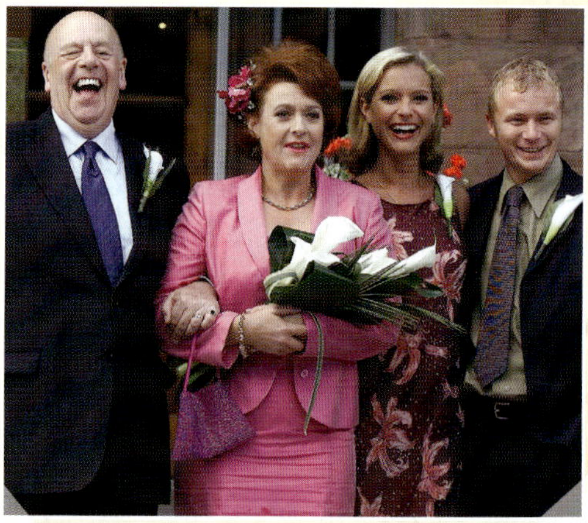

Above: Fred Elliott and Eve Sykes, September 2001

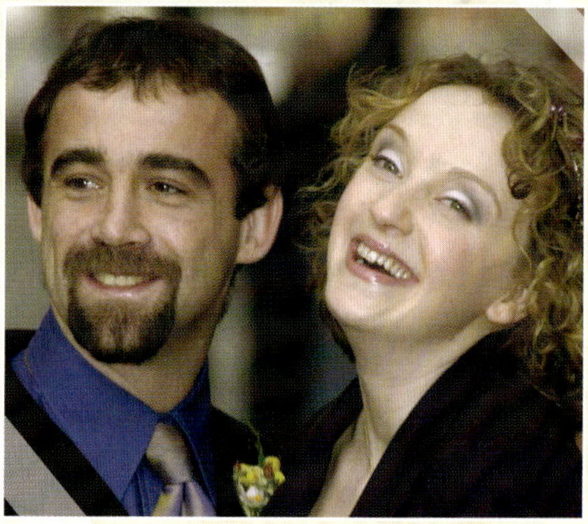

Above: Alison Wakefield and Kevin Webster, January 2000

Left: Alec Gilroy and Bet Lynch, September 1987

Below: Des Barnes and Natalie Horrocks, October 1998

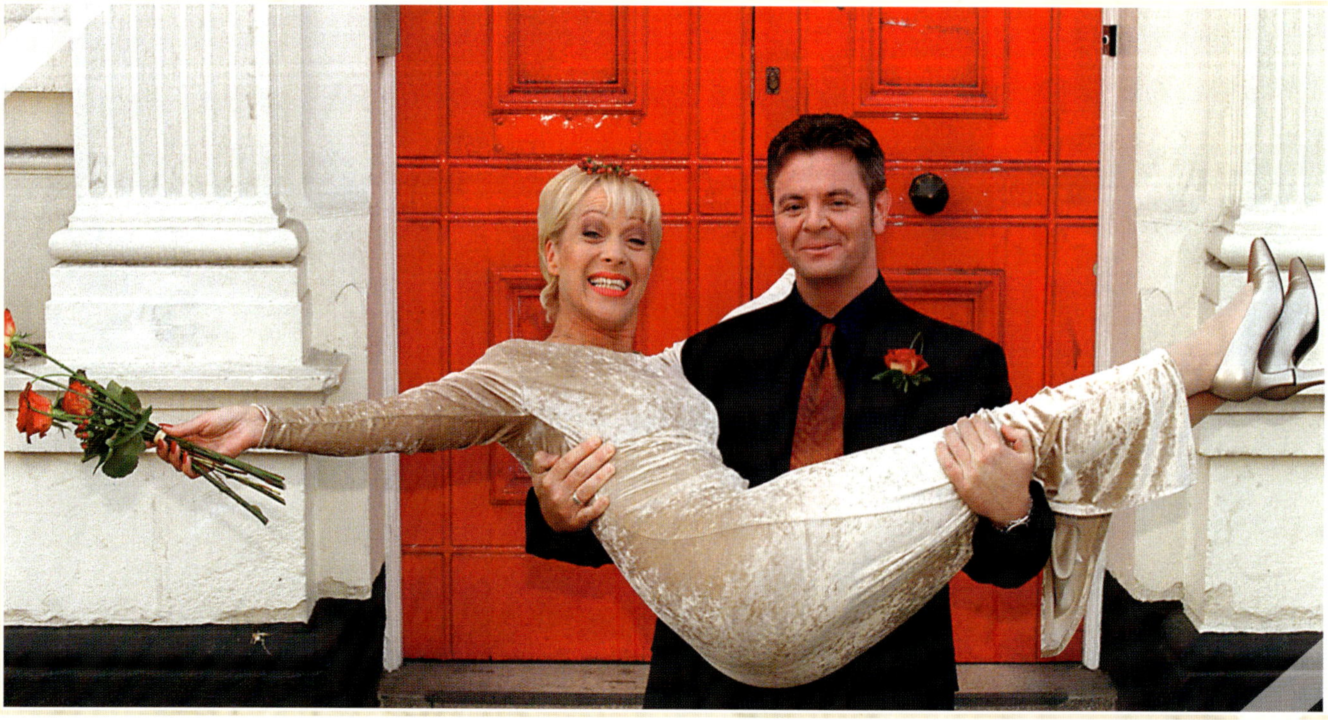

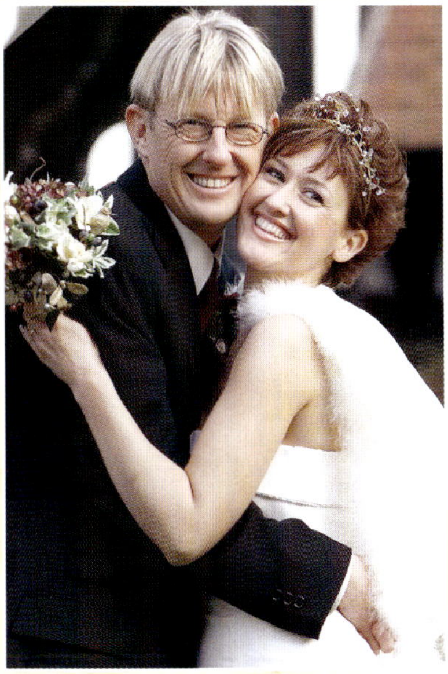

Above: Curly Watts and Emma Taylor, December 2000

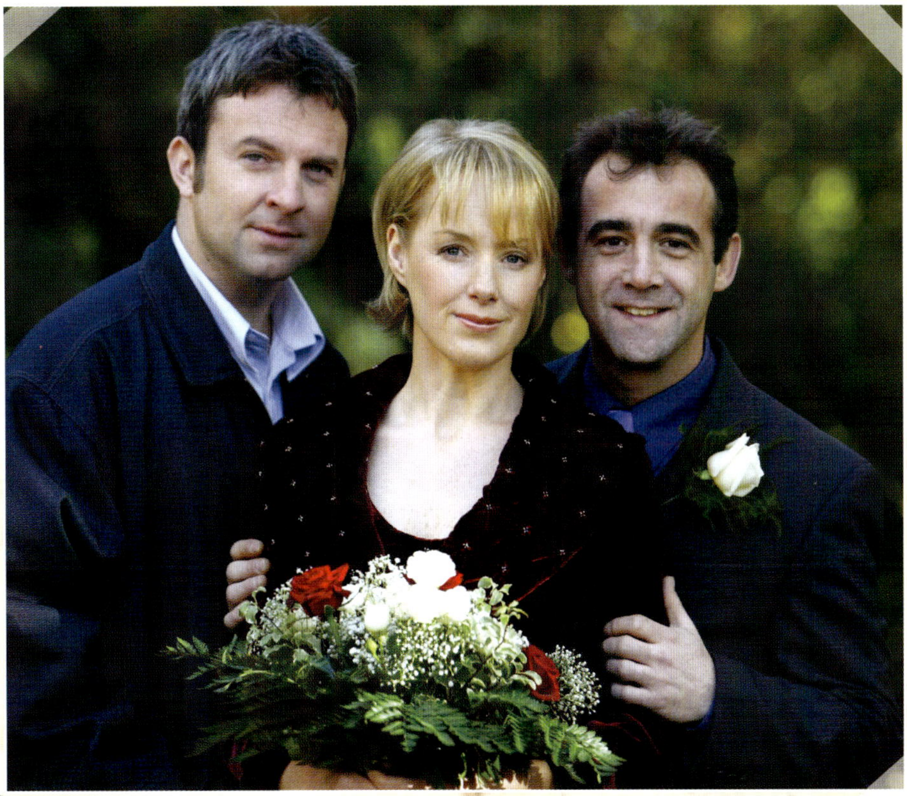

Above: Sally and Kevin Webster (second time around), December 2002

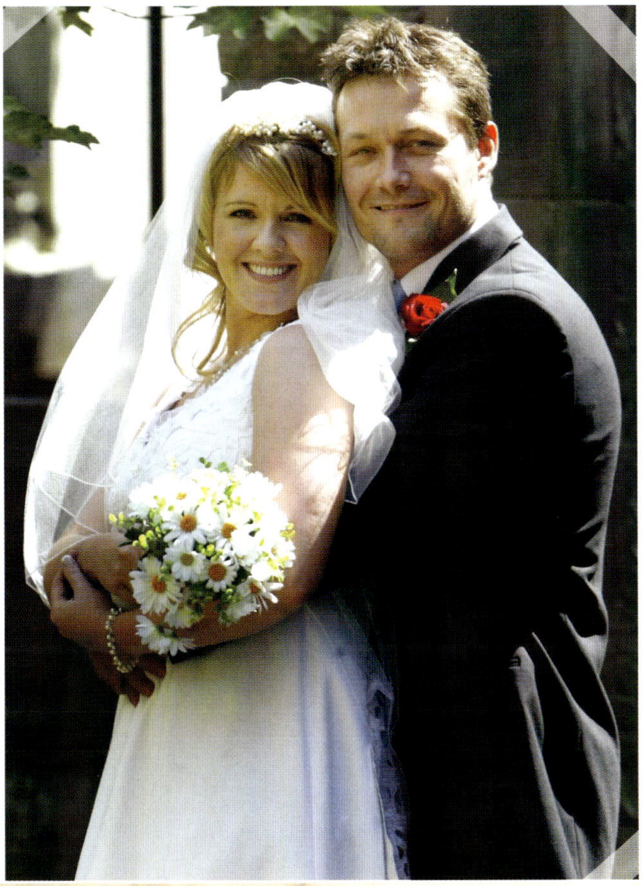

Above: Shelley Unwin and Charlie Stubbs, September 2005

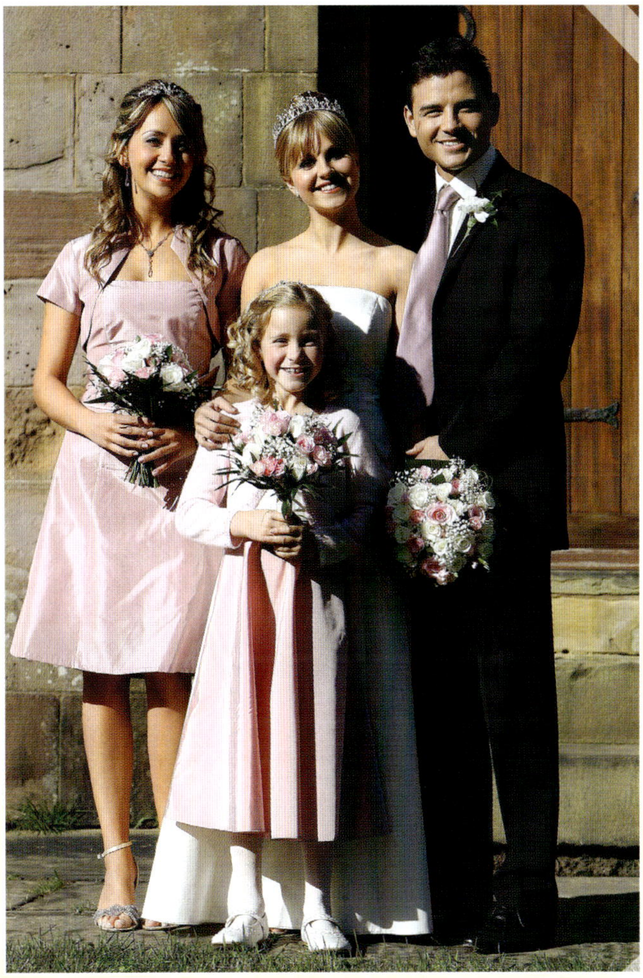

Above: Sarah Platt and Jason Grimshaw, August 2006

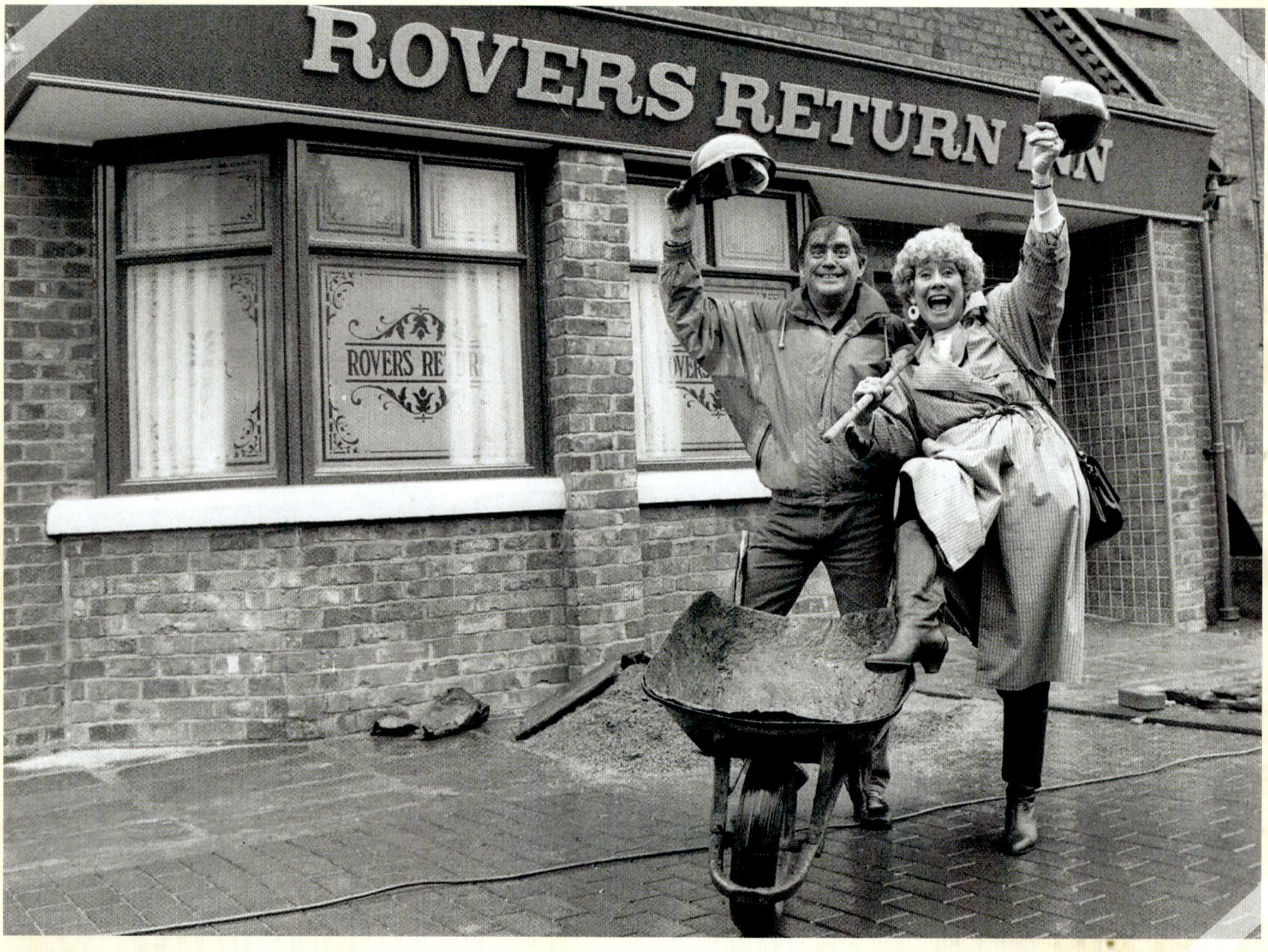

Friday, January 18, 2008

The Street's greatest double act

AND so we say ta-ra to Vera Duckworth. Along with Dot Cotton, Vera was the last of the archetypal long-suffering, tragi-comic, working-class women upon which our soaps are built. Tonight millions will see husband Jack fight back tears as the body of his beloved "little swamp duck" is carried out of their stone-clad home at Number 9 Coronation Street.

Just a few hours earlier the couple had been excitedly planning a new life in Blackpool, but in tonight's double bill those dreams are cruelly shattered by the sudden death of Vera, played by Liz Dawn.

How she dies has been kept a closely guarded secret. Three different endings were shot on a closed set one Sunday in December. But one thing is not in doubt – her passing is a momentous event for Corrie.

After Bet Lynch and Hilda Ogden, Vera was the Street's greatest icon. For 33 years, she has also been half of probably the most popular couple in soap – right up there with Stan and Hilda Ogden, Den and Angie Watts and Bobby and Sheila Grant.

Her status as a true icon is confirmed by the fact that even people who've never watched Corrie know Jack and Vera and what they stand for.

Vera wasn't one of those soap characters who you remember for her meaty storylines. She was, instead, part of the firmament, the day-to-day life that makes Coronation Street such that she was related to the Queen; her insistence on naming their humdrum terraced house The Old Rectory; and that home's famous/hideous stone cladding.

She spent her latter years taking Jack's side, nagging him . . . about his pigeons, his betting, his skiving.

Her distinct cry "Jaaaa-ck!" – like the squawk of an aggrieved magpie – could crack pint glasses at 50 metres.

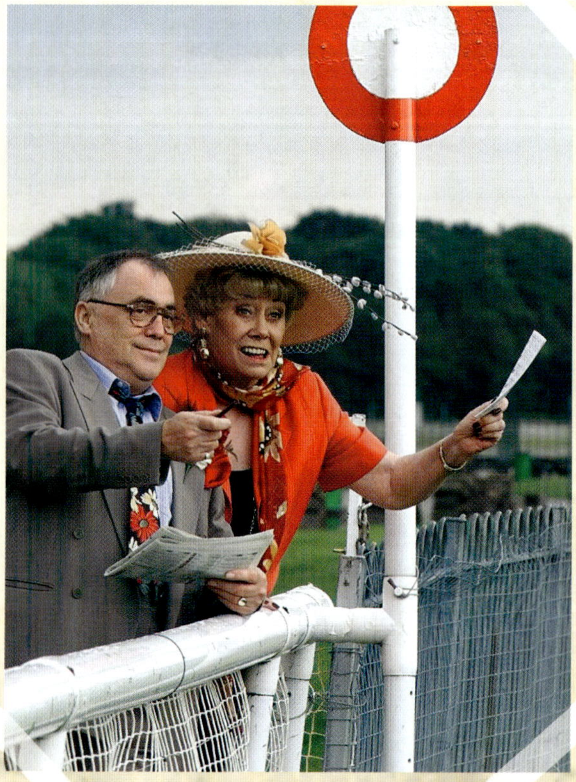

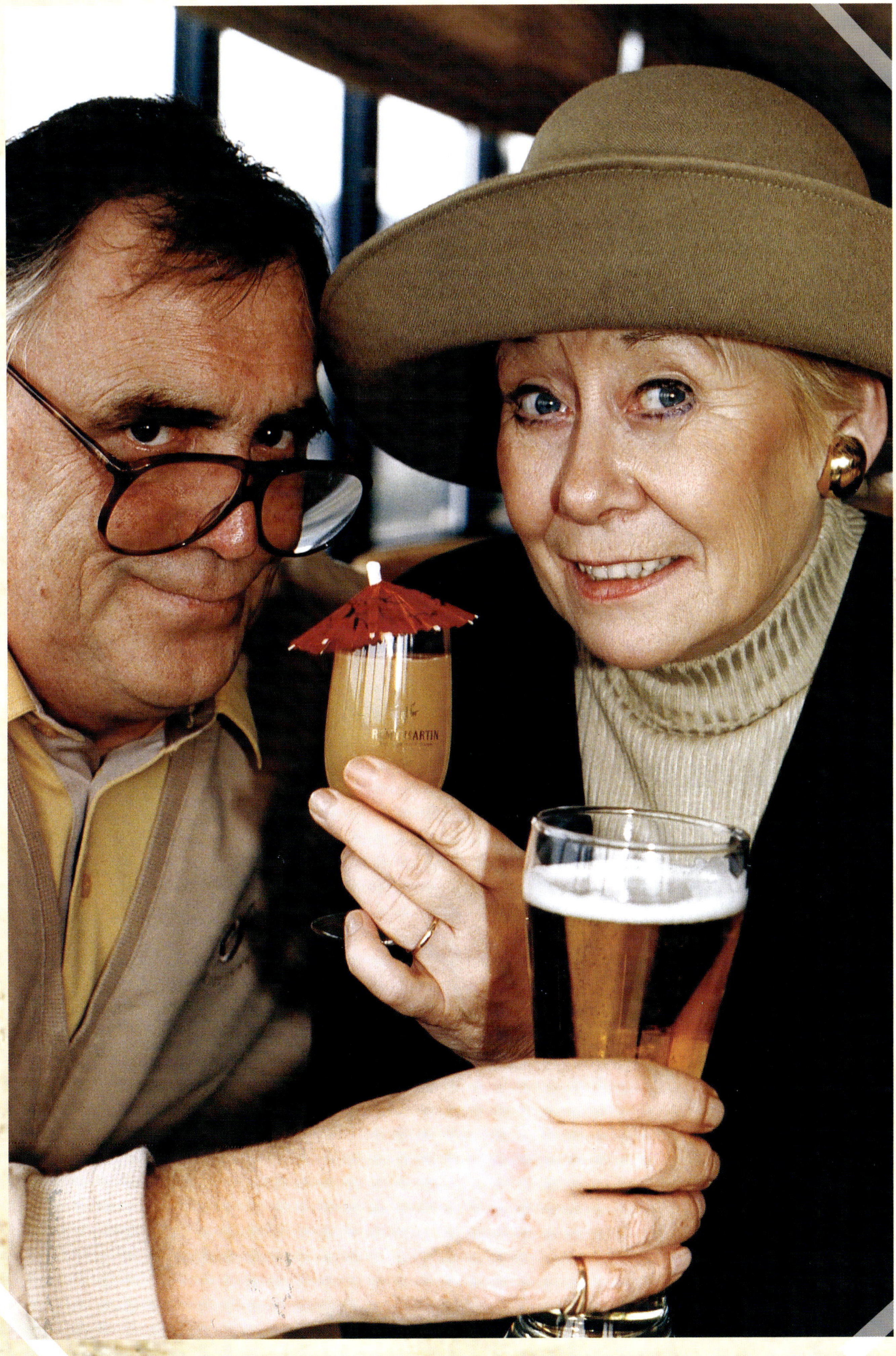

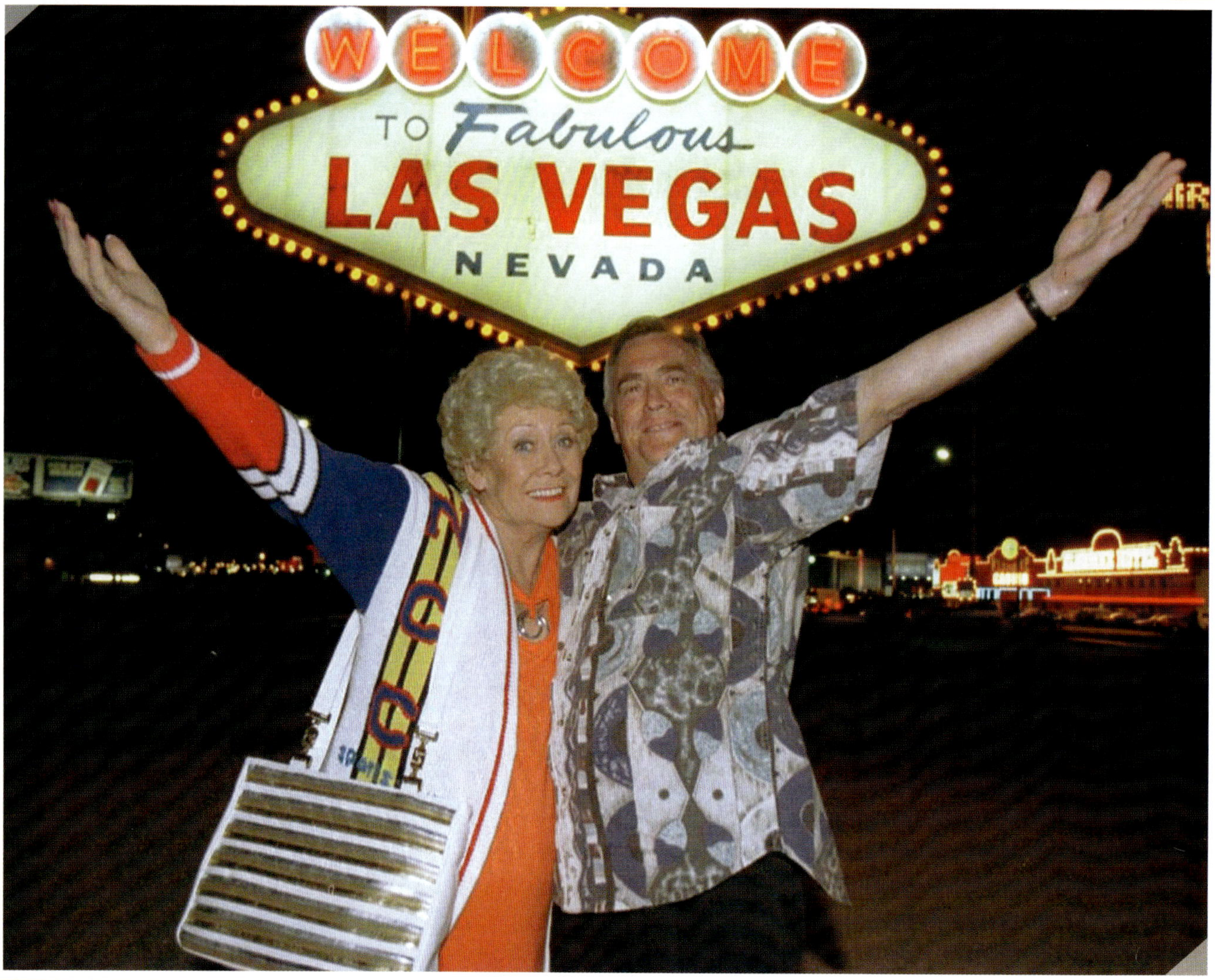

Monday, September 22, 1997

Vegas shocker for Vera

CORONATION STREET'S hen-pecked hubby Jack Duckworth gives wife Vera a shock when he reveals their marriage is a FRAUD.

Rovers landlord Jack lied about his age when they wed in the Sixties, claiming he was 22 instead of 20.

Furious Vera is convinced their marriage is illegal and they have been living in sin for 30 years.

Jack's guilty secret comes to light when the couple dig out their old marriage certificate to have their union blessed at Las Vegas's world famous Little White Wedding Chapel.

But Vera gets her romantic ending when Jack proposes again.

The Duckworths, played by Bill Tarmey and Liz Dawn, are not the only ones in trouble in the 75-minute Christmas video now being filmed in Nevada.

Hairdressers Fiona and Maxine – actresses Angela Griffin and Tracy Shaw – end up in a police cell after getting mixed up with gangsters at a party.

Tracy said: "Vegas is a mad place and everything certainly goes mad in this video. It's so funny because the script is brilliant."

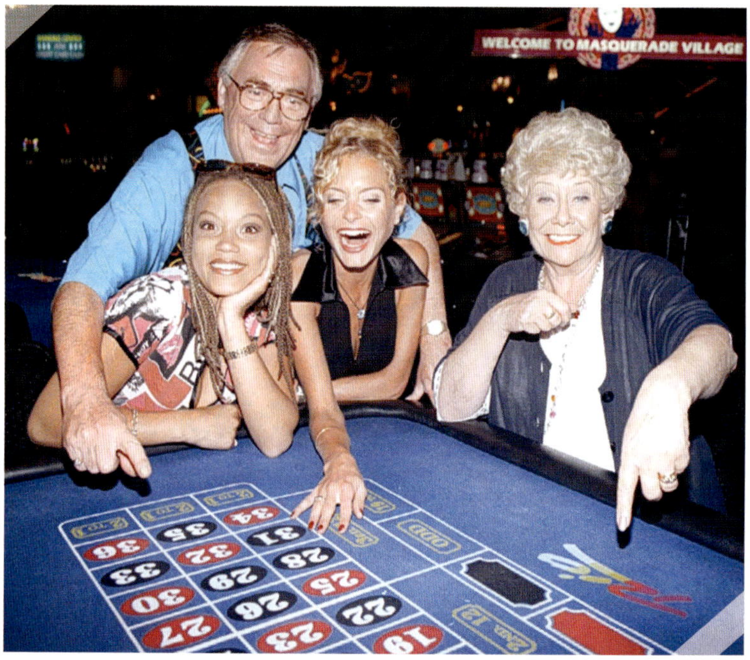

Above: The Duckworths hit Vegas with Fiona and Maxine, for a video special in 1997

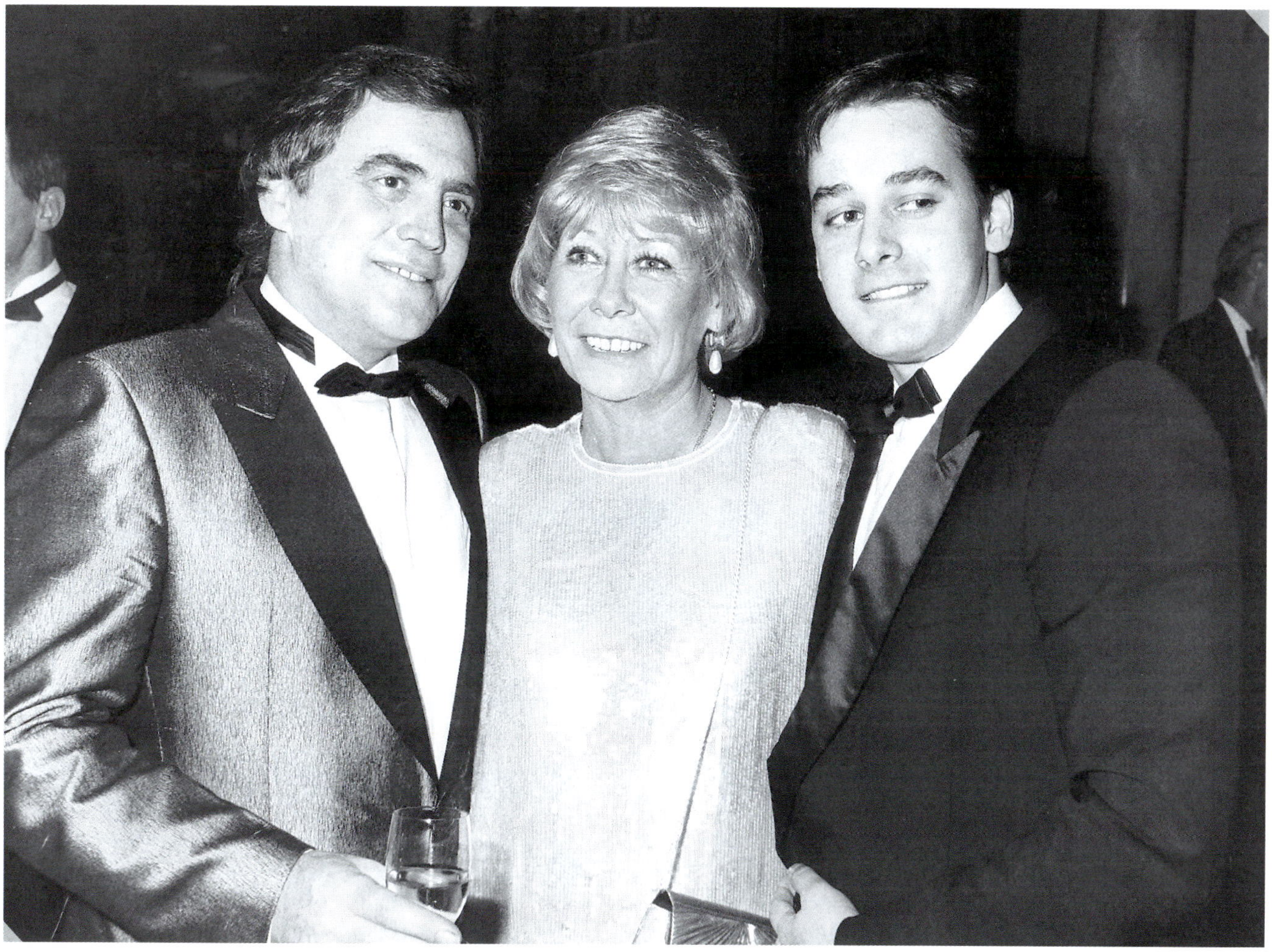

Above: Celebrating 25 years of Coronation Street with their screen son, Terry, played by Nigel Pivaro

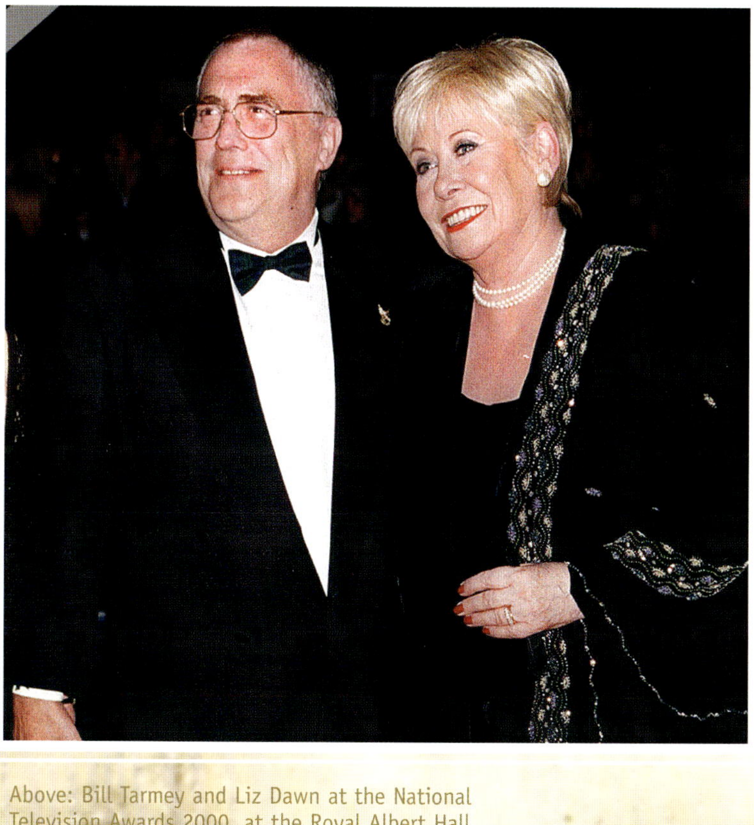

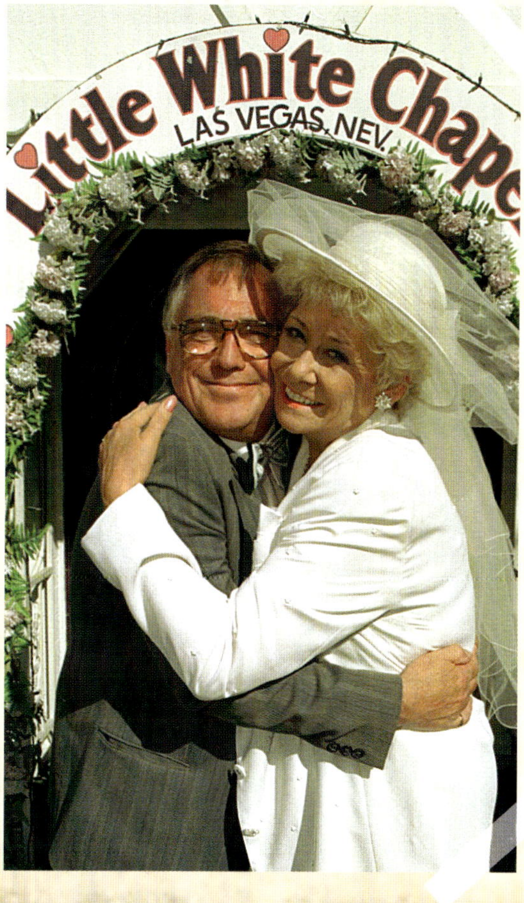

Above: Bill Tarmey and Liz Dawn at the National Television Awards 2000, at the Royal Albert Hall

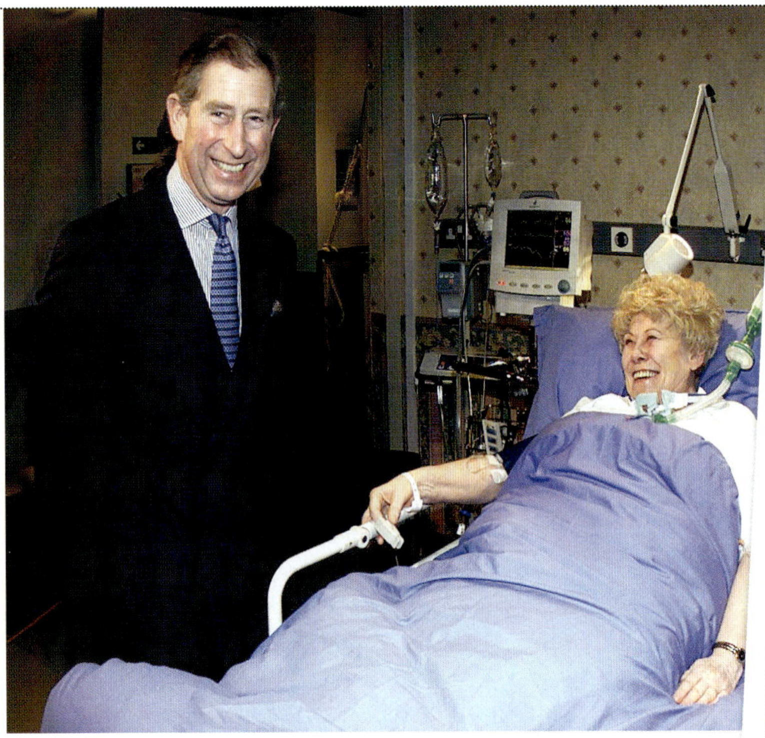

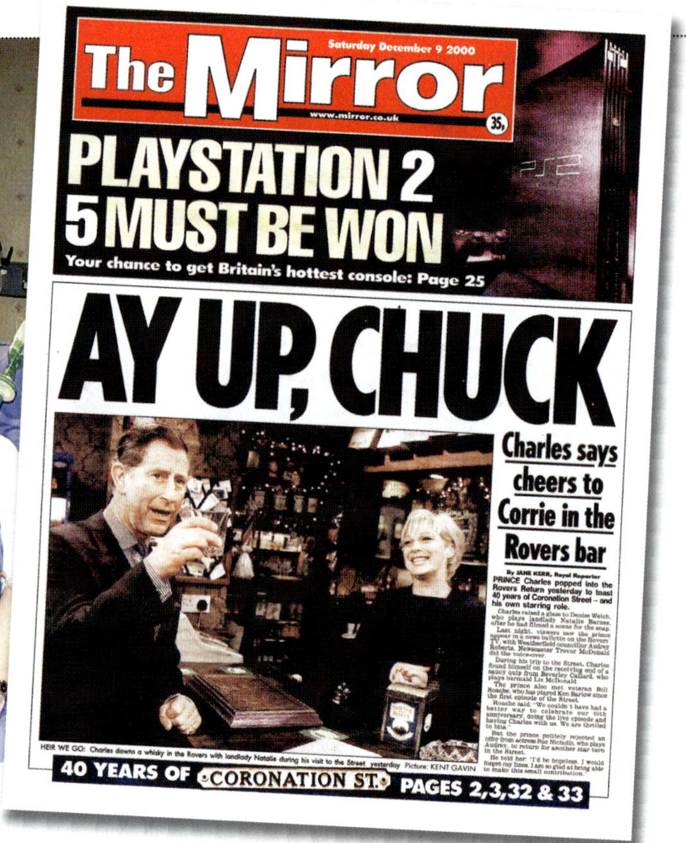
Saturday December 9 2000
The Mirror
www.mirror.co.uk
35p
PLAYSTATION 2
5 MUST BE WON
Your chance to get Britain's hottest console: Page 25

AY UP, CHUCK

Charles says cheers to Corrie in the Rovers bar

By JANE KERR, Royal Reporter

PRINCE Charles popped into the Rovers Return yesterday to toast 40 years of Coronation Street – and his own starring role.

Charles raised a glass to Denise Welch, who plays landlady Natalie Barnes, after he had filmed a scene for the soap.

Last night, viewers saw the prince appear in a news bulletin on the Rovers' TV, with Weatherfield councillor Audrey Roberts. Newscaster Trevor McDonald did the voice-over.

During his trip to the Street, Charles found himself on the receiving end of a saucy quip from Beverley Callard, who plays barmaid Liz McDonald.

The prince also met veteran Bill Roache, who has played Ken Barlow since the first episode of the Street.

Roache said: "We couldn't have had a better way to celebrate our 40th anniversary, doing the live episode and having Charles with us. We are thrilled to bits."

But the prince politely rejected an offer from actress Sue Nicholls, who plays Audrey, to return for another star turn in the Street.

He told her: "I'd be hopeless. I would forget my lines. I am so glad at being able to make this small contribution."

HERE WE GO: Charles downs a whisky in the Rovers with landlady Natalie during his visit to the Street yesterday Picture: KENT GAVIN

40 YEARS OF CORONATION ST. PAGES 2,3,32 & 33

Saturday, December 9, 2000

Chas on day he got star part

PRINCE CHARLES got more than he bargained for yesterday when he joined the cast of Coronation Street.

As he was lured into the Rovers Return by landlady Natalie Barnes for a quick tipple, barmaid Liz McDonald grabbed his arm.

Then she said cheekily: "Originally I ran away with a younger man, so you had better watch out – there's always room for an older one."

Actress Beverley Callard delivered the saucy proposal after Charles agreed to appear in last night's live episode at Granada's studios in Manchester, to mark the soap's 40th anniversary. The prince and the rest of the cast burst out laughing as Bev told him: "Life's never boring in a soap."

Charles filmed a short scene with actress Sue Nicholls, who plays town councillor Audrey Roberts, during an 'official visit' to the offices of Weatherfield Council.

And millions of TV viewers caught a glimpse of him when he was seen on the Rovers Return TV.

Newsreader Trevor McDonald performed the voice-over for the fake news bulletin to add authenticity to the broadcast.

Charles, whose visit to the Street followed one by the Queen in 1982, told the cast: "Having met everybody I understand why everybody is so involved in Coronation Street. It is a wonderful institution, isn't it?"

Charles's visit yesterday also saw him leaning over Vera Duckworth's hospital bed, where she was in a coma following an ill-fated kidney operation.

"Have you brought me any grapes?" quipped Vera – alias actress Liz Dawn – suddenly waking up to greet him.

Although Charles only catches the show occasionally, partner Camilla Parker Bowles is an avid viewer and fan.

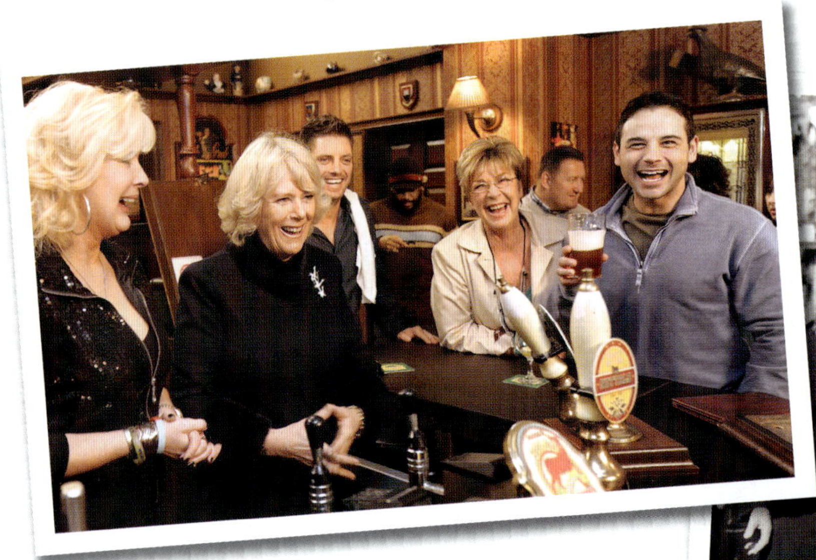

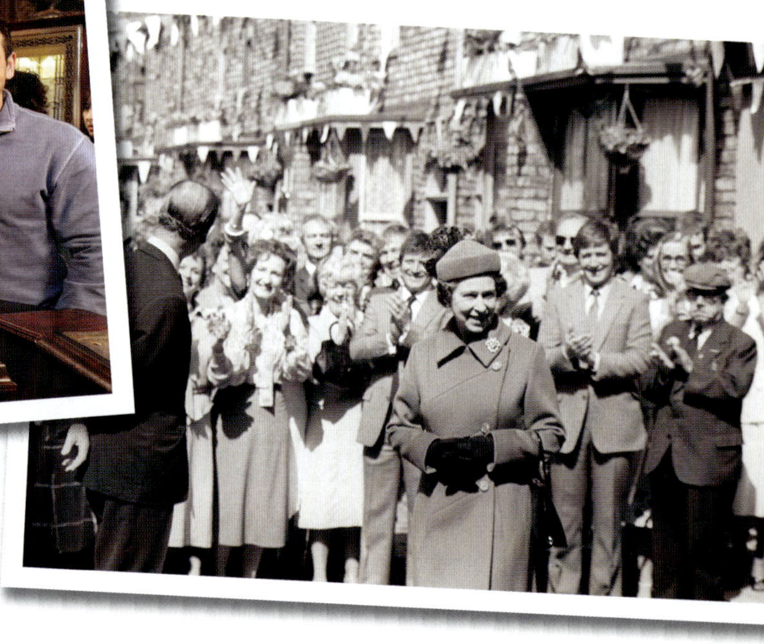

Above: Camilla, Duchess of Conwall, a fan of the show, visited the set in February 2010. The Queen and Prince Philip dropped by in 1982

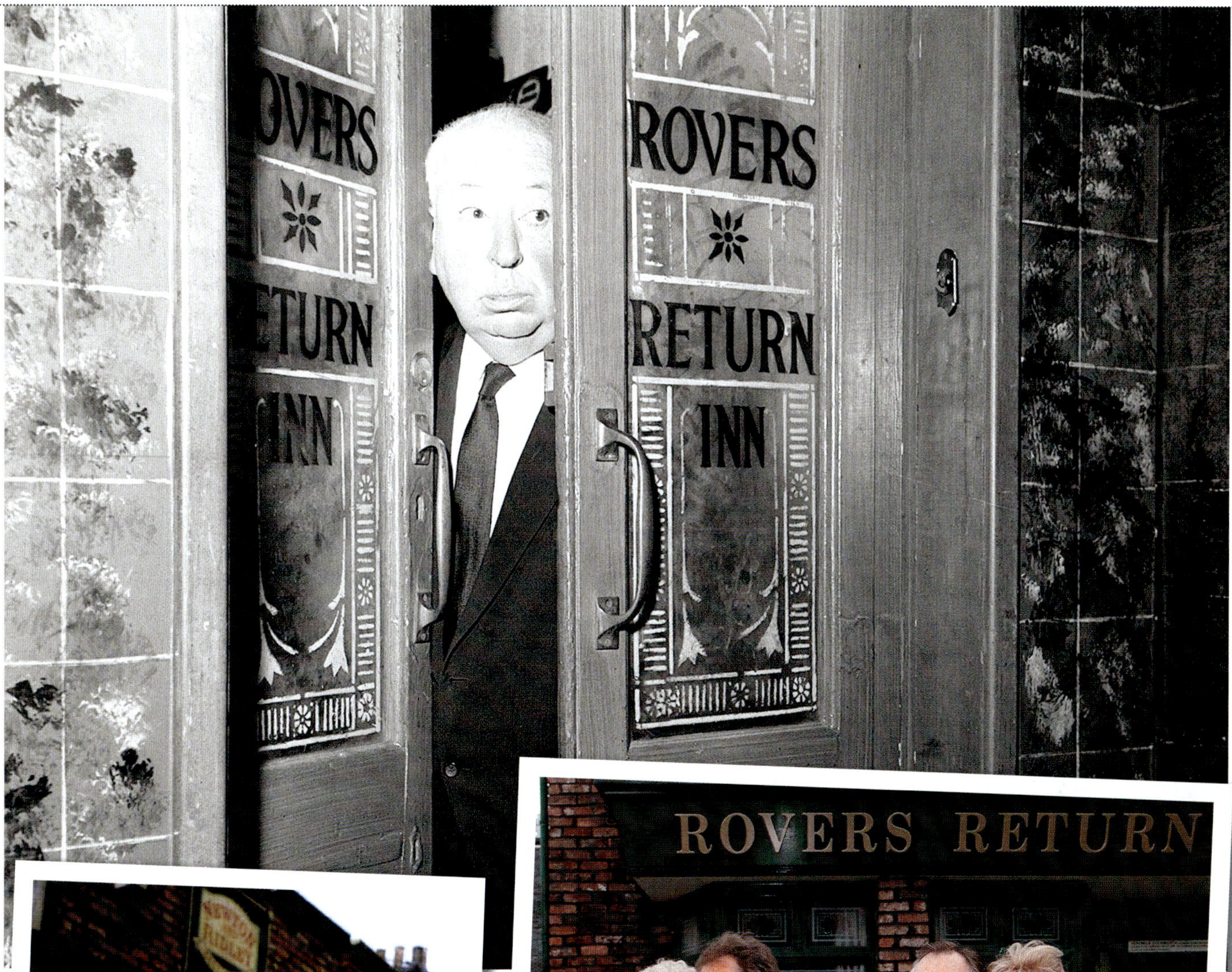

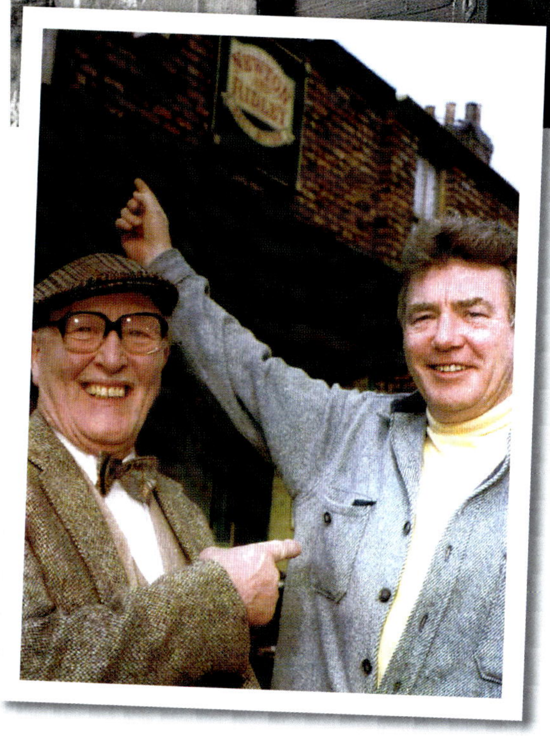

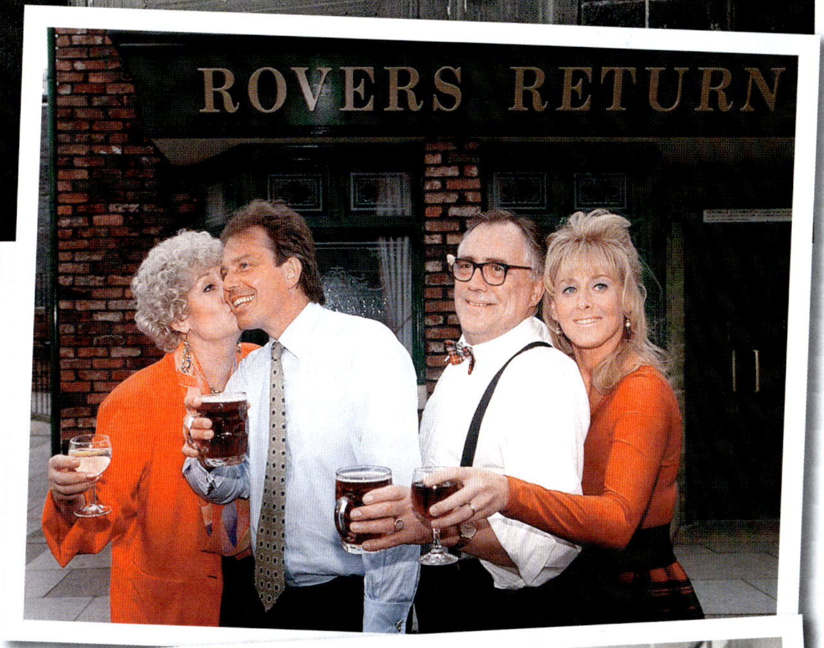

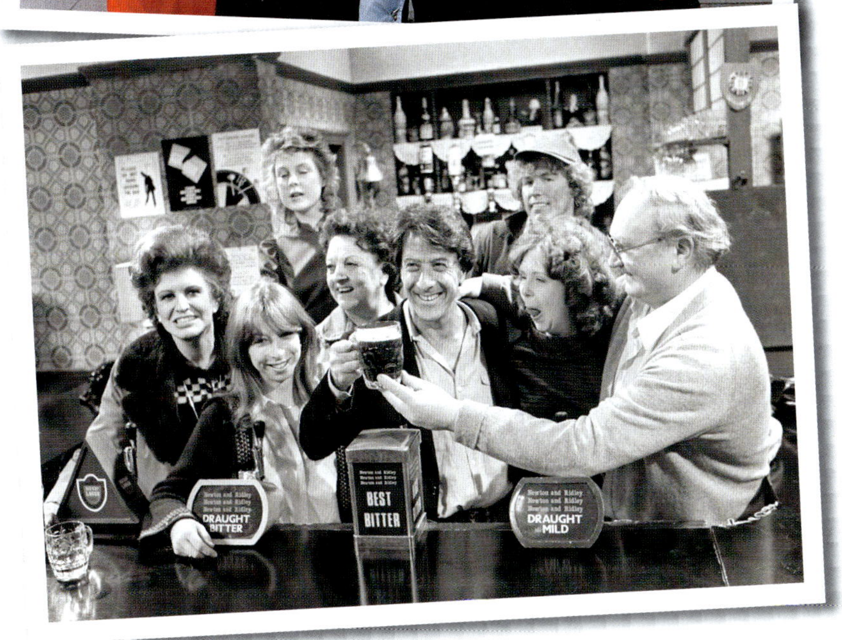

Top picture: Although he didn't appear in the show, film director Alfred Hitchcock did visit the Rovers Return. Other famous faces that can be seen here are Tony Blair (a year before he became Prime Minister), Albert Finney and Dustin Hoffman

★★★ A star

From those starting out on their careers, to those making guest appearances and cameos, here are just some of the famous people who have trod the cobbles over the last 50 years. Do you recognise them all?

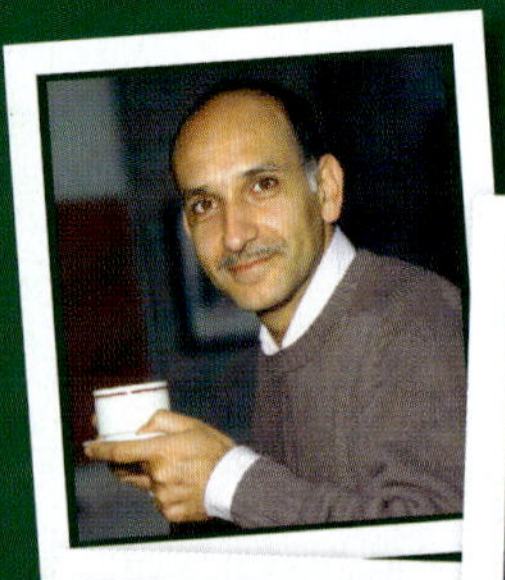
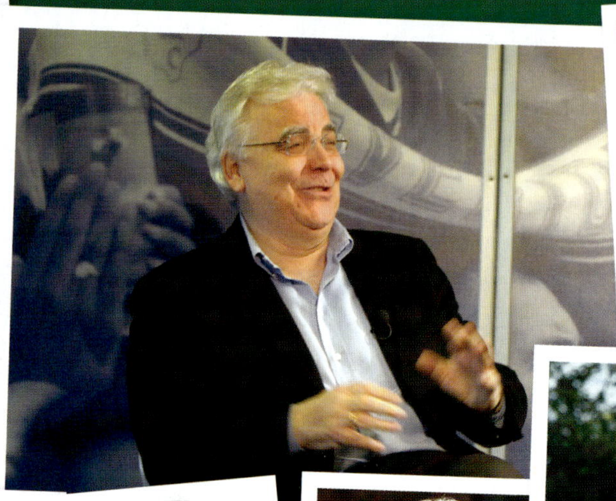
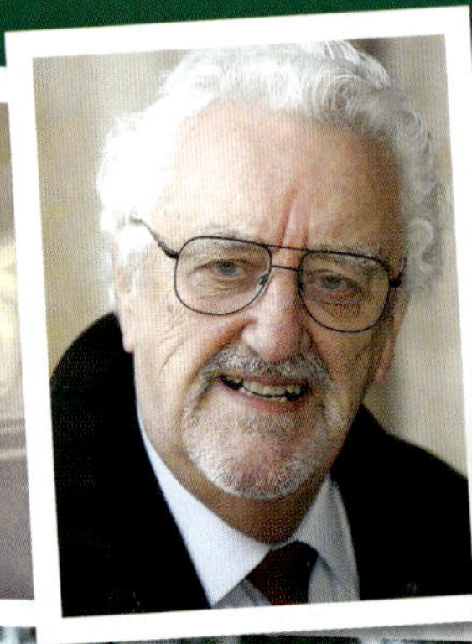
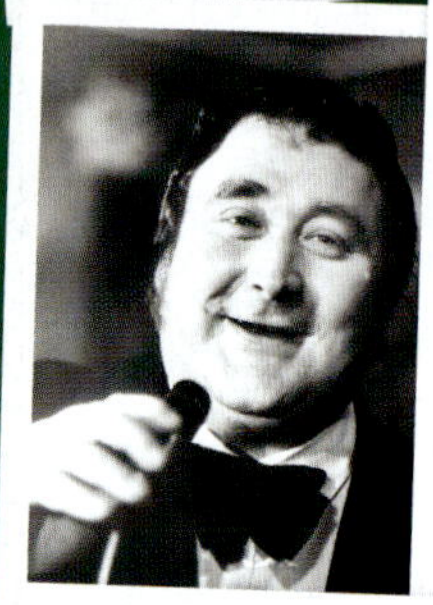
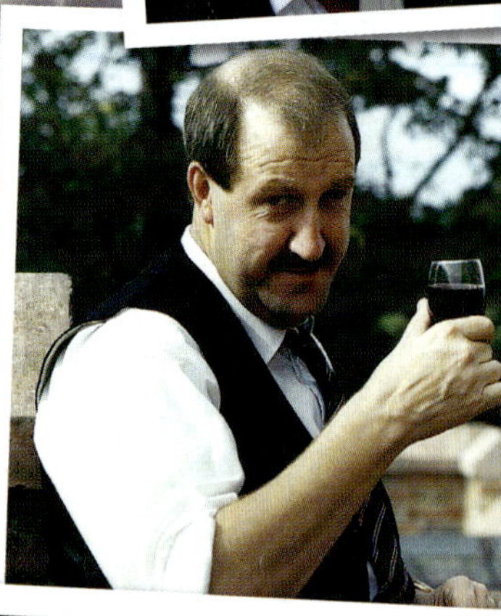
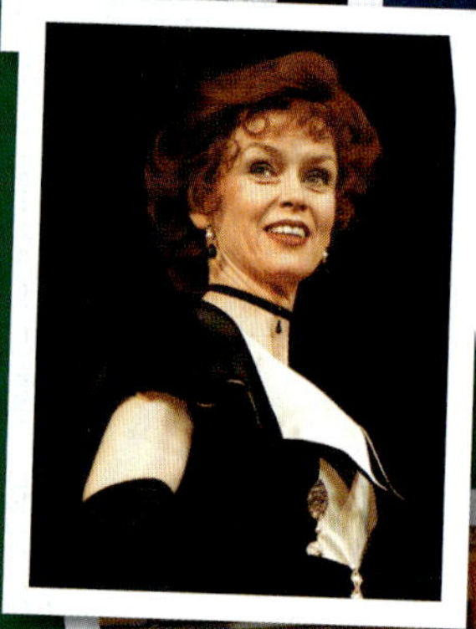
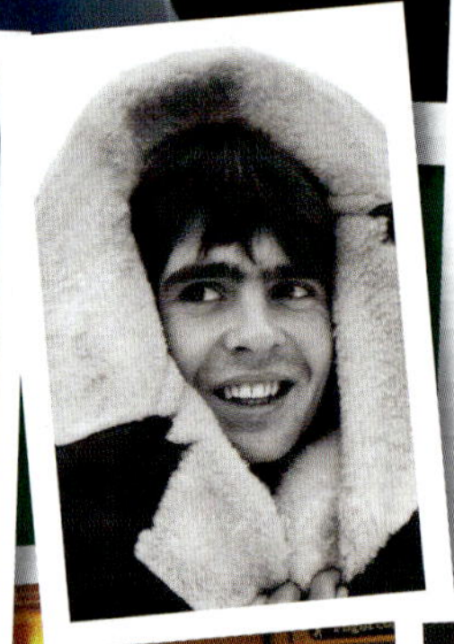
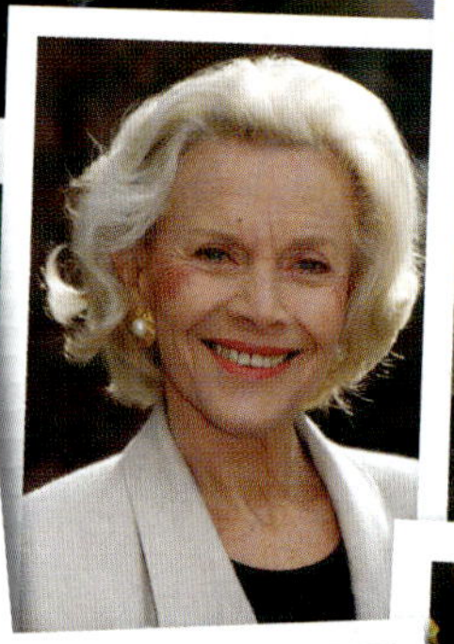
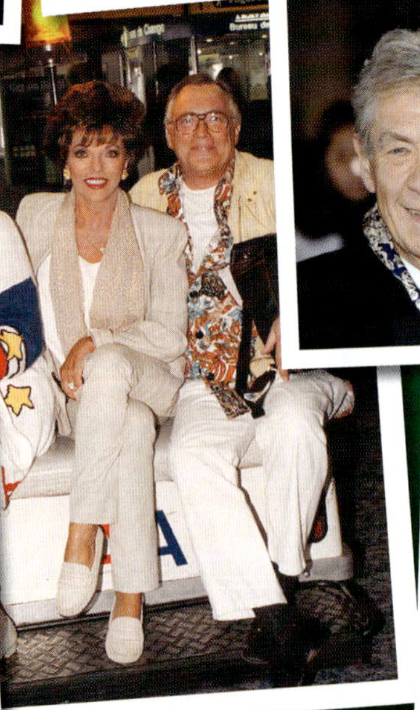
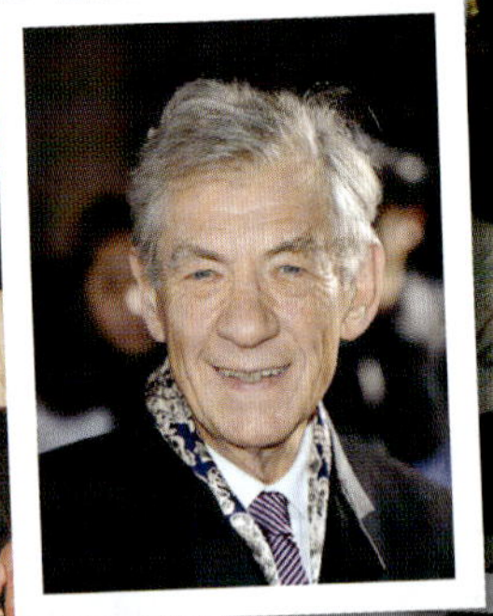
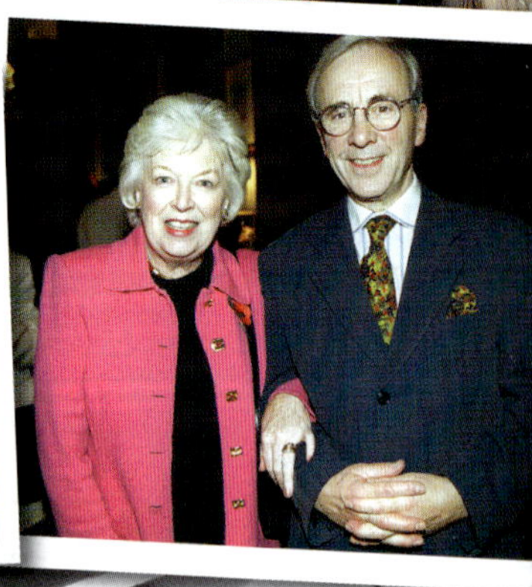
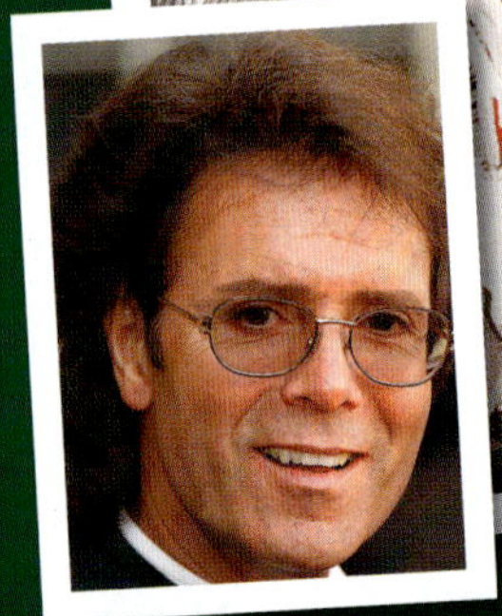
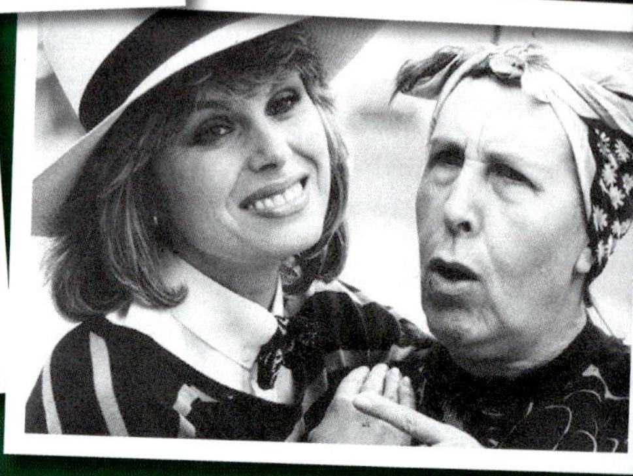

Andrew Sachs
played Norris' brother Ramsay for 27 episodes in 2009

Anna Friel
was in two episodes in 1991 before her stint in Brookside

Ben Kingsley
the Oscar winner played Ron Jenkins in 1966

Bernard Cribbins
played Blanche's friend Wally Bannister in 2003

Bernard Manning
the comedian played himself in an episode in 1971

Bill Kenwright
has played Betty's son Gordon Clegg since 1967

Bill Owen
the Last of the Summer Wine star appeared in 1971

Brenda Fricker
the Oscar winner played a nurse in 1977 for four episodes

Cliff Richard
the pop legend appeared in the Rovers in 1997

Davey Jones
from The Monkees played Colin Lomax in 1961

Gabrielle Drake
first appeared in 1967, returned for two episodes in 2009

Geoffrey Palmer
the British sitcom actor appeared in 1968

Gordon Kaye
played Elsie's nephew Bernard for 38 episodes in 1969

Honor Blackman
played Rula Romanoff for five episodes in 2004

Sir Ian McKellen
stage and screen star played Mel Hutchwright in 2005

Joan Collins
appeared as herself in the 1997 special Viva Las Vegas

Joanna Lumley
played Ken's girlfriend Elaine Perkins in 1973

Joanne Whalley-Kilmer
appeared in three episodes in 1974 and 1976

June Whitfield
played Blanche's friend May Penn in 2010

Kathy Staff
played Vera Hopkins in 1973 after three previous small roles

Kenneth Cope
a long stint as Jed Stone in the 1960s, then again in 2008

Kevin Whately
played lorry driver Kevin for two episodes in 1981

Linus Roache
a young Peter Barlow in the '70s, Ken's son Lawrence in 2010

Lynda La Plante
the crime writer appeared in two episodes in 1965

Martin Shaw
played Robert Croft for five episodes in 1967

is born ★★★

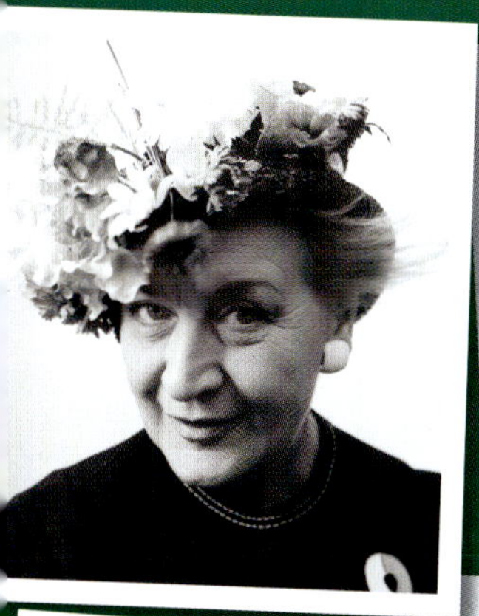
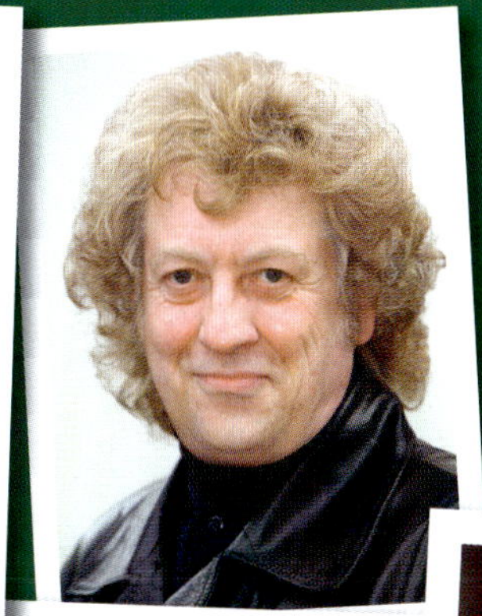
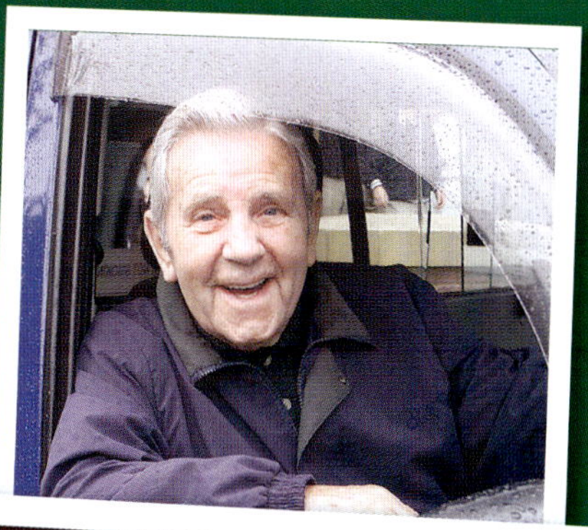
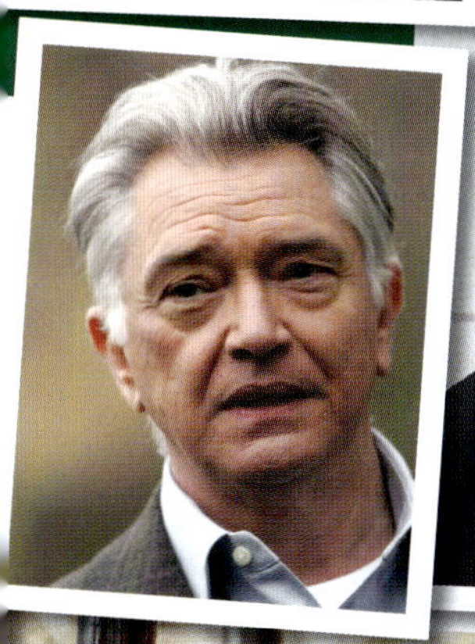
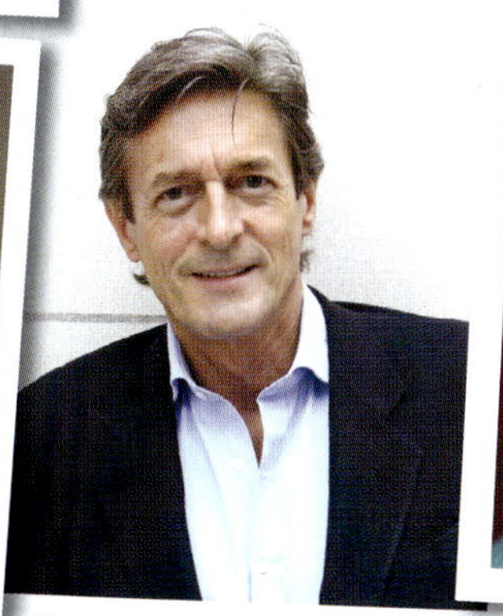
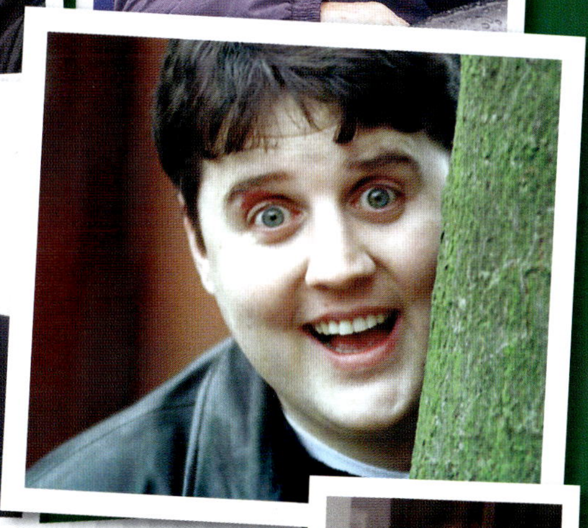
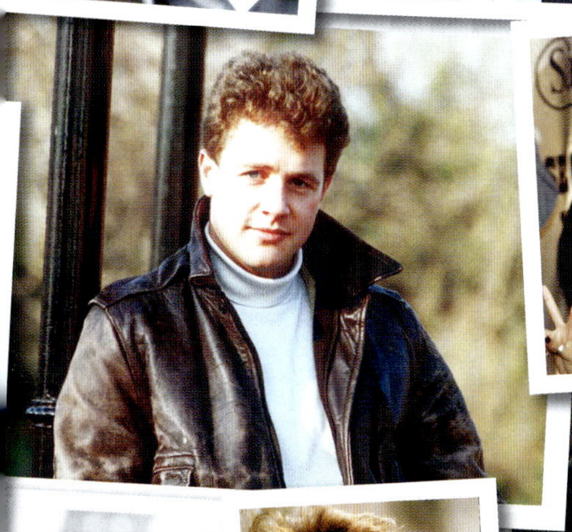
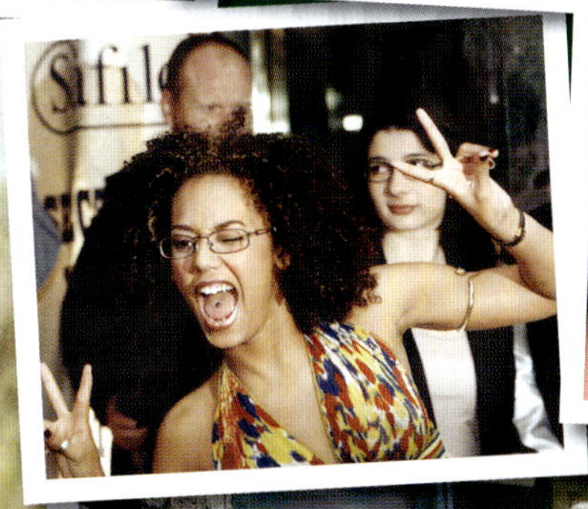
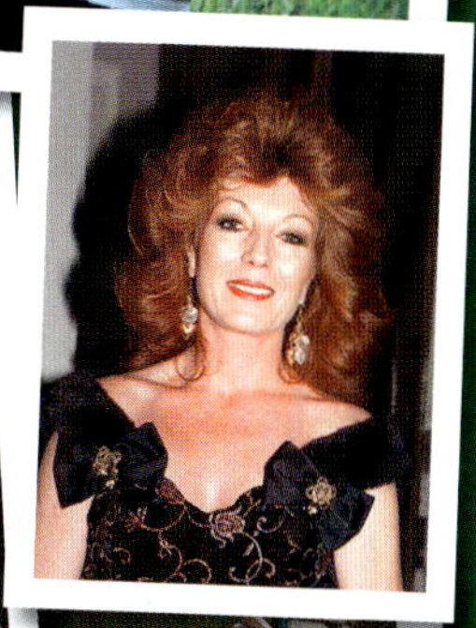
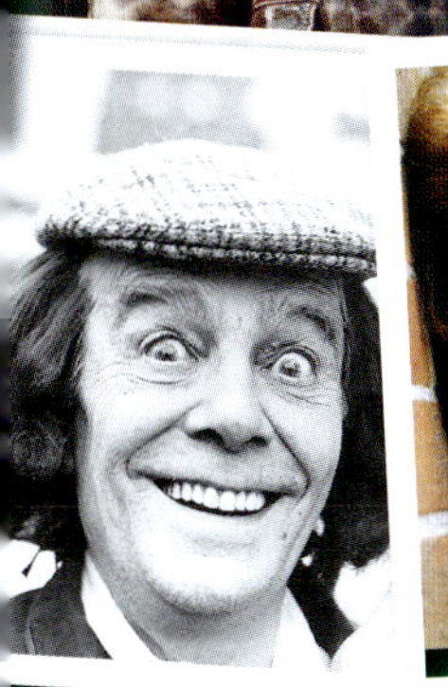
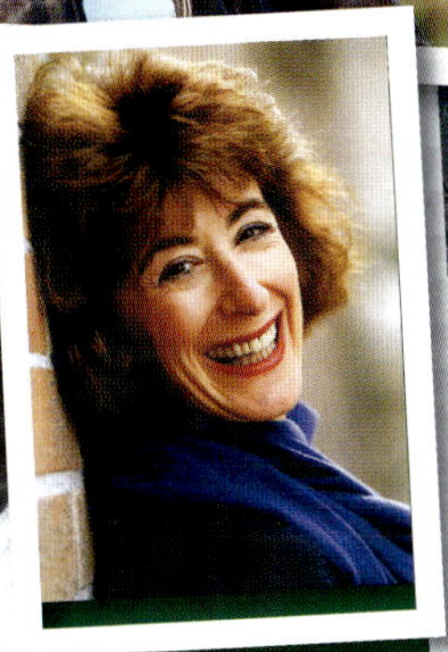
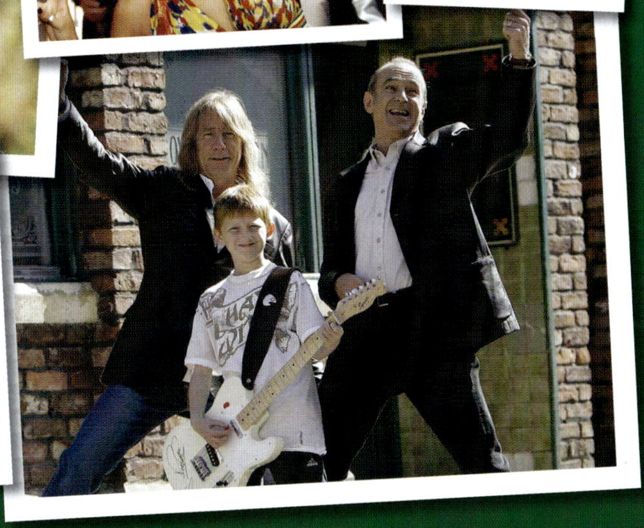

Maureen Lipman
was relief Rovers manageress Lillian Spencer in 2002

Max Wall
the comedian appeared in an episode in 1978

Maxine Peake
appeared in one episode in 1999 as Belinda Peach

Mel B
the Spice Girl did a stint on the checkouts at Bettabuys in 1993

Michael Ball
the musical star appeared in two episodes in 1985

Mollie Sugden
played Nellie Harvey for 16 episodes from 1965

Nigel Havers
played escort Lewis Archer in 2009 and 2010

Noddy Holder
the Slade star appeared in the live episode in 2000

Norman Wisdom
the comedian appeared in one episode in 2004

Patricia Routledge
played Sylvia Snape for four episodes in 1961

Patrick Stewart
of Star Trek and X-Men fame appeared in 1967

Pete Postlethwaite
acclaimed British actor played a detective in 1981

Peter Kay
appeared in 1997, and then played Shelley's date Eric Gartside in 2004

Peter Schmeichel
the goalkeeper was seen in the Rovers in 1999

Phil 'The Power' Taylor
the darts star played Disco Dave in 2009

HRH Prince Charles
graced the screen as himself in 2000

Prunella Scales
the Fawlty Towers star played Eileen Hughes in 1961

Richard Beckinsale
played a PC who arrested Ena Sharples in 1967

Rula Lenska
plays Claudia, a friend of Audrey, 2009 to present day

Roy Hudd
has appeared as undertaker Archie Shuttleworth since 2002

Status Quo
the rock group played at Les Battersby's wedding in 2005

Stephanie Beacham
played Ken's actress girlfriend Martha in 2009

Tim Healy
seen in 1976 before playing Brian Tully, Sean's dad, in 2006

Tony Booth
appeared in two episodes in 1960, another two in 1987

Tony Slattery
played bookie Eric in 2005

Queen of the Street

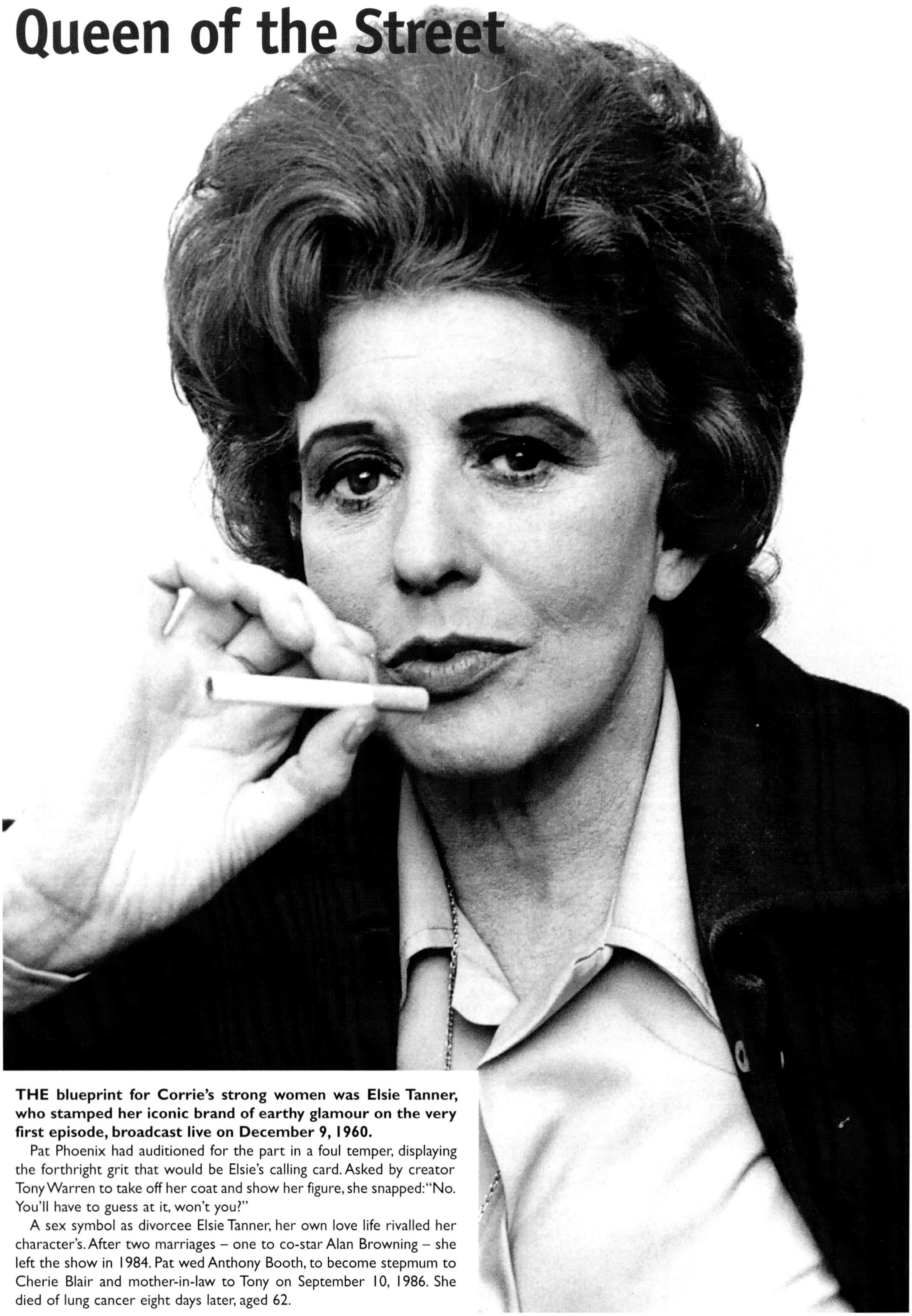

THE blueprint for Corrie's strong women was Elsie Tanner, who stamped her iconic brand of earthy glamour on the very first episode, broadcast live on December 9, 1960.

Pat Phoenix had auditioned for the part in a foul temper, displaying the forthright grit that would be Elsie's calling card. Asked by creator Tony Warren to take off her coat and show her figure, she snapped: "No. You'll have to guess at it, won't you?"

A sex symbol as divorcee Elsie Tanner, her own love life rivalled her character's. After two marriages – one to co-star Alan Browning – she left the show in 1984. Pat wed Anthony Booth, to become stepmum to Cherie Blair and mother-in-law to Tony on September 10, 1986. She died of lung cancer eight days later, aged 62.

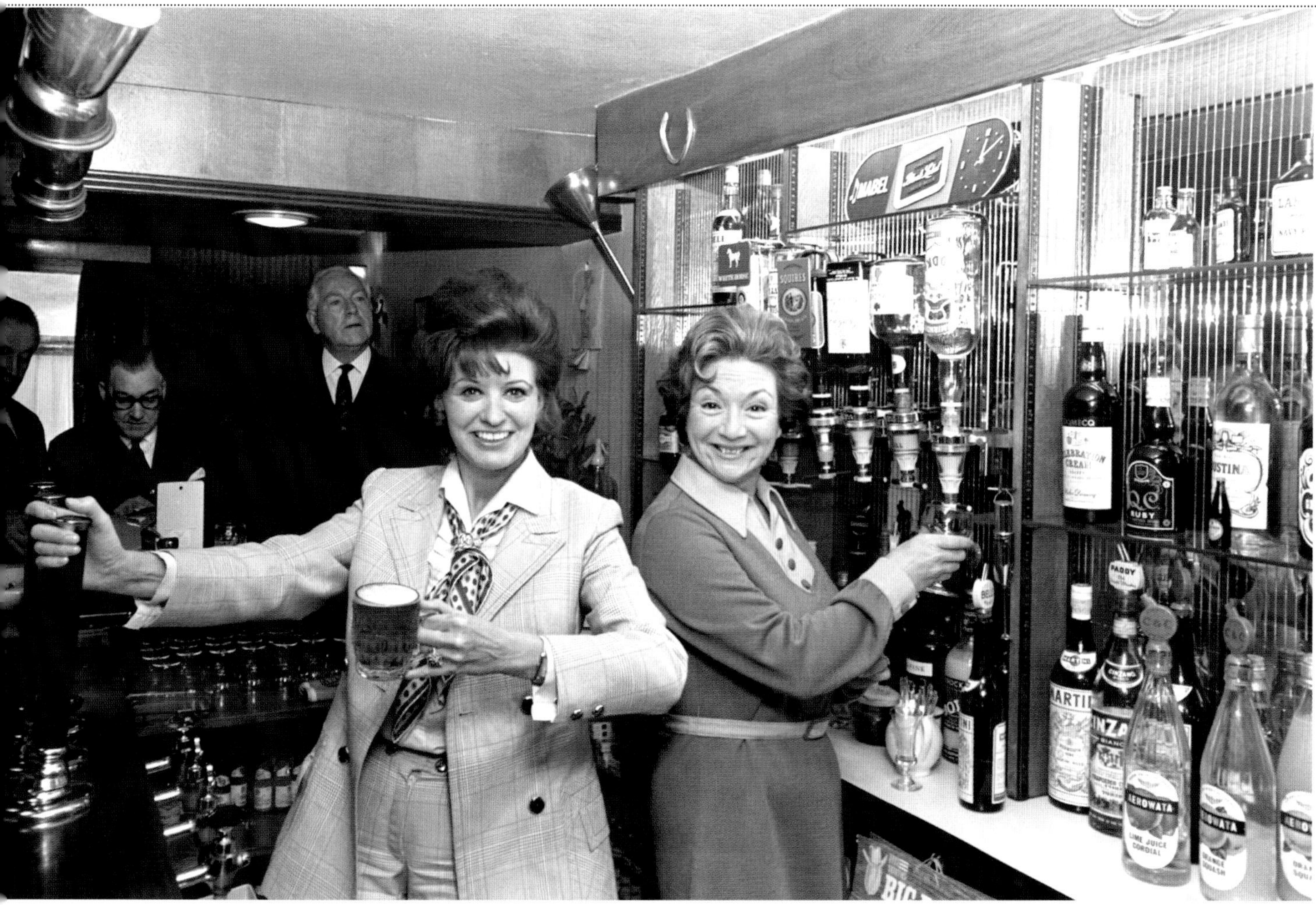

Above: Although her character never ran the Rovers Return, Pat did become licencee of the Navigation Hotel in Derbyshire, in 1969, with help from Joan Francis – who played Dot Greenhalgh. Below, Elsie celebrates Christmas with love interest Len Fairclough and son Dennis

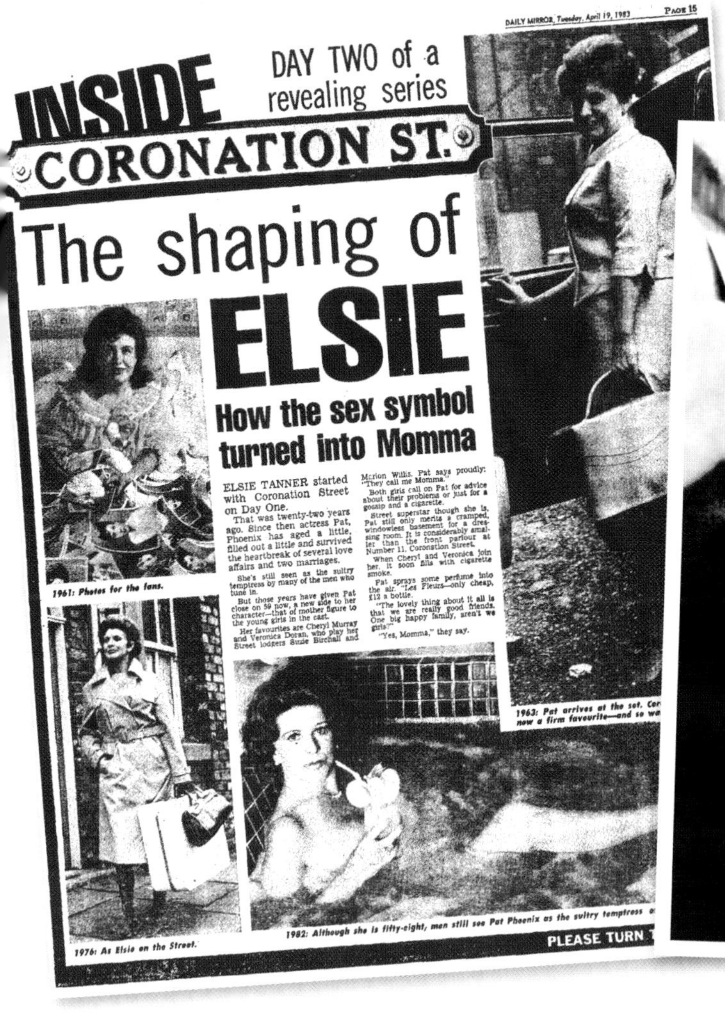

DAILY MIRROR, Tuesday, April 19, 1983 PAGE 15

INSIDE CORONATION ST.

DAY TWO of a revealing series

The shaping of ELSIE

How the sex symbol turned into Momma

ELSIE TANNER started with Coronation Street on Day One.

That was twenty-two years ago. Since then actress Pat, Phoenix has aged a little, filled out a little and survived the heartbreak of several love affairs and two marriages.

She's still seen as the sultry temptress by many of the men who tune in.

But those years have given Pat close on 59 now, a new side to her character—that of mother figure to the young girls in the cast.

Her favourites are Cheryl Murray and Veronica Doran, who play her Street lodgers Suzie Birchall and Marion Willis. Pat says proudly: "They call me Momma."

Both girls call on Pat for advice about their problems or just for a gossip and a cigarette.

Street superstar though she is, Pat still only merits a cramped, windowless basement for a dressing room. It is considerably smaller than the front parlour at Number 11, Coronation Street.

When Cheryl and Veronica join her, it soon fills with cigarette smoke.

Pat sprays some perfume into the air. "Les Fleurs—only cheap, £12 a bottle.

"The lovely thing about it all is that we are really good friends. One big happy family, aren't we girls?"

"Yes, Momma," they say.

1961: Photos for the fans.

1963: Pat arrives at the set. Cor... now a firm favourite—and so wa...

1976: As Elsie on the Street.

1982: Although she is fifty-eight, men still see Pat Phoenix as the sultry temptress a...

PLEASE TURN T

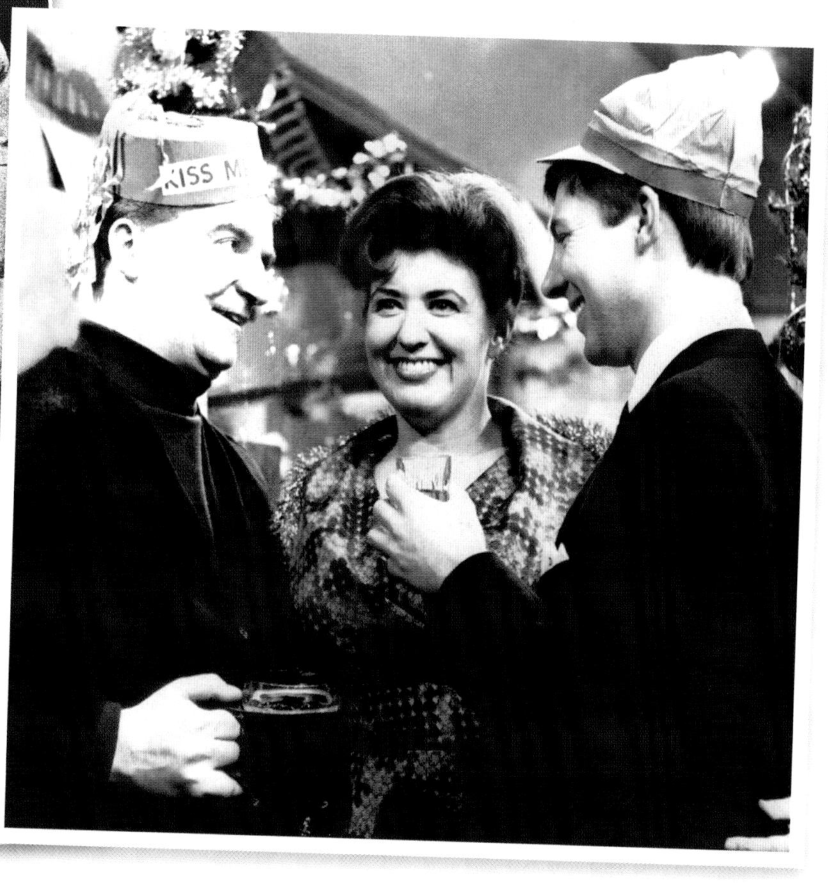

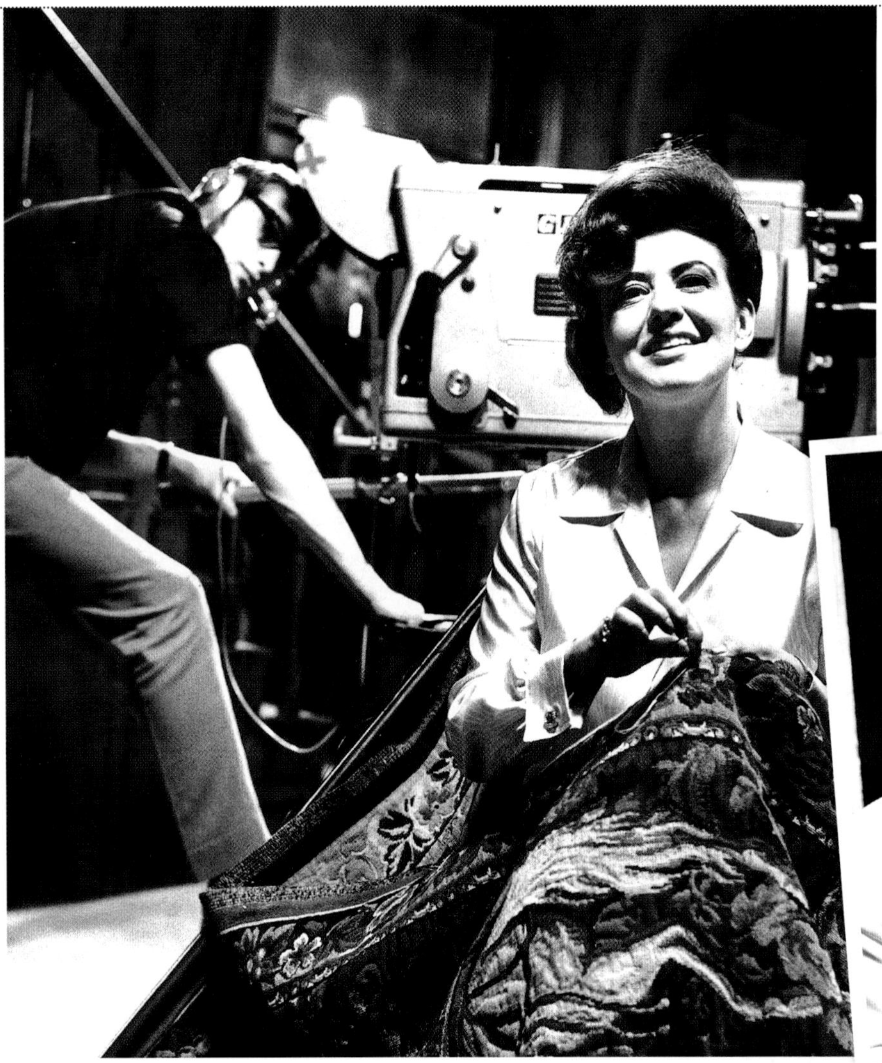

Left: Relaxing with some needlework in a break from shooting scenes. Below, singing with Peter Adamson, who played Len Fairclough. The picture at the bottom of the page shows Elsie's wedding to American serviceman Steve Tanner. Len Fairclough, Ken Barlow and Emily Nugent (later Bishop) are among those watching on

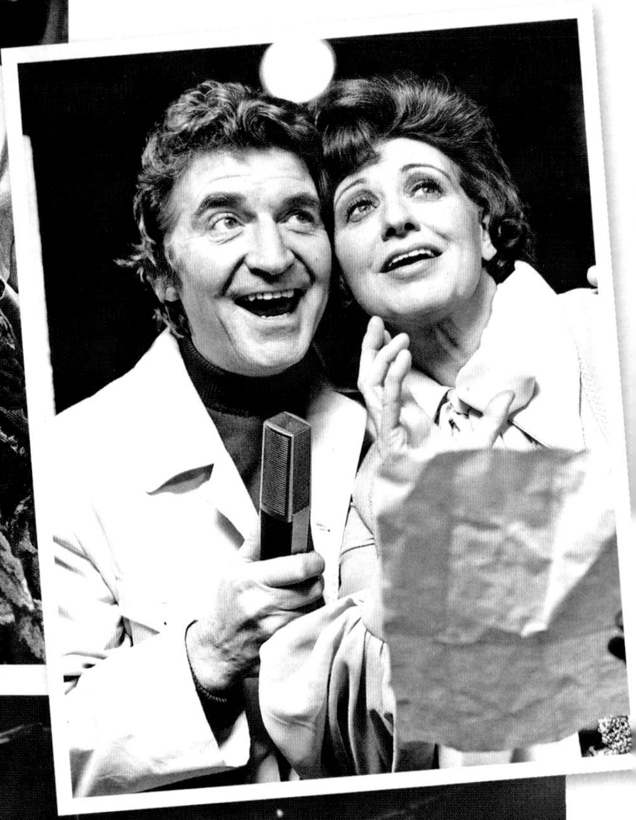

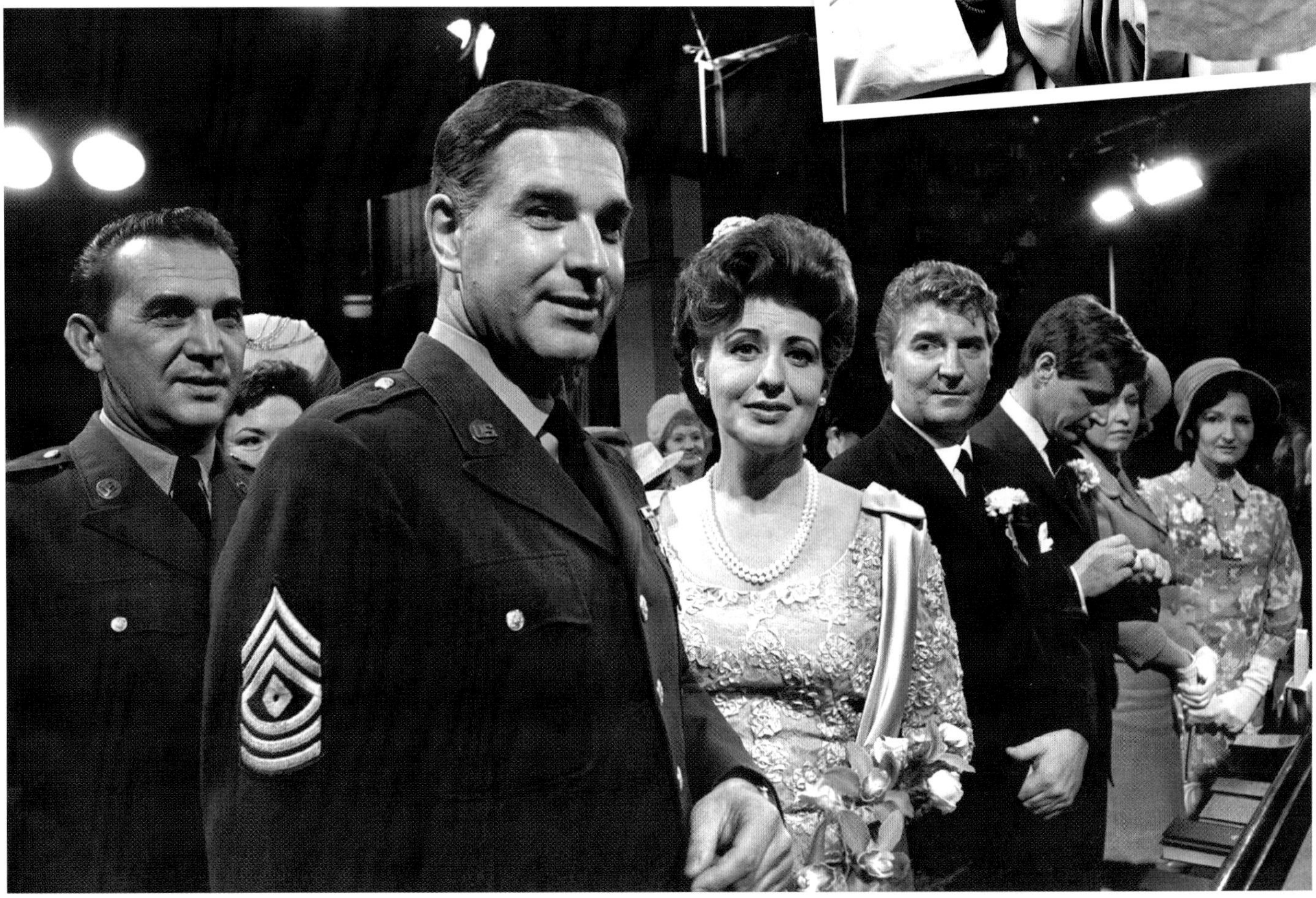

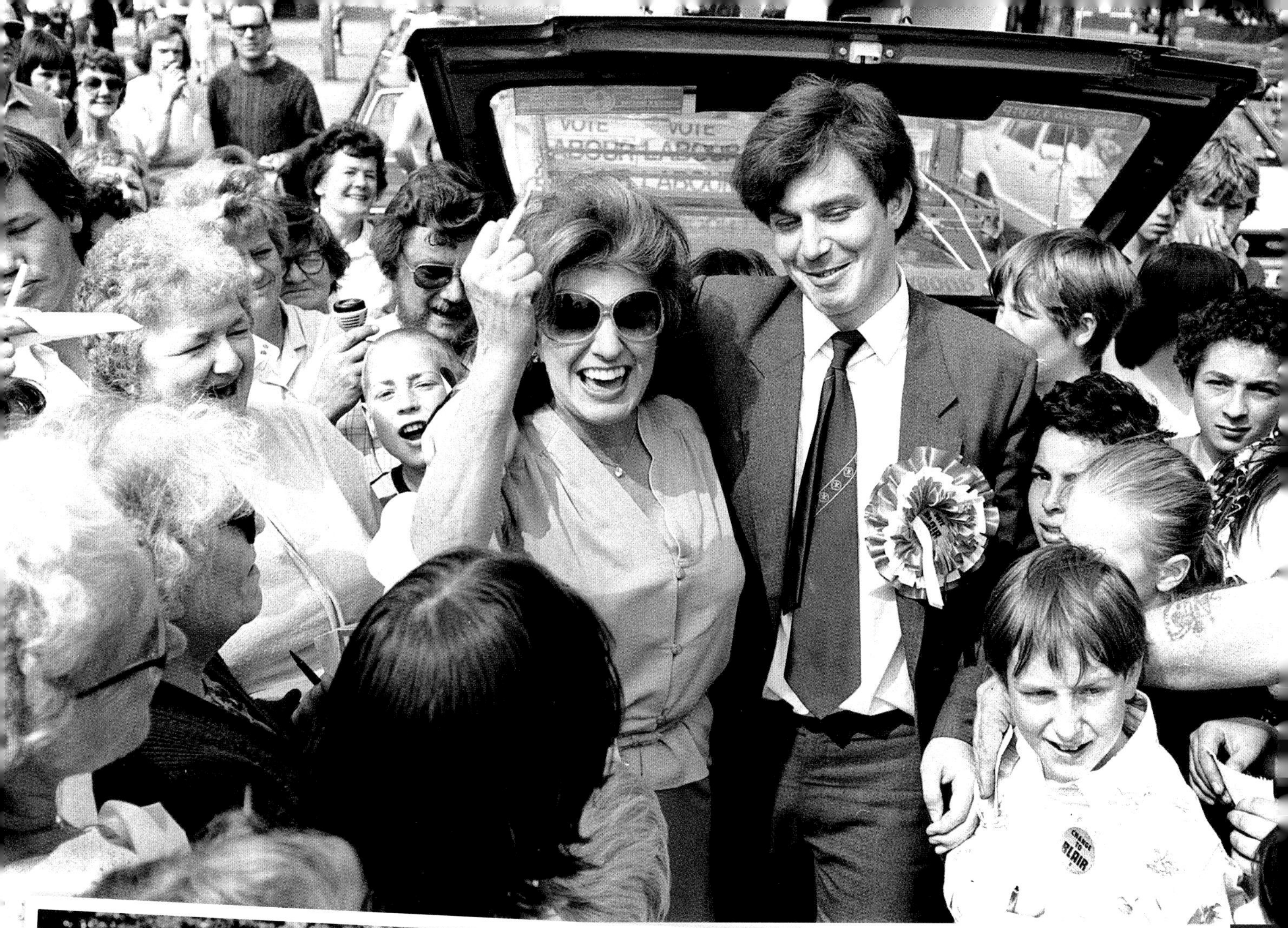

Above: Campaigning with Labour candidate, and future Prime Minister, Tony Blair during the Slough by-election in May 1982. Blair lost, but was elected in Sedgefield a year later during the General Election. Pat is shown (left) canvassing for him again with her then boyfriend (and future husband) Anthony Booth, plus his daughter Cherie

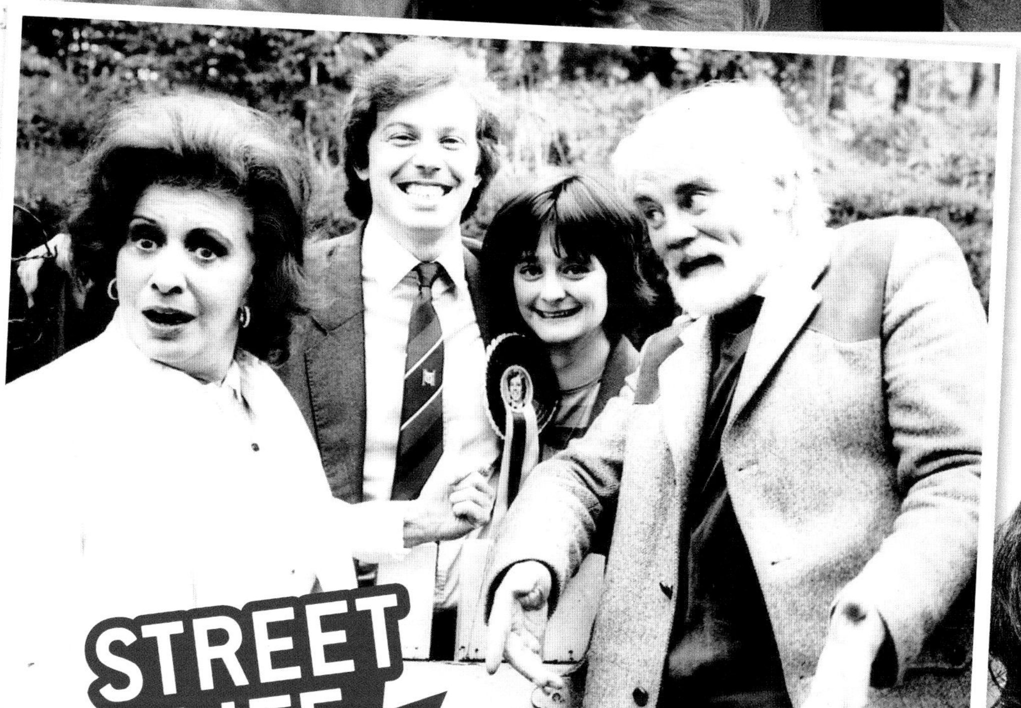

STREET LIFE

The show was originally called Florizel Street. It was changed when somebody said it sounded like a disinfectant

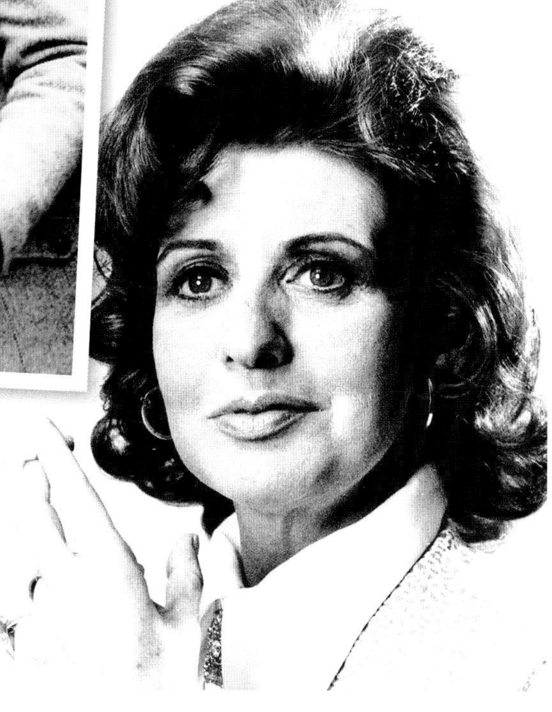

Right: A trademark character pose, February 1977

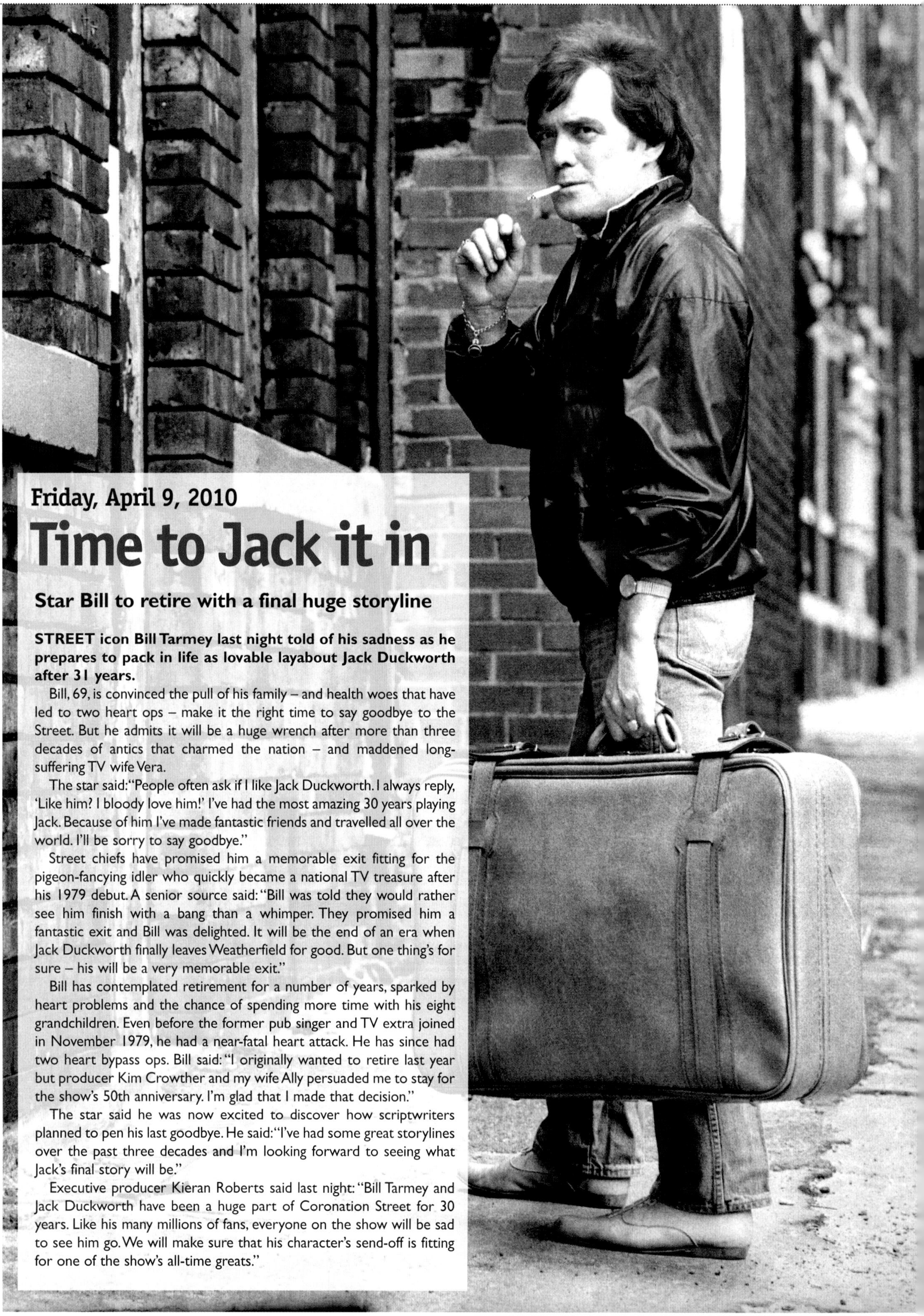

Friday, April 9, 2010

Time to Jack it in

Star Bill to retire with a final huge storyline

STREET icon Bill Tarmey last night told of his sadness as he prepares to pack in life as lovable layabout Jack Duckworth after 31 years.

Bill, 69, is convinced the pull of his family – and health woes that have led to two heart ops – make it the right time to say goodbye to the Street. But he admits it will be a huge wrench after more than three decades of antics that charmed the nation – and maddened long-suffering TV wife Vera.

The star said: "People often ask if I like Jack Duckworth. I always reply, 'Like him? I bloody love him!' I've had the most amazing 30 years playing Jack. Because of him I've made fantastic friends and travelled all over the world. I'll be sorry to say goodbye."

Street chiefs have promised him a memorable exit fitting for the pigeon-fancying idler who quickly became a national TV treasure after his 1979 debut. A senior source said: "Bill was told they would rather see him finish with a bang than a whimper. They promised him a fantastic exit and Bill was delighted. It will be the end of an era when Jack Duckworth finally leaves Weatherfield for good. But one thing's for sure – his will be a very memorable exit."

Bill has contemplated retirement for a number of years, sparked by heart problems and the chance of spending more time with his eight grandchildren. Even before the former pub singer and TV extra joined in November 1979, he had a near-fatal heart attack. He has since had two heart bypass ops. Bill said: "I originally wanted to retire last year but producer Kim Crowther and my wife Ally persuaded me to stay for the show's 50th anniversary. I'm glad that I made that decision."

The star said he was now excited to discover how scriptwriters planned to pen his last goodbye. He said: "I've had some great storylines over the past three decades and I'm looking forward to seeing what Jack's final story will be."

Executive producer Kieran Roberts said last night: "Bill Tarmey and Jack Duckworth have been a huge part of Coronation Street for 30 years. Like his many millions of fans, everyone on the show will be sad to see him go. We will make sure that his character's send-off is fitting for one of the show's all-time greats."

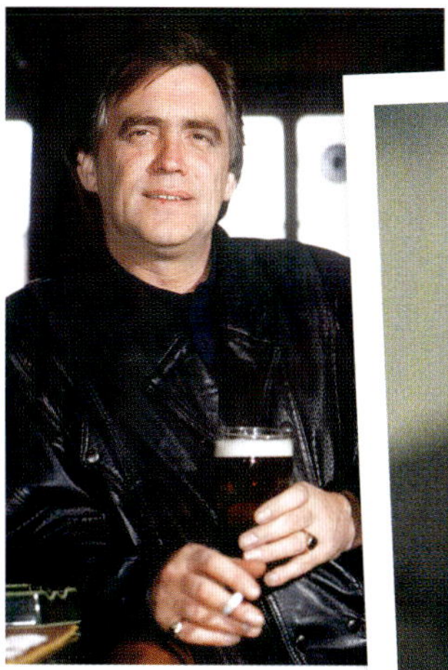

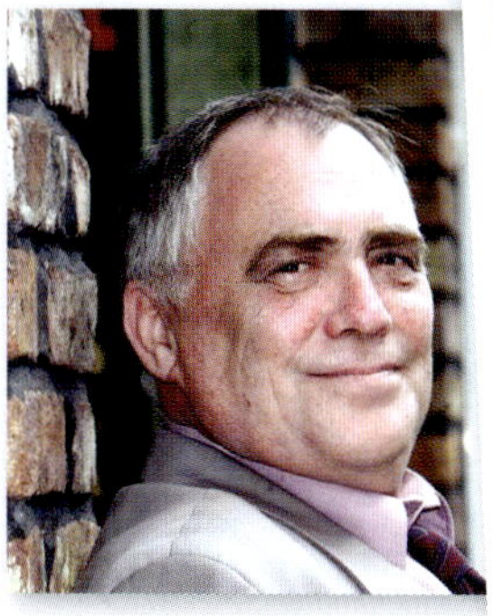

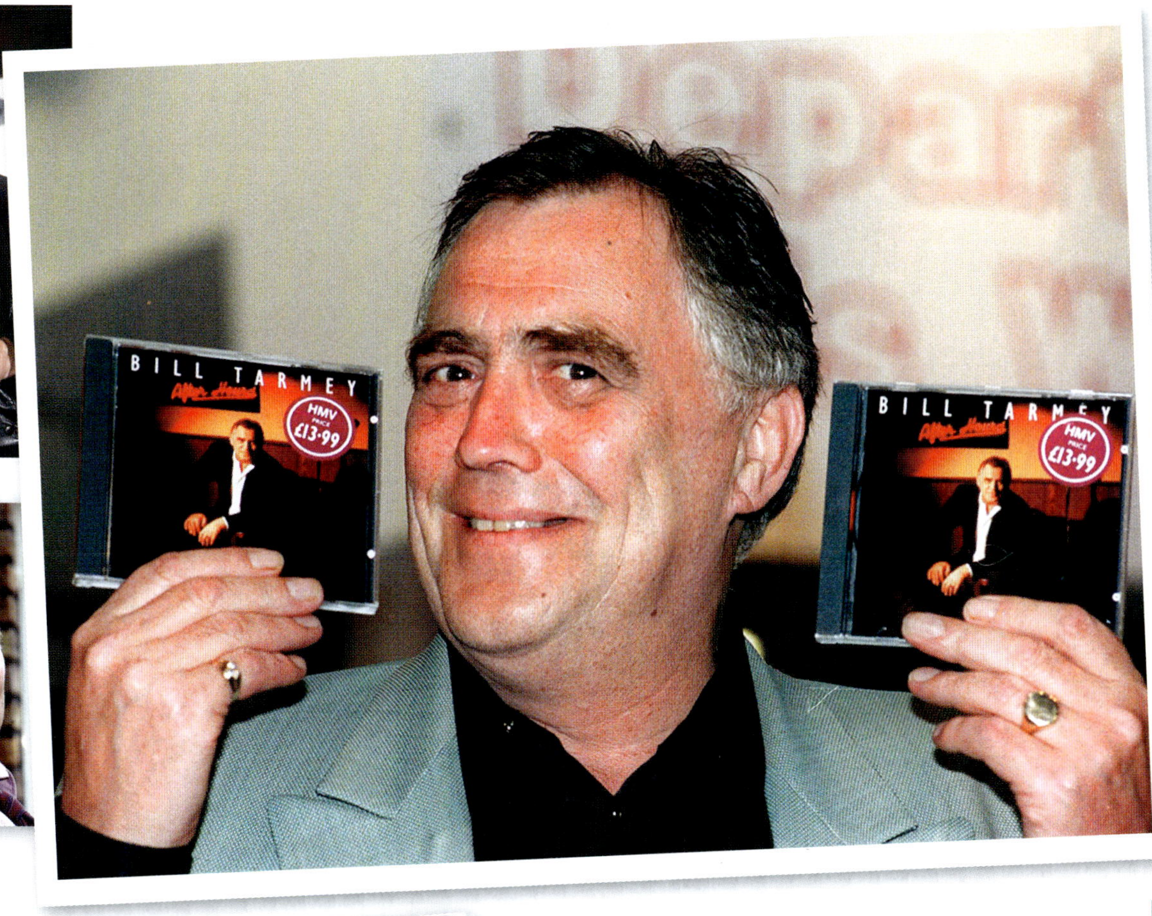

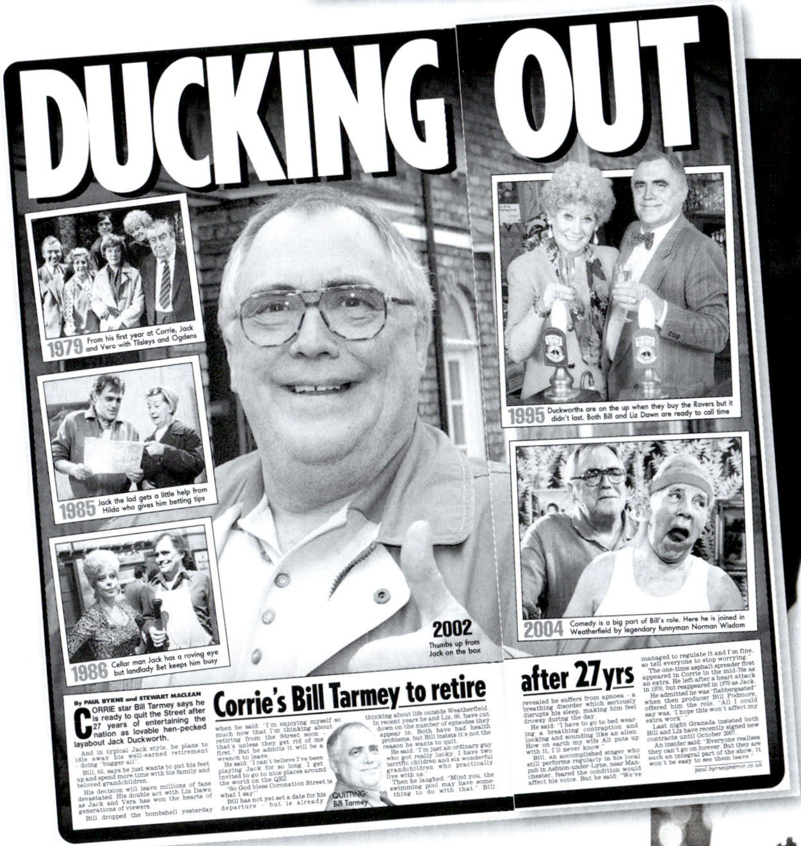

DUCKING OUT

1979 From his first year at Corrie, Jack and Vera with Tilsleys and Ogdens

1985 Jack the lad gets a little help from Hilda who gives him betting tips

1986 Cellar man Jack has a roving eye but landlady Bet keeps him busy

2002 Thumbs up from Jack on the box

1995 Duckworths are on the up when they buy the Rovers but it didn't last. Both Bill and Liz Dawn are ready to call time

2004 Comedy is a big part of Bill's role. Here he is joined in Weatherfield by legendary funnyman Norman Wisdom

Corrie's Bill Tarmey to retire after 27yrs

By PAUL BYRNE and STEWART MACLEAN

CORRIE star Bill Tarmey says he is ready to quit the Street after 27 years of entertaining the nation as lovable hen-pecked layabout Jack Duckworth.

And in typical Jack style, he plans to idle away his well-earned retirement - doing "bugger all".

Bill, 65, says he just wants to put his feet up and spend more time with his family and beloved grandchildren.

His decision will leave millions of fans devastated. His double act with Liz Dawn as Jack and Vera has won the hearts of generations of viewers.

Bill dropped the bombshell yesterday when he said: "I'm enjoying myself so much now that I'm thinking about retiring from the Street soon - that's unless they get rid of me first." But he admits it will be a wrench to leave.

He said: "I can't believe I've been playing Jack for so long. I get invited to go to nice places around the world on the QE2.

"So God bless Coronation Street is what I say!"

Bill has not yet set a date for his departure - but is already thinking about life outside Weatherfield.

In recent years he and Liz, 66, have cut down on the number of episodes they appear in. Both have had health problems, but Bill insists it's not the reason he wants to quit.

He said: "I'm just an ordinary guy who got really lucky. I have two terrific children and six wonderful grandchildren who practically live with us."

Then he laughed: "Mind you, the swimming pool may have something to do with that." Bill revealed he suffers from apnoea - a breathing disorder which seriously disrupts his sleep, making him feel drowsy during the day.

He said: "I have to go to bed wearing a breathing contraption and looking and sounding like an alien. How on earth my wife Ali puts up with it, I'll never know."

Bill, an accomplished singer who still performs regularly in his local pub in Ashton-under-Lyne, near Manchester, feared the condition would affect his voice. But he said: "We've managed to regulate it and I'm fine, so tell everyone to stop worrying."

The one-time asphalt spreader first appeared in Corrie in the mid-70s as an extra. He left after a heart attack in 1976, but reappeared in 1979 as Jack.

He admitted he was "flabbergasted" when then producer Bill Podmore offered him the role. "All I could say was, 'I hope this won't affect my extra work'."

Last night Granada insisted both Bill and Liz have recently signed new contracts until October 2007.

An insider said: "Everyone realises they can't go on forever. But they are such an integral part of the show, it won't be easy to see them leave."

paul.byrne@mirror.co.uk

QUITTING: Bill Tarmey

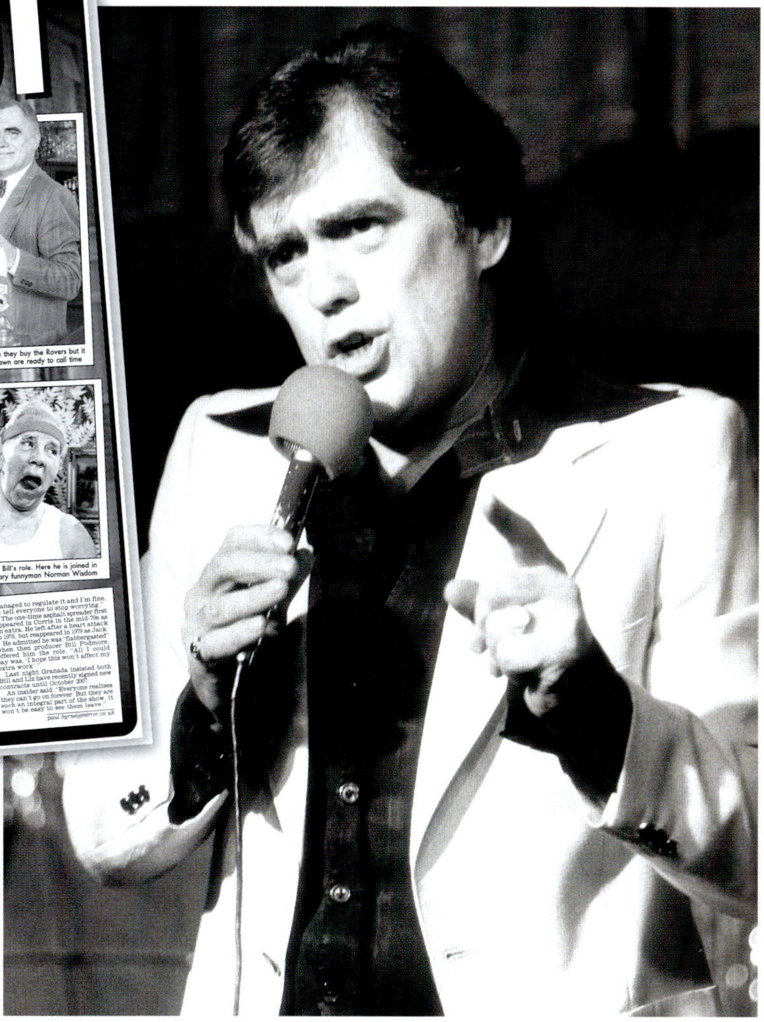

Above: Bill Tarmey, who played Jack, has released several albums and is seen with microphone in hand while performing in Leeds in March 1983 (right)

Right: Making a point to Rita in January 1981

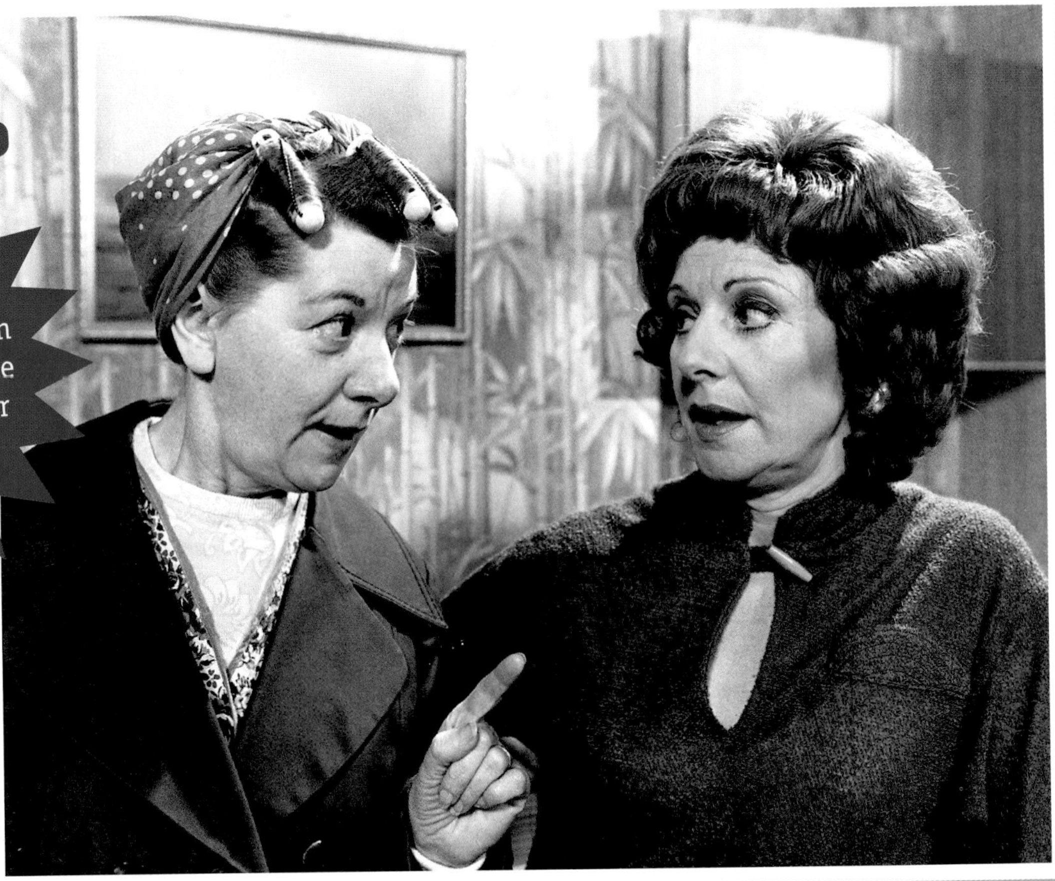

STREET LIFE

Hilda Ogden was chosen by the Task Force in the South Atlantic as their pin-up during the Falklands War

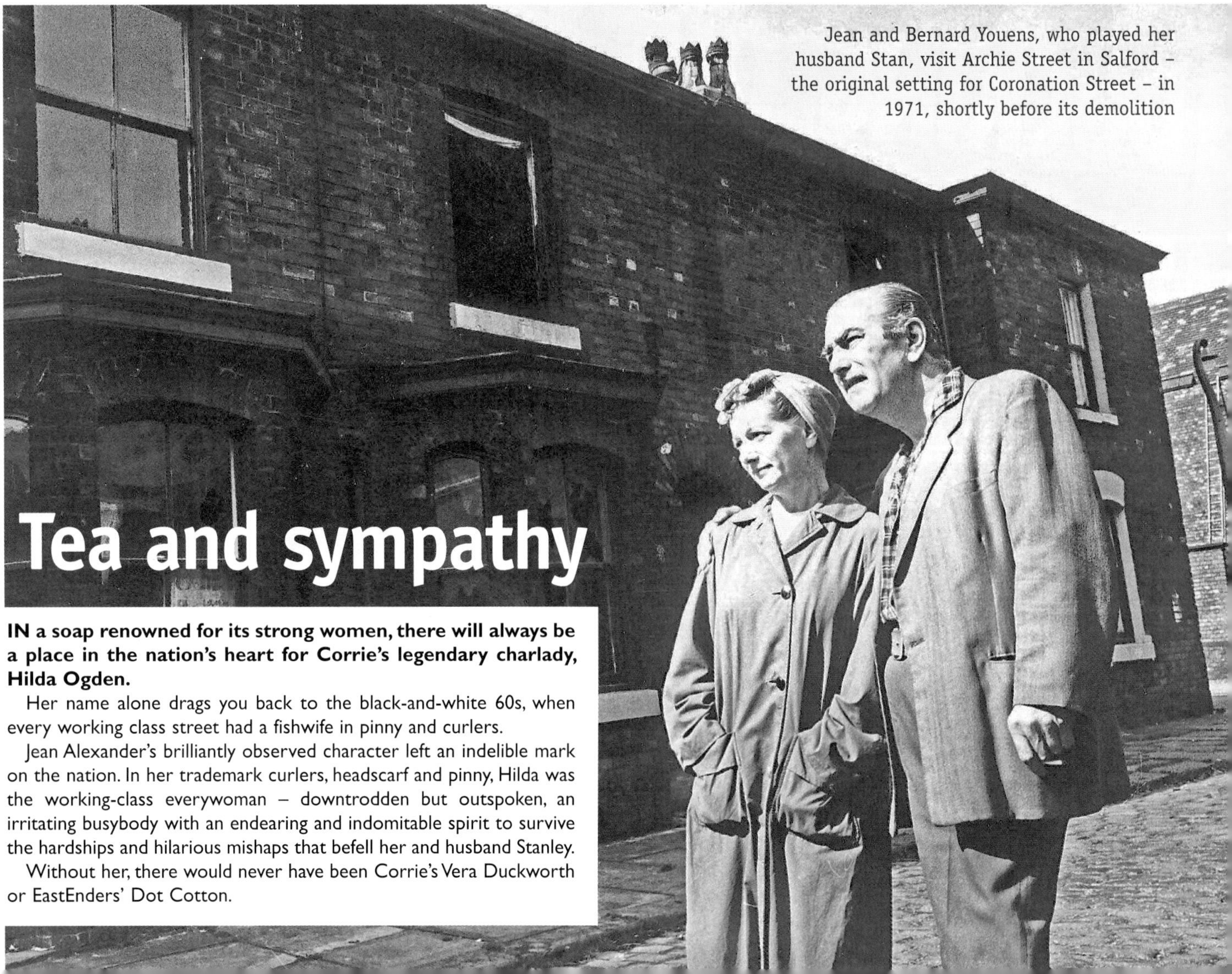

Jean and Bernard Youens, who played her husband Stan, visit Archie Street in Salford – the original setting for Coronation Street – in 1971, shortly before its demolition

Tea and sympathy

IN a soap renowned for its strong women, there will always be a place in the nation's heart for Corrie's legendary charlady, Hilda Ogden.

Her name alone drags you back to the black-and-white 60s, when every working class street had a fishwife in pinny and curlers.

Jean Alexander's brilliantly observed character left an indelible mark on the nation. In her trademark curlers, headscarf and pinny, Hilda was the working-class everywoman – downtrodden but outspoken, an irritating busybody with an endearing and indomitable spirit to survive the hardships and hilarious mishaps that befell her and husband Stanley.

Without her, there would never have been Corrie's Vera Duckworth or EastEnders' Dot Cotton.

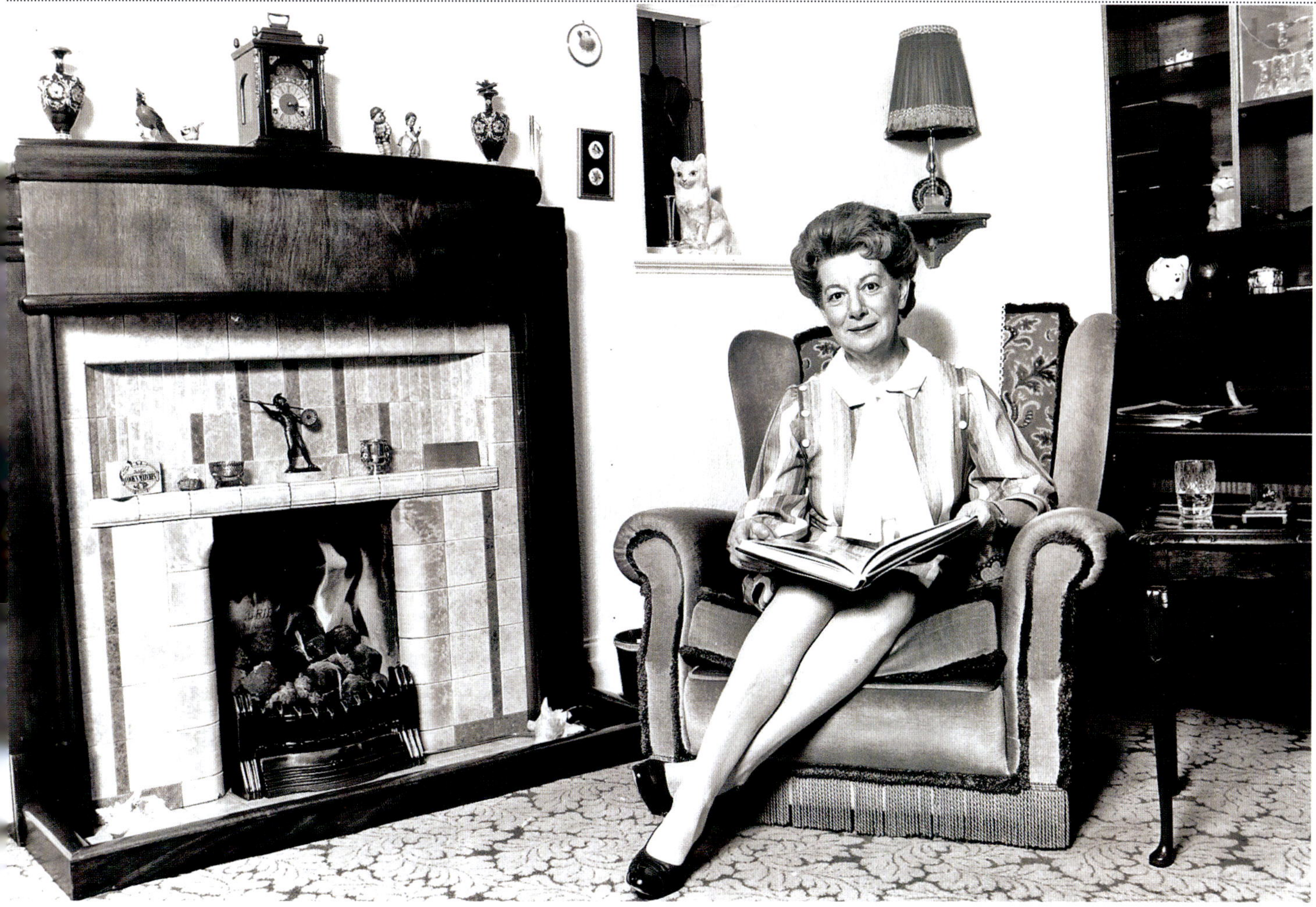

Above: Pictured at home in December 1987, the month that Hilda said goodbye to the Street

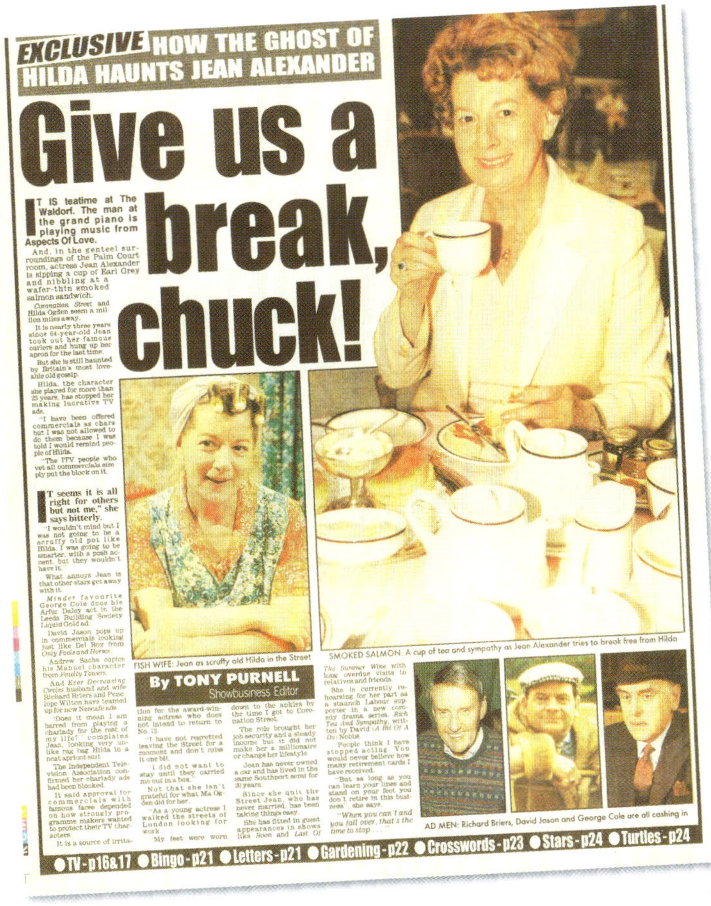

EXCLUSIVE HOW THE GHOST OF HILDA HAUNTS JEAN ALEXANDER

Give us a break, chuck!

IT IS teatime at The Waldorf. The man at the grand piano is playing music from Aspects Of Love.

And, in the genteel surroundings of the Palm Court room, actress Jean Alexander is sipping a cup of Earl Grey and nibbling at a wafer-thin smoked salmon sandwich.

Coronation Street and Hilda Ogden seem a million miles away.

It is nearly three years since 64-year-old Jean took out her famous curlers and hung up her apron for the last time.

But she is still haunted by Britain's most loveable old gossip.

Hilda, the character she played for more than 23 years, has stopped her making lucrative TV ads.

"I have been offered commercials as chars but I was not allowed to do them because I was told I would remind people of Hilda.

"The ITV people who vet all commercials simply put the block on it.

IT seems it is all right for others but not me," she says bitterly.

"I wouldn't mind but I was not going to be a scruffy old pot like Hilda. I was going to be smarter, with a posh accent, but they wouldn't have it."

What annoys Jean is that other stars get away with it.

Minder favourite George Cole does his Arfur Daley act in the Leeds Building Society Liquid Gold ad.

David Jason pops up in commercials looking just like Del Boy from *Only Fools and Horses*.

Andrew Sachs copies his Manuel character from *Fawlty Towers*.

And *Ever Decreasing Circles* husband and wife Richard Briers and Penelope Wilton have teamed up for new Nescafe ads.

"Does it mean I am barred from playing a charlady for the rest of my life?" complains Jean, looking very unlike rag bag Hilda in a neat apricot suit.

The Independent Television Association confirmed her charlady ads had been blocked.

It said approval for commercials with famous faces depended on how strongly programme makers wanted to protect their TV characters.

It is a source of irritation for the award-winning actress who does not intend to return to No. 13.

"I have not regretted leaving the Street for a moment and don't miss it one bit.

"I did not want to stay until they carried me out in a box."

Not that she isn't grateful for what Ma Ogden did for her.

"As a young actress I walked the streets of London looking for work.

"My feet were worn down to the ankles by the time I got to Coronation Street."

The role brought her job security and a steady income but it did not make her a millionaire or change her lifestyle.

Jean has never owned a car and has lived in the same Southport semi for 20 years.

Since she quit the Street Jean, who has never married, has been taking things easy.

She has fitted in guest appearances in shows like *Boon* and *Last Of The Summer Wine* with long overdue visits to relatives and friends.

She is currently rehearsing for her part as a staunch Labour supporter in a new comedy drama series, *Rich Tea And Sympathy*, written by David (*A Bit Of A Do*) Nobbs.

"People think I have stopped acting. You would never believe how many retirement cards I have received.

"But as long as you can learn your lines and stand on your feet you don't retire in this business", she says.

"When you can't and you fall over, that's the time to stop . . ."

By TONY PURNELL
Showbusiness Editor

FISH WIFE: Jean as scruffy old Hilda in the Street

SMOKED SALMON: A cup of tea and sympathy as Jean Alexander tries to break free from Hilda

AD MEN: Richard Briers, David Jason and George Cole are all cashing in

●TV-p16&17 ●Bingo-p21 ●Letters-p21 ●Gardening-p22 ●Crosswords-p23 ●Stars-p24 ●Turtles-p24

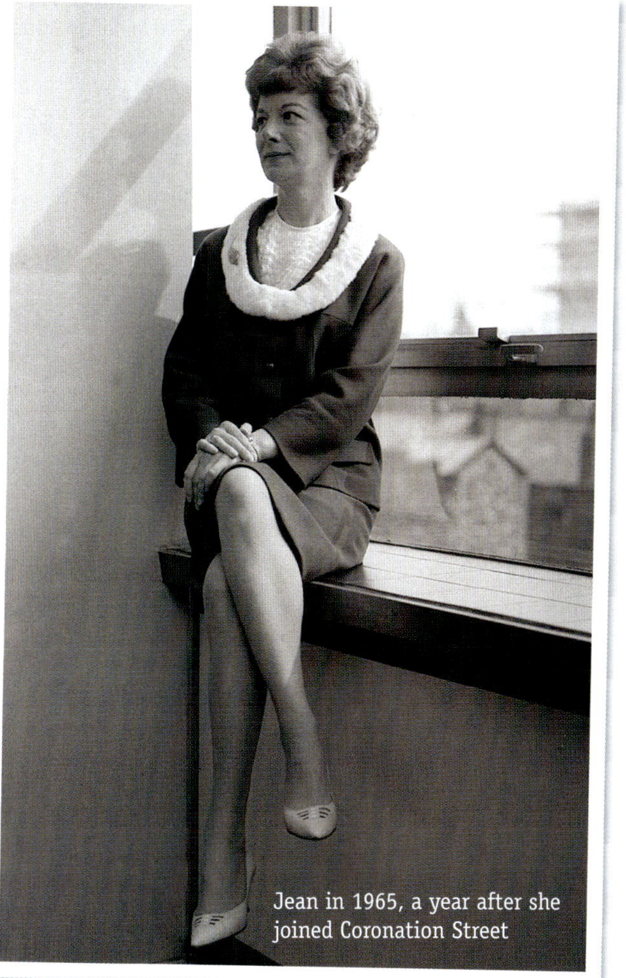

Jean in 1965, a year after she joined Coronation Street

Tuesday, March 31, 1998

Don't panic . . . Deirdre gets out in three months

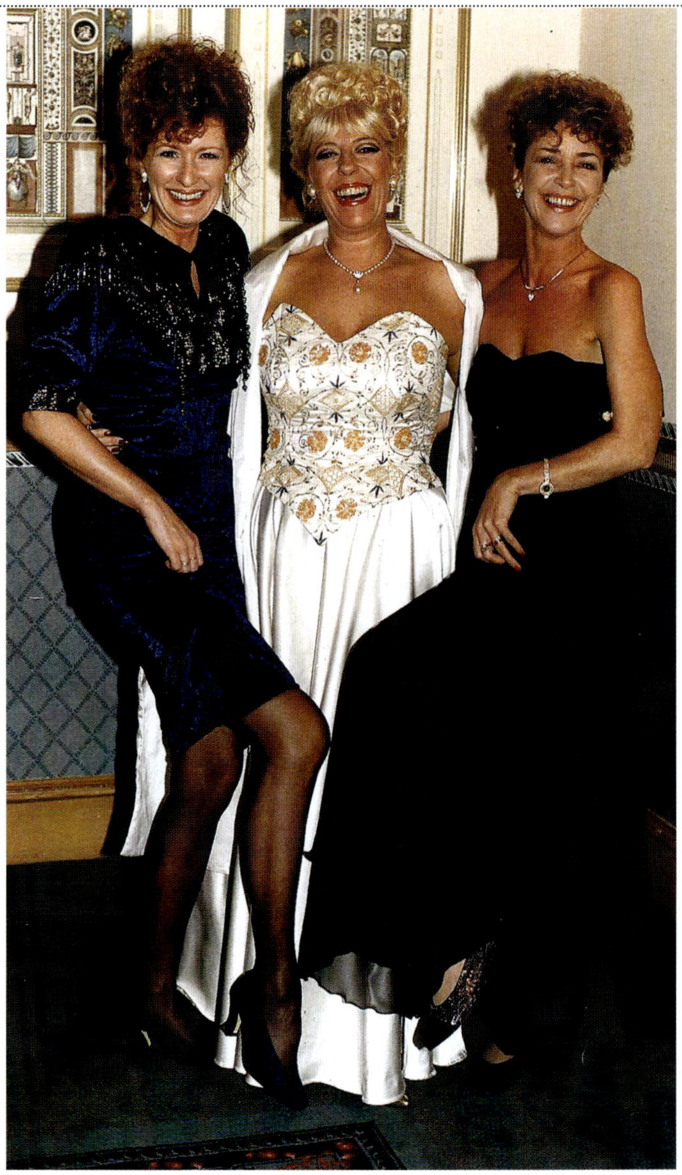

Above: Anne Kirkbride, right, with co-stars Beverley Callard and Julie Goodyear. Below, fighting a council election campaign against Alf Roberts in 1987

RELAX, Coronation Street fans – jailed Deirdre Rachid will soon walk free.

The Mirror can today reassure millions of worried viewers that justice will be done within three months. The nation went into shock on Sunday night when luckless Deirdre was sentenced to 18 months for mortgage and credit card fraud.

Granada's phone lines were swamped by tearful viewers. And Labour MP Fraser Kemp vowed to launch a 'Free The Weatherfield One' campaign. The dramatic episode, watched by an audience of about 19 million, saw Deirdre – actress Anne Kirkbride – draw all the short straws.

Her ex-lover Jon Lindsay, bogus airline pilot and the real crook, duped the judge and jury and escaped with a suspended sentence. Poor Deirdre was close to fainting as she was led from the dock and into a white prison van to begin her jail term.

The filthy stench of her tiny cell and being banged up with violent Jackie Dobbs, actress Margi Clarke, completed her misery.

But put away your hankies, folks – she'll be savouring freedom and sipping a gin and tonic in the Rovers by summertime.

In coming weeks viewers will see the wife of villain Lindsay become wracked with guilt. She goes to Ken Barlow to confess her husband's wrongdoings. Delighted Ken reckons he has enough for an appeal. And when the case goes to court again, relieved Deirdre walks free.

The soap's phone lines buzzed "red hot" for 90 minutes after Sunday's episode.

A Street insider said: "We expected some kind of response, but nothing like we received. We've always known there are people who think what happens in the Street is real, but this Deirdre business has taken the biscuit.

"Viewers are so wrapped up in it all that they are genuinely calling for her release – it's frightening."

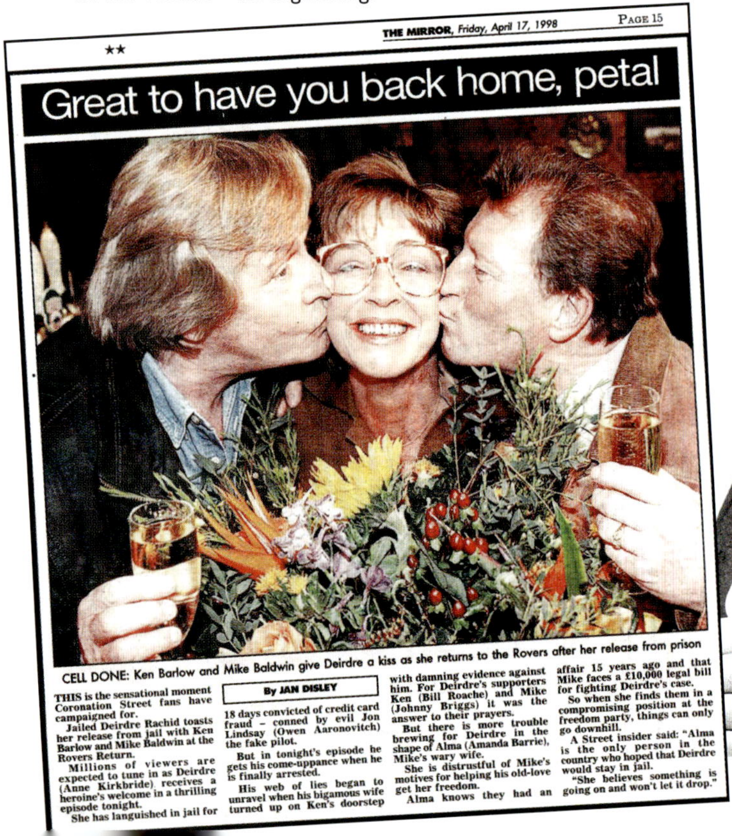

★★ THE MIRROR, Friday, April 17, 1998 PAGE 15

Great to have you back home, petal

CELL DONE: Ken Barlow and Mike Baldwin give Deirdre a kiss as she returns to the Rovers after her release from prison

By JAN DISLEY

THIS is the sensational moment Coronation Street fans have campaigned for.

Jailed Deirdre Rachid toasts her release from jail with Ken Barlow and Mike Baldwin at the Rovers Return.

Millions of viewers are expected to tune in as Deirdre (Anne Kirkbride) receives a heroine's welcome in a thrilling episode tonight.

She has languished in jail for 18 days convicted of credit card fraud – conned by evil Jon Lindsay (Owen Aaronovitch) the fake pilot.

But in tonight's episode he gets his come-uppance when he is finally arrested.

His web of lies began to unravel when his bigamous wife turned up on Ken's doorstep with damning evidence against him. For Deirdre's supporters Ken (Bill Roache) and Mike (Johnny Briggs) it was the answer to their prayers.

But there is more trouble brewing for Deirdre in the shape of Alma (Amanda Barrie), Mike's wary wife.

She is distrustful of Mike's motives for helping his old-love get her freedom.

Alma knows they had an affair 15 years ago and that Mike faces a £10,000 legal bill for fighting Deirdre's case.

So when she finds them in a compromising position at the freedom party, things can only go downhill.

A Street insider said: "Alma is the only person in the country who hoped that Deirdre would stay in jail.

"She believes something is going on and won't let it drop."

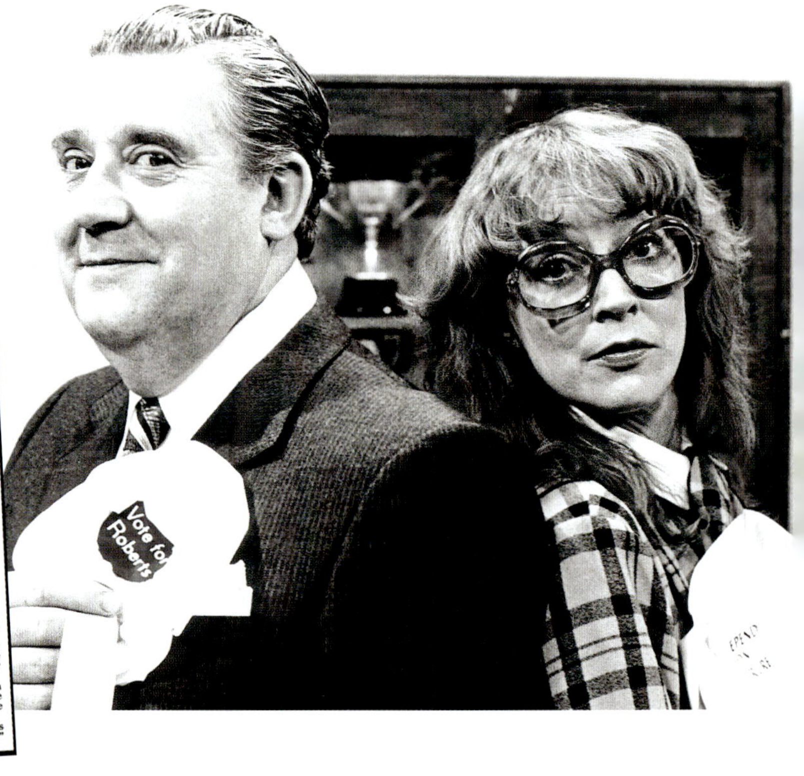

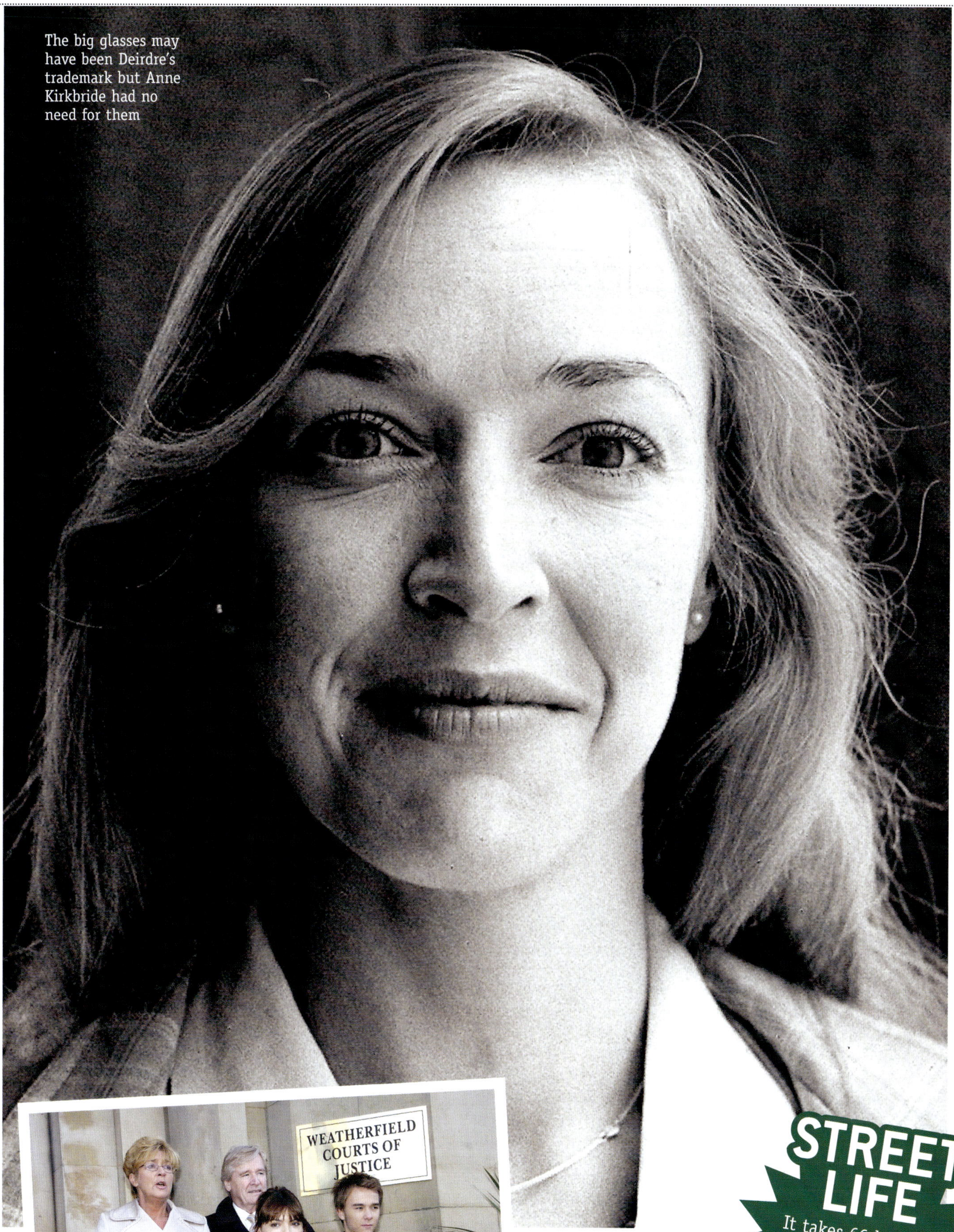

The big glasses may have been Deirdre's trademark but Anne Kirkbride had no need for them

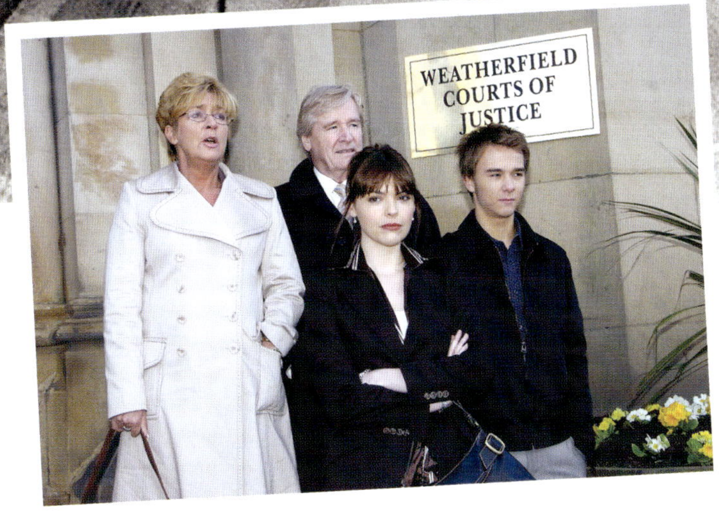

Left: With husband Ken Barlow during daughter Tracy's murder trial in 2007. David Platt joins them on the court steps

STREET LIFE

It takes 66 hours to make 5 episodes of Coronation Street. That's six days a week, 52 weeks of the year

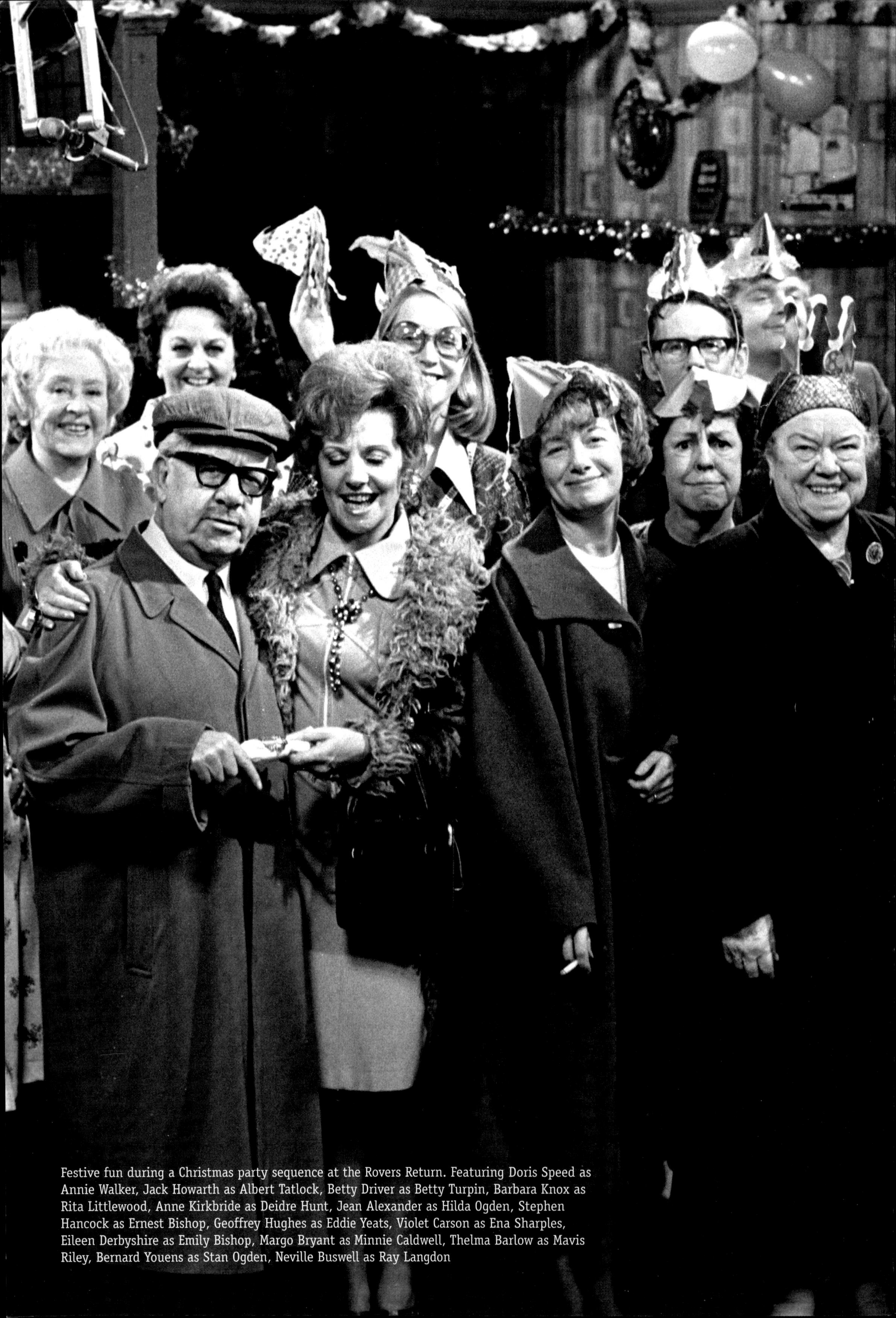

Festive fun during a Christmas party sequence at the Rovers Return. Featuring Doris Speed as Annie Walker, Jack Howarth as Albert Tatlock, Betty Driver as Betty Turpin, Barbara Knox as Rita Littlewood, Anne Kirkbride as Deidre Hunt, Jean Alexander as Hilda Ogden, Stephen Hancock as Ernest Bishop, Geoffrey Hughes as Eddie Yeats, Violet Carson as Ena Sharples, Eileen Derbyshire as Emily Bishop, Margo Bryant as Minnie Caldwell, Thelma Barlow as Mavis Riley, Bernard Youens as Stan Ogden, Neville Buswell as Ray Langdon

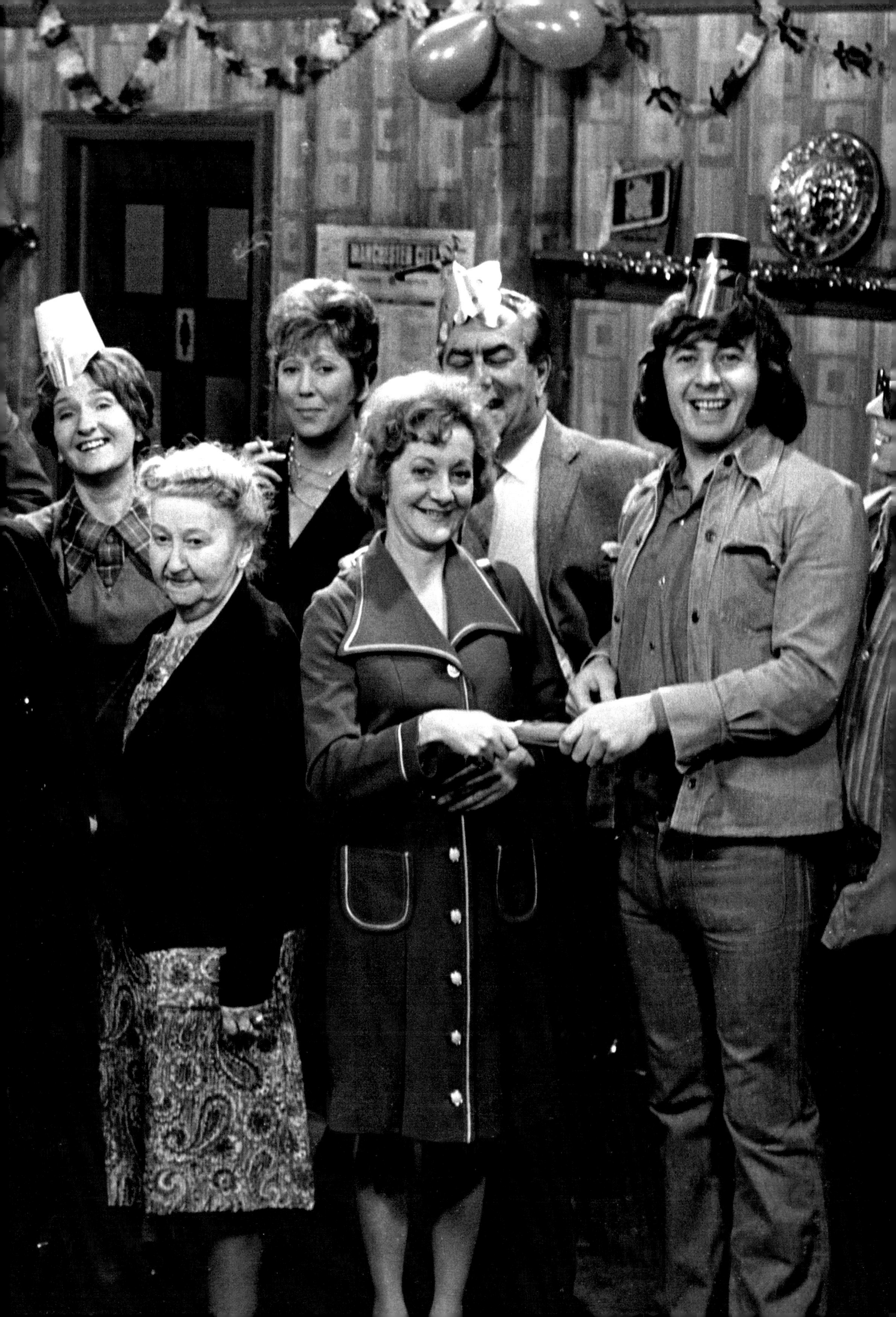

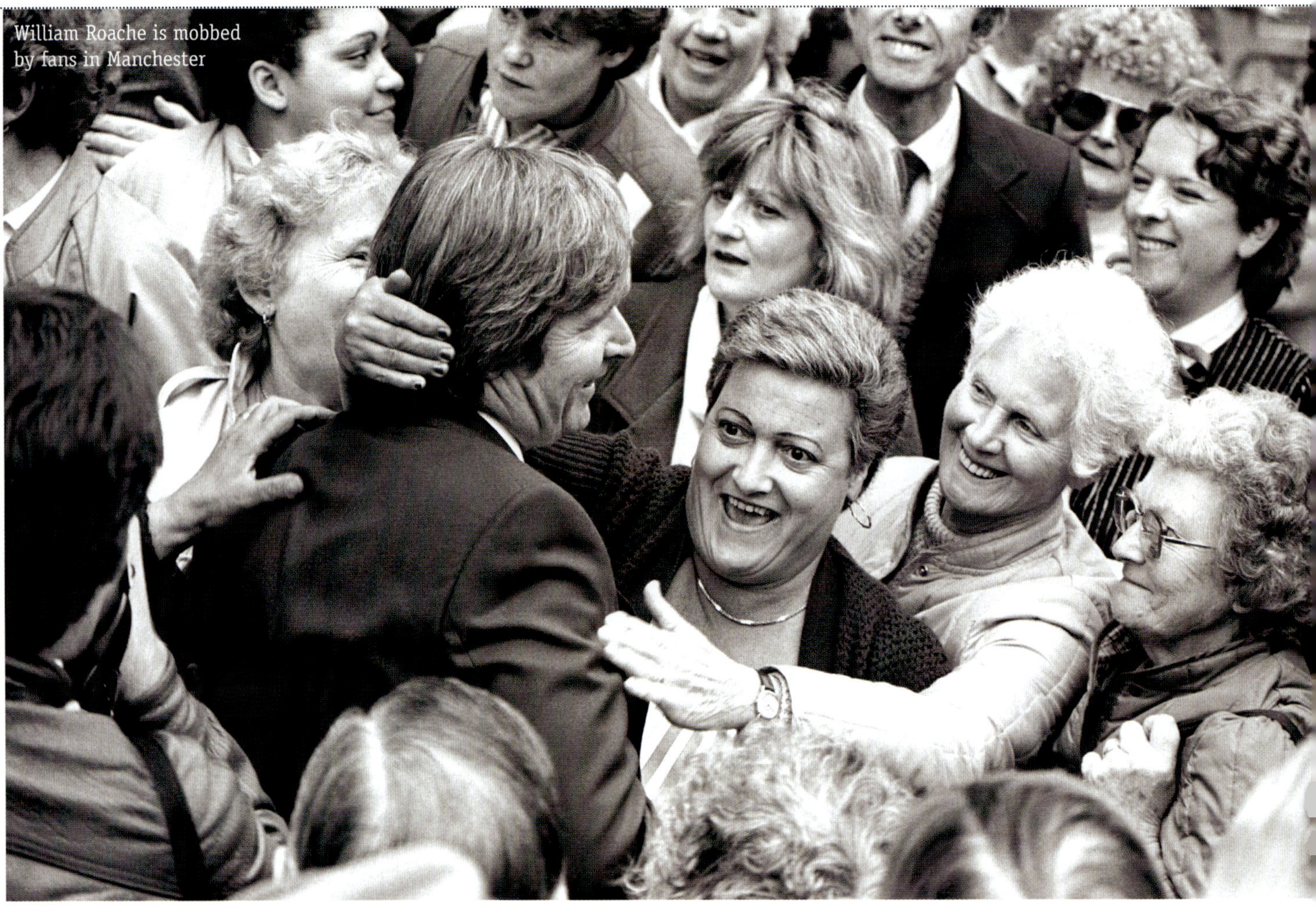
William Roache is mobbed by fans in Manchester

Thursday, April 15, 2010

The love of his life

27 women in 50 years and Ken Barlow is still up for more . . .

HE'S romanced nearly 30 women and notched up four marriages during his time on the cobbles. And despite nudging 80, Coronation Street legend Ken Barlow is not quite ready to say goodbye to his lothario image just yet.

Incredibly, actor William Roache, who has been in our living rooms for 50 years playing Ken, is begging scriptwriters to sex up his storylines even more. William, the only remaining character from the first episode in 1960, wants a racy romance to celebrate the soap's 50th anniversary this autumn.

"I thought it was great last year having a girlfriend, especially at my age. A few more would be great. I've lost count of romances I've had in the show not to mention the four weddings. The lovely Joanna Lumley being one of my girlfriends was a particular highlight.

"Not a bad life is it? Ken did misbehave last year with Stephanie Beacham. I'm pleased about that too. I love my job. I don't want to retire. While they want me, while I'm useful – I'd love to stay. With my dysfunctional family I'm still useful to the show. An alcoholic son, a murderess daughter . . . it's good drama."

Incredibly, he will be the world's longest-serving soap character this winter.

"There's a guy in New York in 'As The World Turns' who beats me by two months, but his show is not being commissioned this year. So I'll be in the Guinness Book of Records as longest-serving TV actor."

And the dad-of-four says of staying young: "I'm 78 this month. I don't exercise but I don't smoke or drink much. It's in the genes.

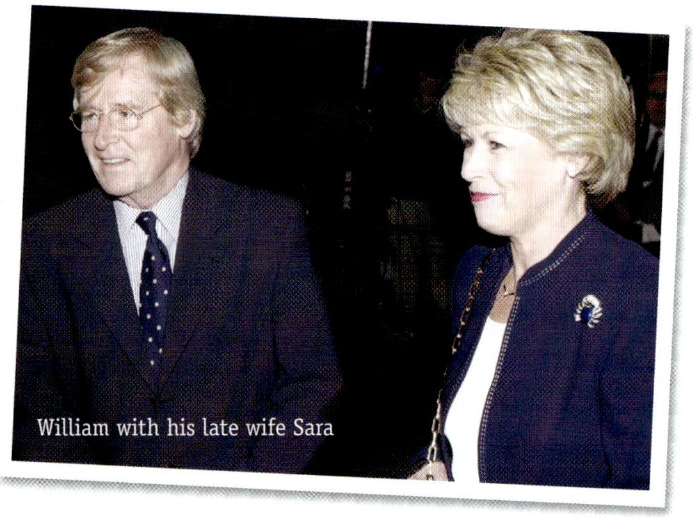
William with his late wife Sara

"However, I do like champagne. I'll celebrate my birthday with a glass or two and have dinner with my children."

It is surprising how upbeat he is, considering the tragedy he suffered last year. His wife Sara died suddenly at their home in Wilmslow, Cheshire, aged 58. Speaking softly, he said: "I'm just looking after the family, dealing with things, taking life as it comes. We're coping and life is going forward. I'm trying to get my two children settled in London.

"The fans are wonderful. People are very caring. I'd like to thank them all as I didn't manage to answer all the letters – there were a tremendous amount."

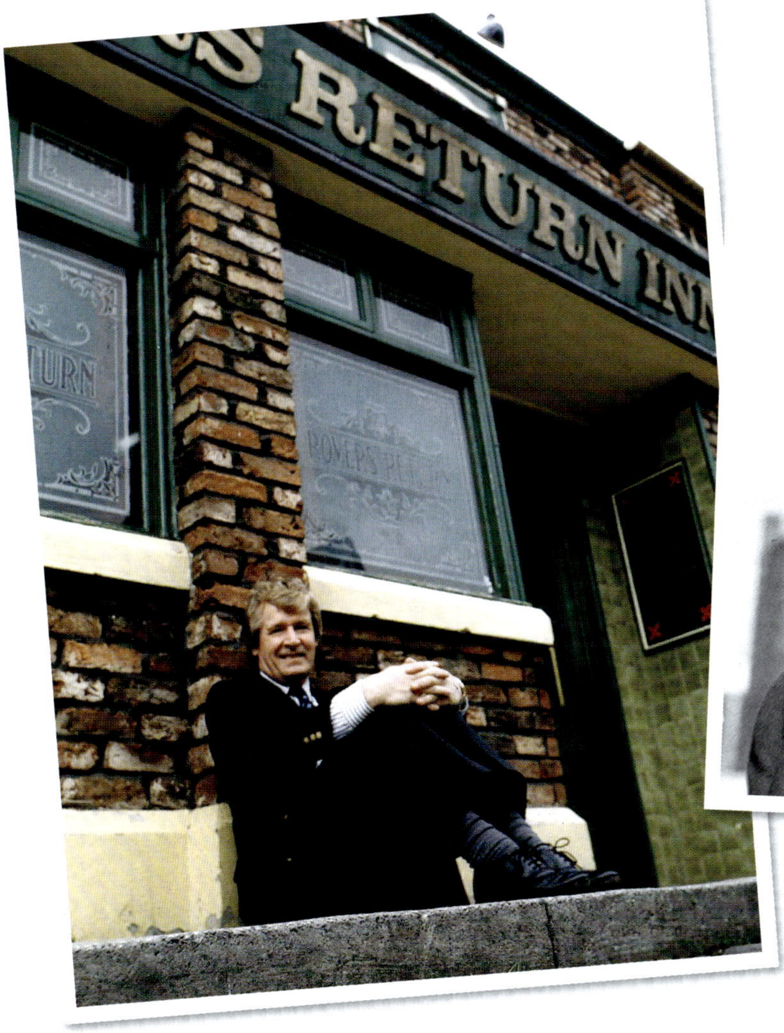

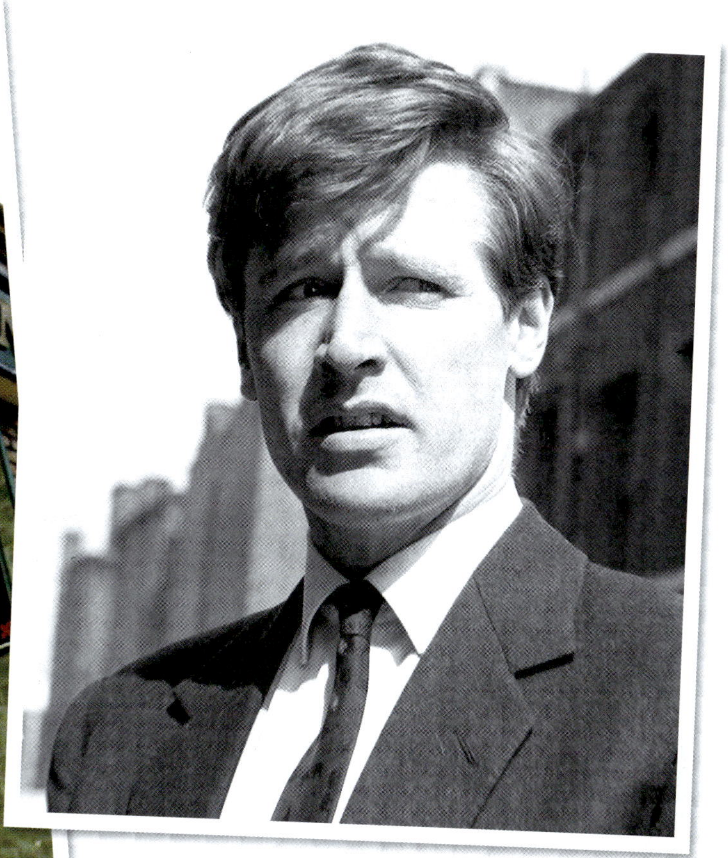

Above: Ken Barlow in an early episode of the soap
Below: On set in 2000, the Prince of Wales talks with Bill Roache and Jacqueline Pirie during the show's 40th anniversary celebrations

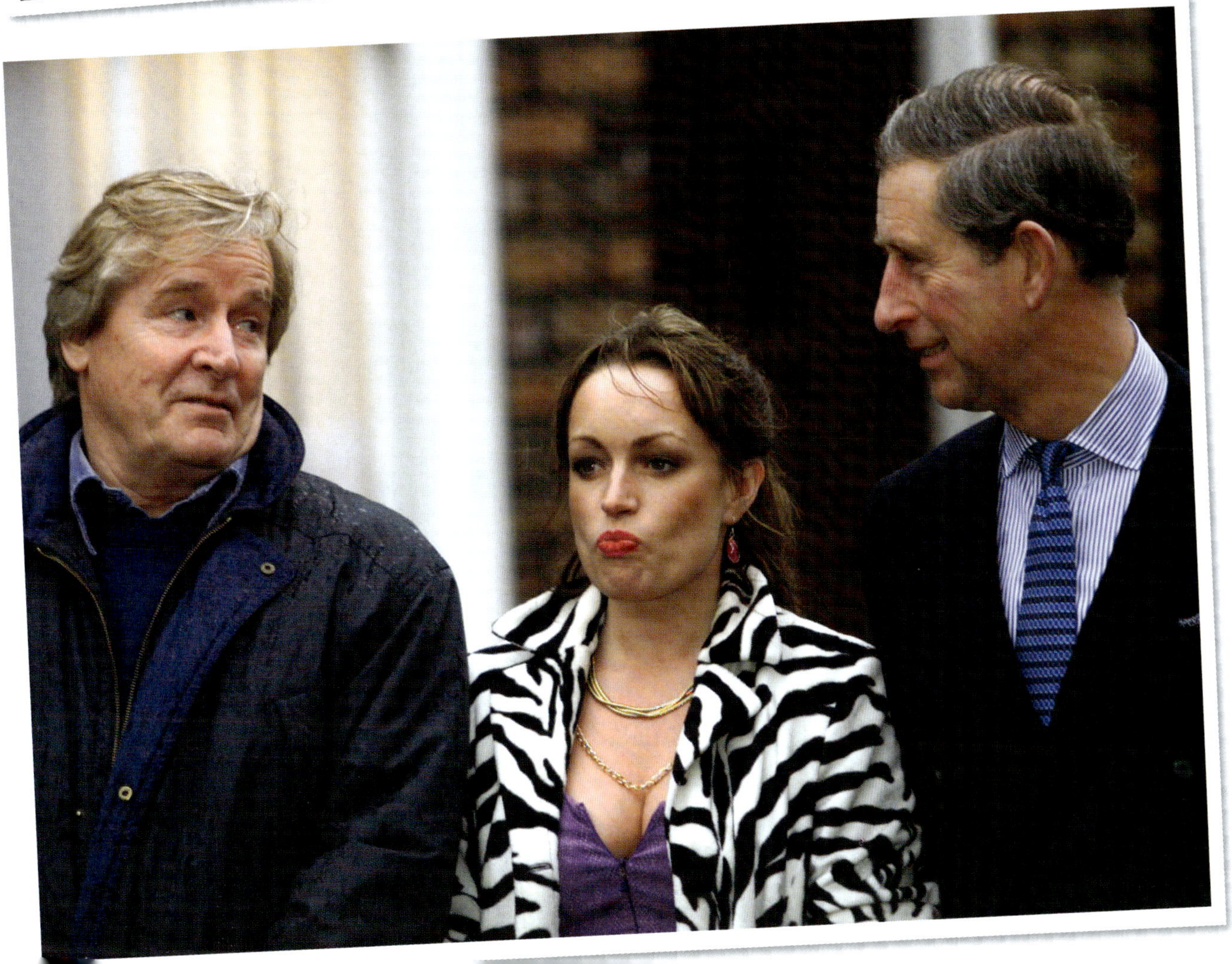

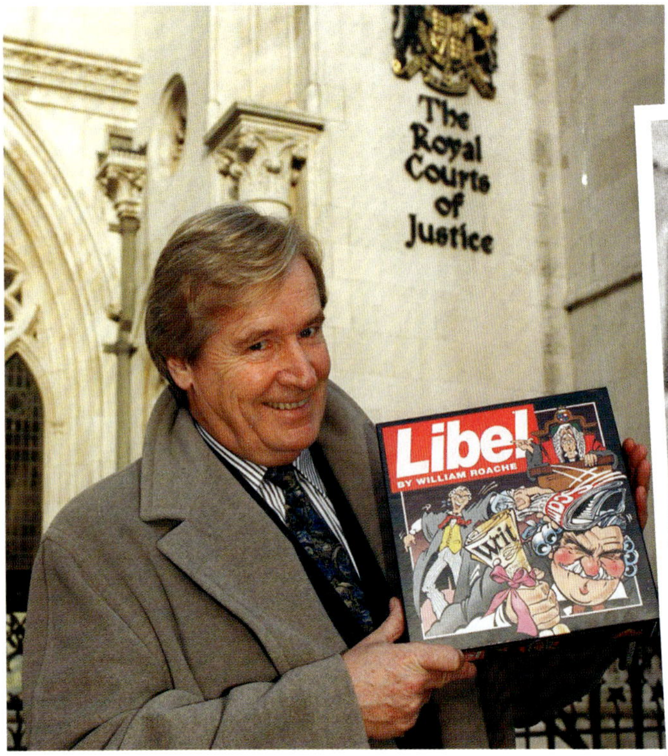
The Royal Courts of Justice
Libel
BY WILLIAM ROACHE
writ

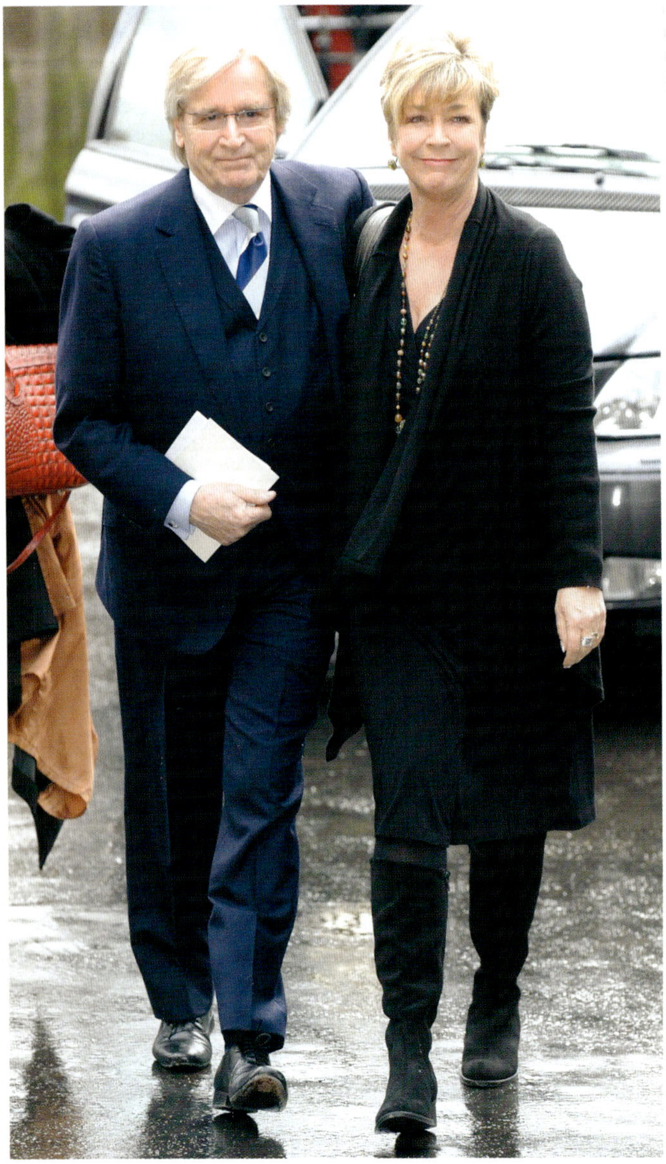

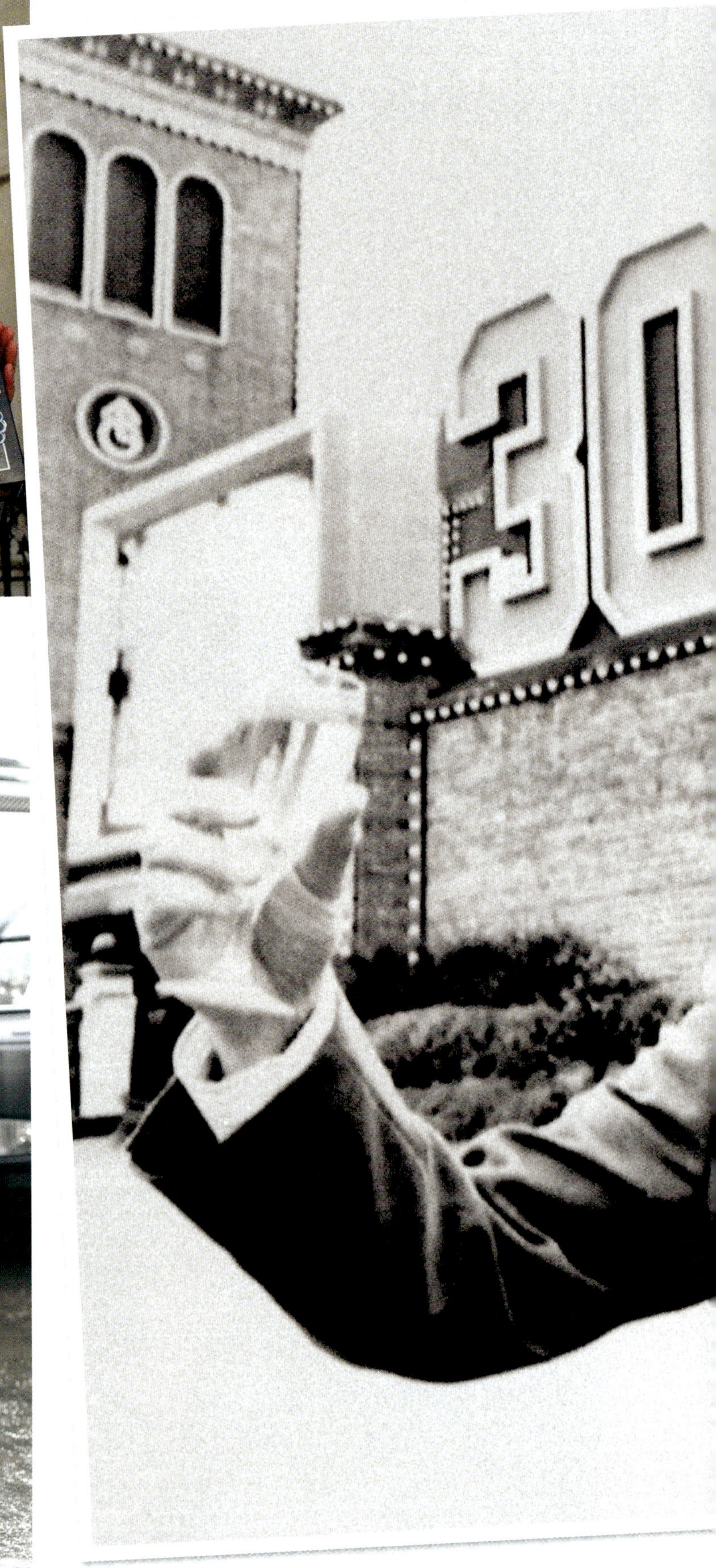
30

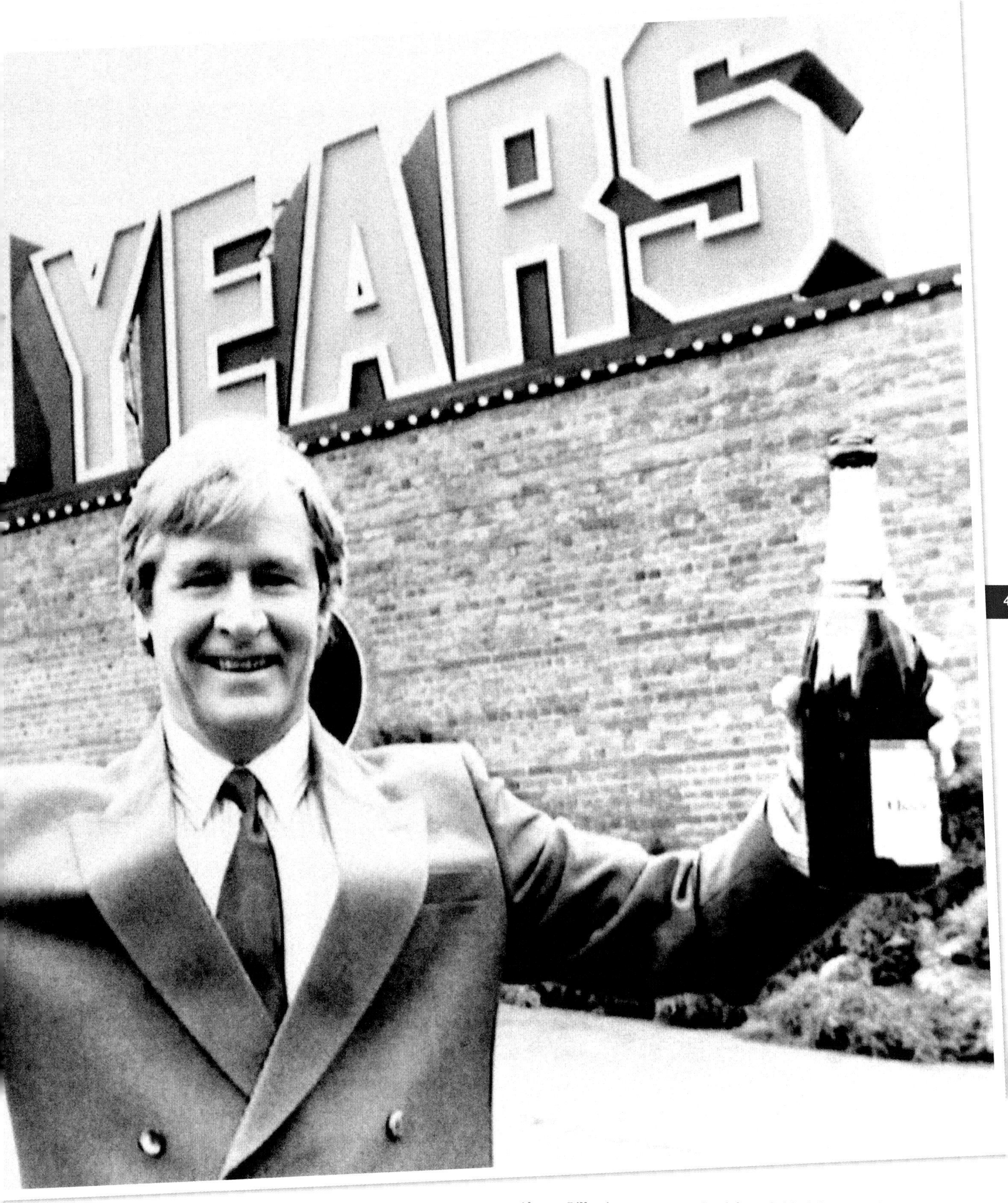

Above: Bill raises a toast to Corrie's 30th birthday outside the show's production studio in Manchester
Left: With his board game 'Libel', which he invented during his high-profile legal action against The Sun newspaper; pictured with Anne Kirkbride at Maggie Jones's memorial, Salford Cathedral

Johnny Briggs: My farewell story

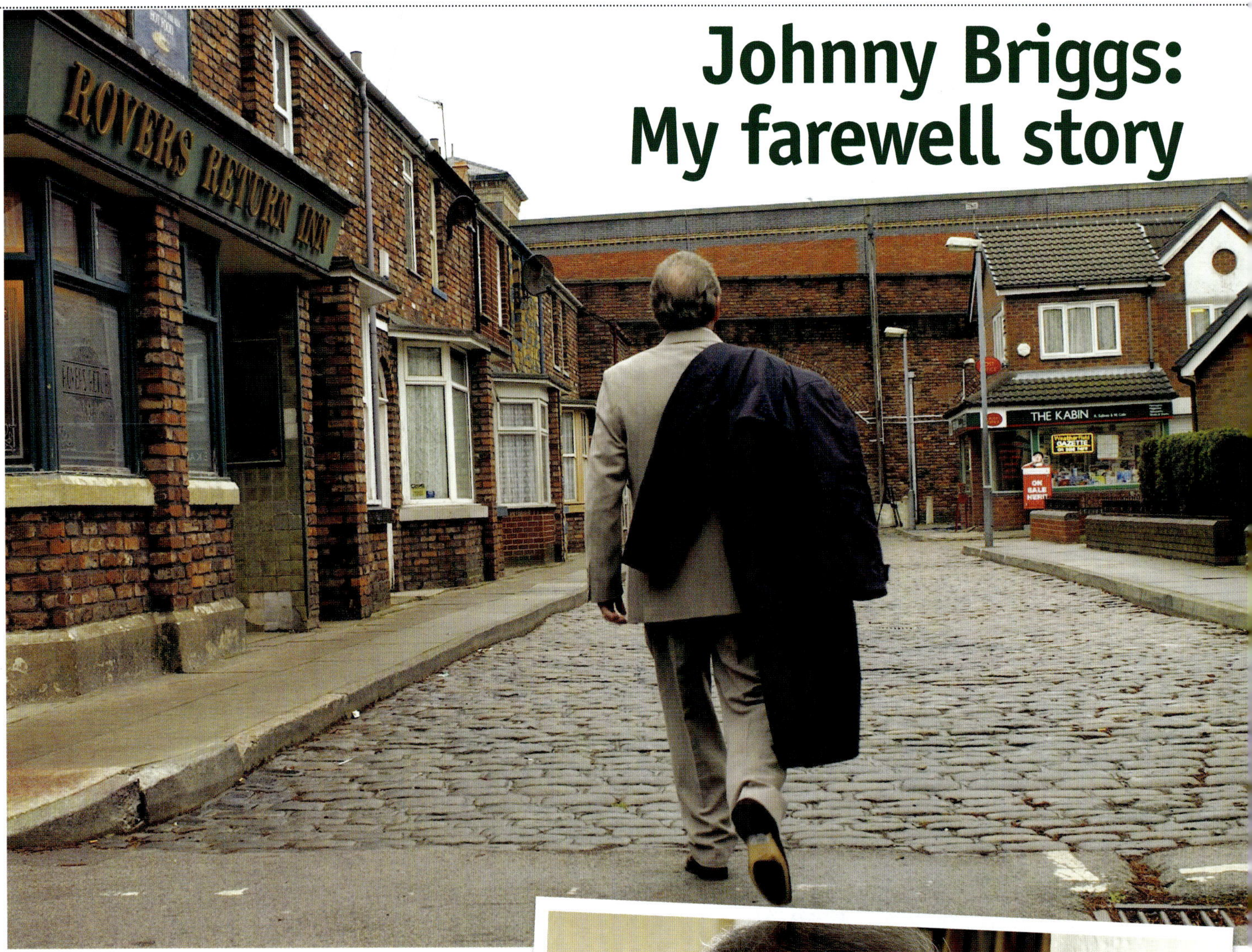

Monday, March 20, 2006

"Saying goodbye was one of the hardest things I've ever had to do."

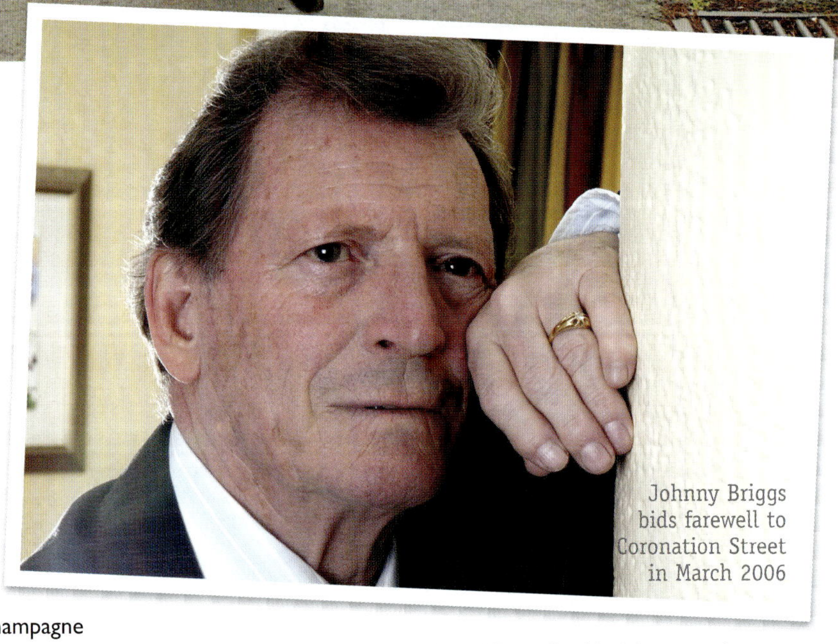

Johnny Briggs bids farewell to Coronation Street in March 2006

AS he stepped on to the cobbles for the final time, Johnny Briggs knew it was going to be an emotional day.

After 30 years playing Mike Baldwin, he had one last, harrowing scene to film.

Mike, the cockney factory boss who has been suffering from Alzheimer's disease, was about to close his eyes and fall unconscious into the arms of his daughter-in-law Frankie.

As the scene ended and Johnny looked up, he was stunned to see 150 cast and crew – including Street creator Tony Warren – gathered around him.

Led by Bill Roache, who has played Mike's arch-rival Ken Barlow for more than three decades, his colleagues had crept on set to mark his exit with a standing ovation and a champagne party.

Speaking to the Daily Mirror, the 70-year-old actor fights back tears as he says: "I was stunned and completely overwhelmed.

"I was overcome by all the love and affection. I hadn't expected to see anyone. But when I opened my eyes, all these people were there. There must have been about 150 – I've played to smaller audiences.

"Some of the crew are real tough guys and even they were struggling not to cry. I know I was weeping."

Around him friends, including Sally Whittaker, who plays Sally Webster, were crying too.

But the most emotional moment came when he got a text from his daughter Stephanie, 23, who told him: "Dear Daddy, I hope you're okay. One day I hope you're as proud of me as I am of you."

"So I wanted to say a few words but didn't get very far," he says. "I was too choked. It's been such a huge part of my life for so long I was bowled over by how I felt.

"Saying goodbye to Mike was one of the hardest things I've ever done."

Johnny never watches himself on TV – but for once he will join the millions of viewers glued to his final scenes as Mike passes away in his old rival Ken's arms next month.

And he'll drink to the character who made him a household name.

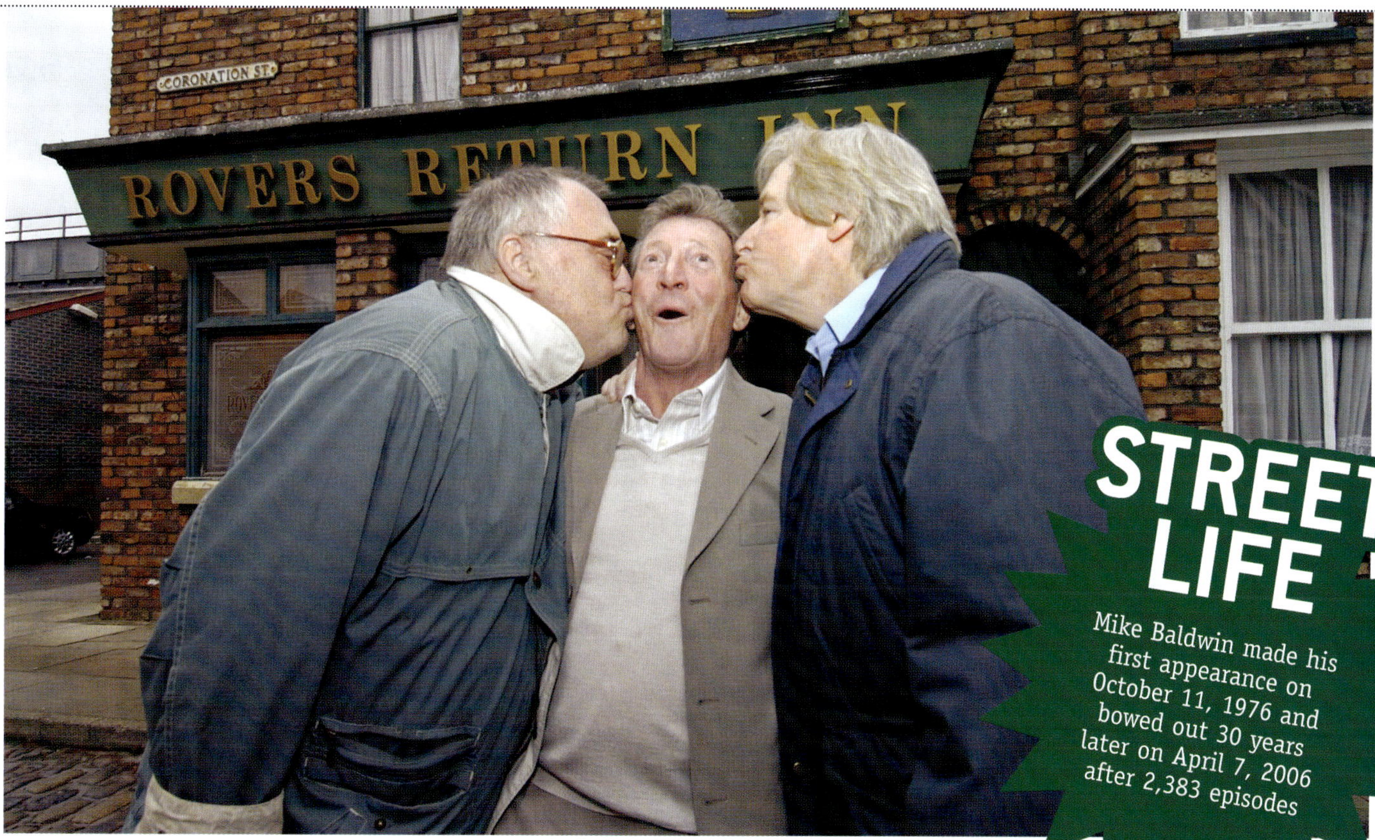

A fond farewell from Bill Tarmey (Jack) and Bill Roache (Ken)

STREET LIFE

Mike Baldwin made his first appearance on October 11, 1976 and bowed out 30 years later on April 7, 2006 after 2,383 episodes

After so long in the show Johnny agonised over his decision to leave. Finally, he asked bosses if he could go – as long as Mike went out in style.

"I asked if it was okay not to renew my contract," he says. "I didn't want to be talked into doing any longer than I wanted to.

"They asked me how I wanted Mike to go and I was very definite about it. I wanted to go out with a bang. I wanted a good storyline to end on and the Alzheimer's is the best I've ever done.

"Alzheimer's affects a lot of people, but equally it affects their families very hard. It is very distressing for everyone involved and we had to think about that when we were first formulating the idea."

Johnny's long stint on Coronation Street nearly didn't happen. He told producers an earlier role in Crossroads had left him never wanting do a soap again. He says: "They'd put me, a Londoner, in Crossroads to see if it would boost the ratings and it sent them flying up, so they decided to do the same in Coronation Street.

"They phoned me up and asked me to do three months.

"When I asked what Mike was like, they said: 'Just be yourself.' Men want to be him and women want to be with him."

Assuming he didn't want to stay on after his initial stint, bosses almost let him go.

"When I explained I loved it, the producer said: 'You berk, why didn't you tell us?' So I signed up for another three months – and ended up staying for 30 years."

Soon he was starring alongside Street greats Ena Sharples, Elsie Tanner and Albert Tatlock. He has charmed his way through 25 girlfriends and four wives and enjoyed four punch-ups with his nemesis Ken. He has also mingled with royalty, meeting the Queen and Prince Charles when they visited the set.

Now he is quitting acting – his livelihood since he was 12.

"If you're in the best show in the world, where do you go?" he says. "The only way is down after Coronation Street."

Flashing a typical Baldwin grin, he smiles: "I'm looking forward to a well-deserved break.

"I think I deserve it now, don't you?"

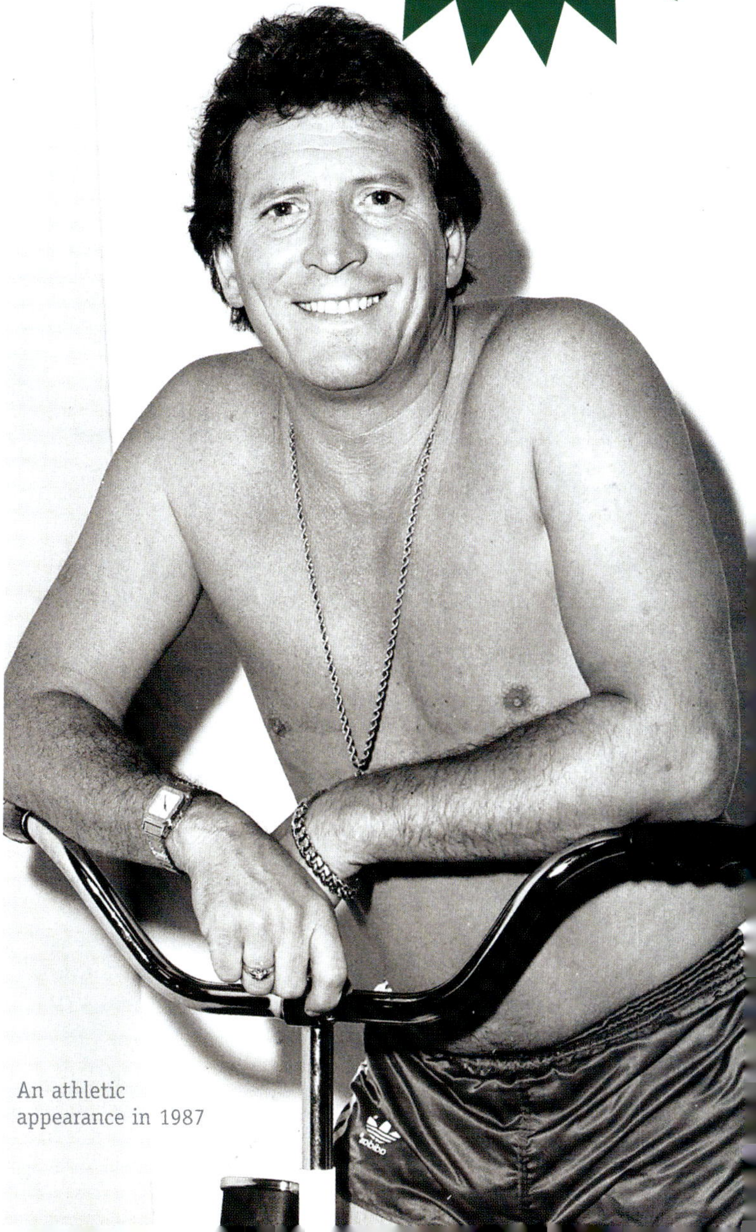

An athletic appearance in 1987

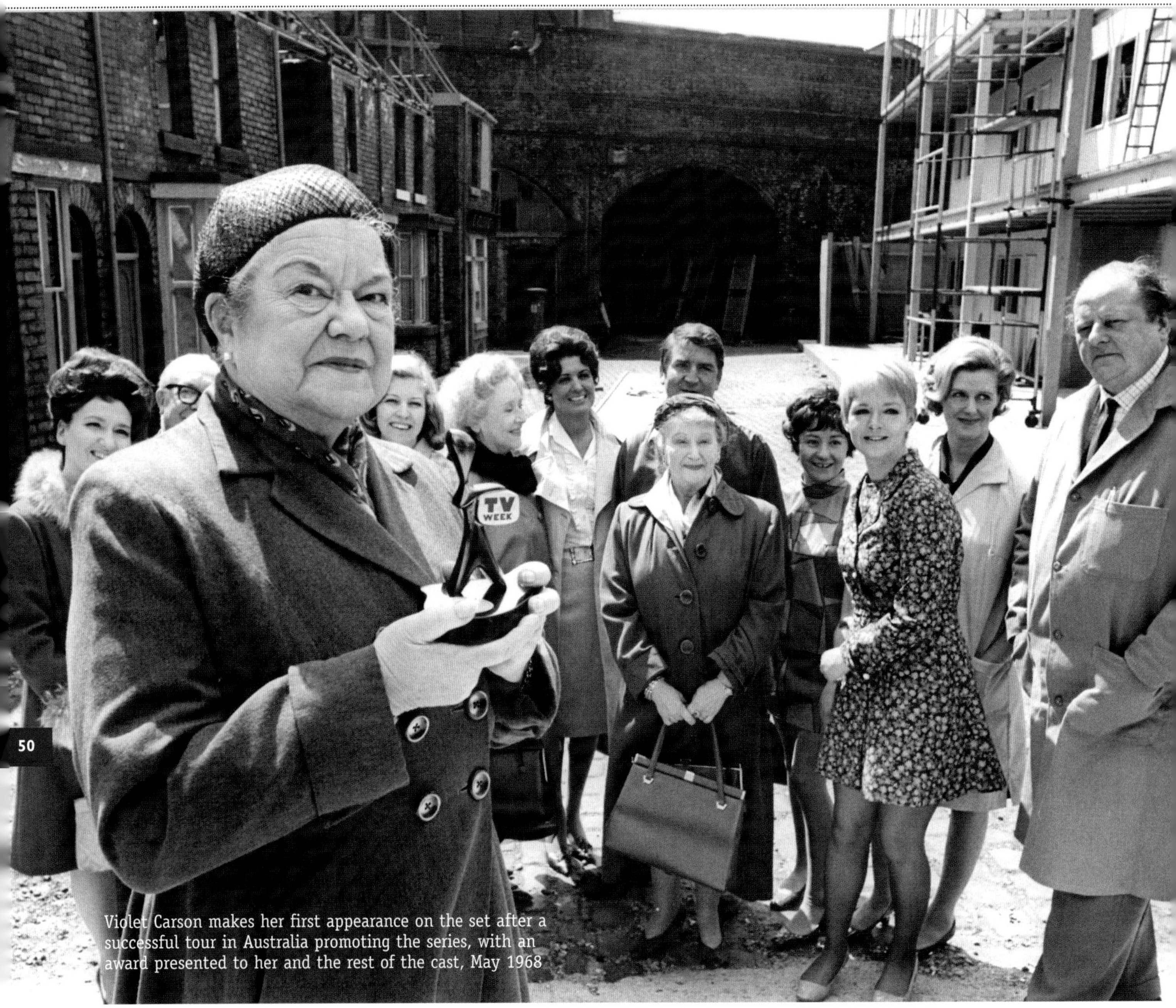

Violet Carson makes her first appearance on the set after a successful tour in Australia promoting the series, with an award presented to her and the rest of the cast, May 1968

Saturday, June 12, 1965

It's Ena Sharples, OBE

ENA SHARPLES can begin practising a curtsy . . . and Police-Sergeant George Dixon can rehearse his salute. For today they are both booked – along with the Beatles – for an appearance at Buckingham Palace to receive honours.

Actress Violet Carson, 62, who plays Ena in Granada TV's Coronation Street, and actor Jack Warner – Dixon of Dock Green – are both made Officers of the Order of the British Empire (OBE) in the Queen's Birthday Honours list.

They will be in the same Order as the four Beatles – who are made Members (MBE).

Showbiz really gets 'star billing' . . . singer Frankie Vaughan, 37, is another star who gets the OBE for his services to youth welfare.

Violet Carson and Jack Warner are among the most famous TV faces of the times – Coronation Street and Dock Green have become 'real' places to millions of viewers.

Violet – born in Manchester – has been playing the formidable Ena Sharples for four years. She used to play the piano for Wilfred Pickles in 'Have a Go'.

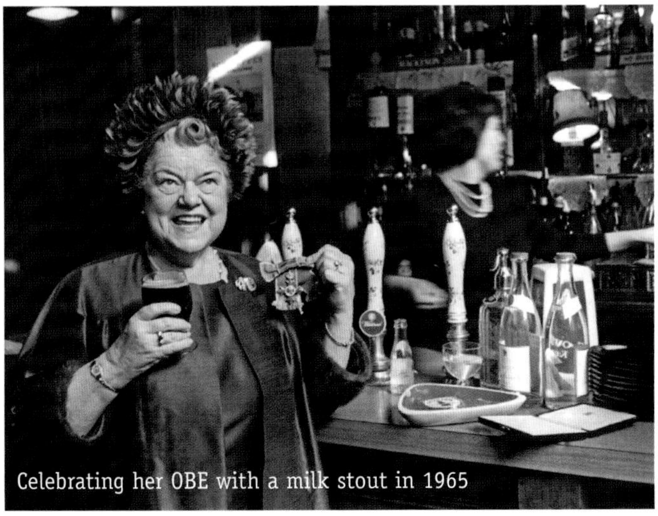

Celebrating her OBE with a milk stout in 1965

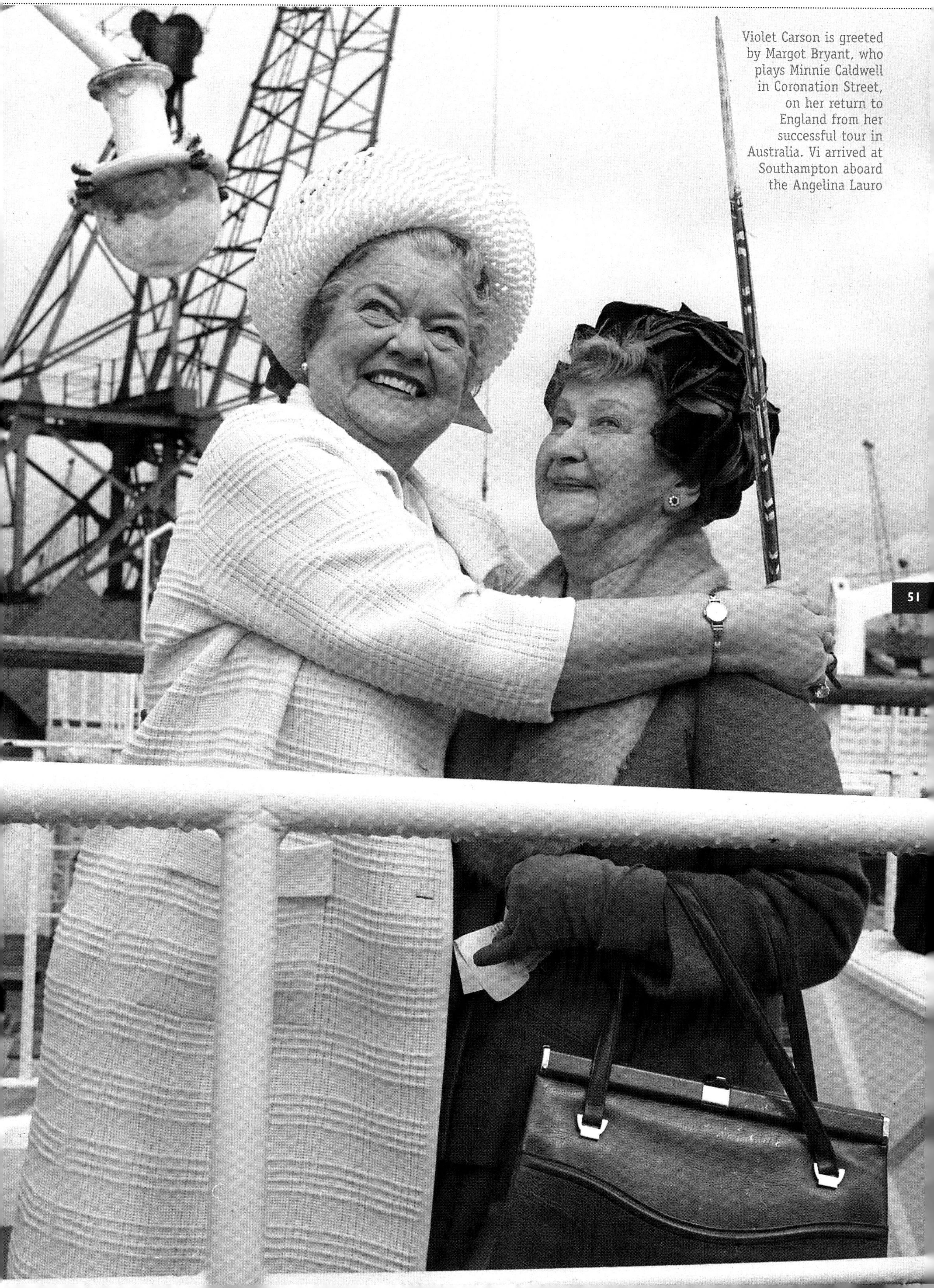

Violet Carson is greeted by Margot Bryant, who plays Minnie Caldwell in Coronation Street, on her return to England from her successful tour in Australia. Vi arrived at Southampton aboard the Angelina Lauro

Wednesday, February 29, 1984

The Street's fond farewell to Ena

THEY came from far and near yesterday to say a last, fond farewell to the grand old lady of Coronation Street.

There were familiar faces like Ken Barlow, busty Bet Lynch and Rita Fairclough, as well as hundreds of ordinary folk.

They were all there at the memorial service for Violet Carson, the actress who created Britain's best-known battle-axe, Ena Sharples.

But the ceremony at Manchester Cathedral was not an occasion for tears.

Friends and colleagues were there to pay an affectionate, smiling tribute to a woman they loved and respected.

Violet, who died on Boxing Day aged 85, spent 20 years as the hair-netted harridan of the Street. But off-screen she was kindly 'Auntie Vi'.

William Roache, who played alongside her as Ken Barlow from the start of the series, said: "We have all been touched by her magic."

He recalled the time she had a rose named after her.

At rehearsal she told the cast – "I'm described in the catalogue as 'a good bedder – does well against a north wall.'"

Among the stars, including the 'ghosts' of many ex-Street characters, was Violet's closest friend Lynne Carol.

She played Ena's pal Martha Longhurst until she was 'killed off' in 1964. Lynne, who arrived with Violet's sister, Mrs Nellie Kelly, revealed that Violet threatened to resign when she was written out.

Other old Street faces included Alan Rothwell (David Barlow), Stephen Hancock (Ernie Bishop) and Anne Reid (Valerie Barlow).

But unlike their characters, old Ena will not die.

Not yet, anyway. Producer Bill Podmore said references would continue to be made to her in the script.

"We can't kill dear old Ena off," he said.

"Her presence will always be felt somewhere in the Street."

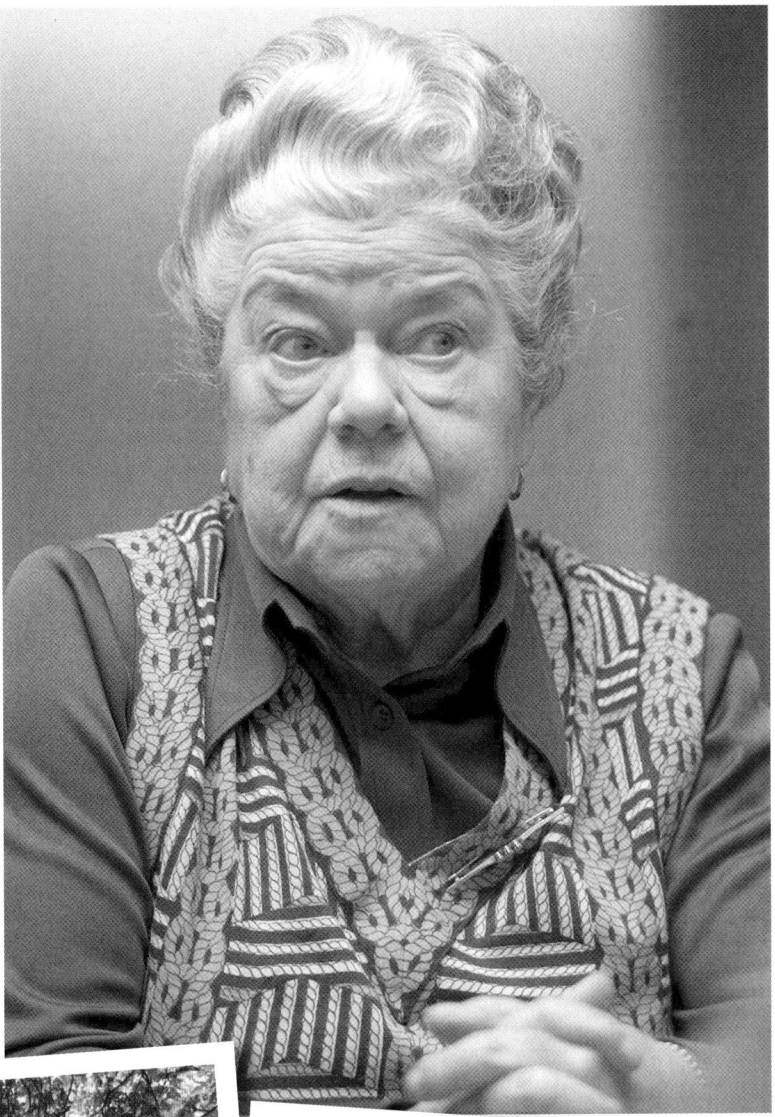

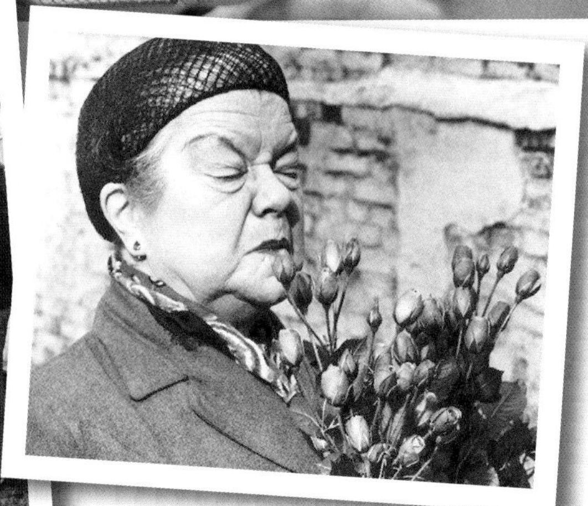

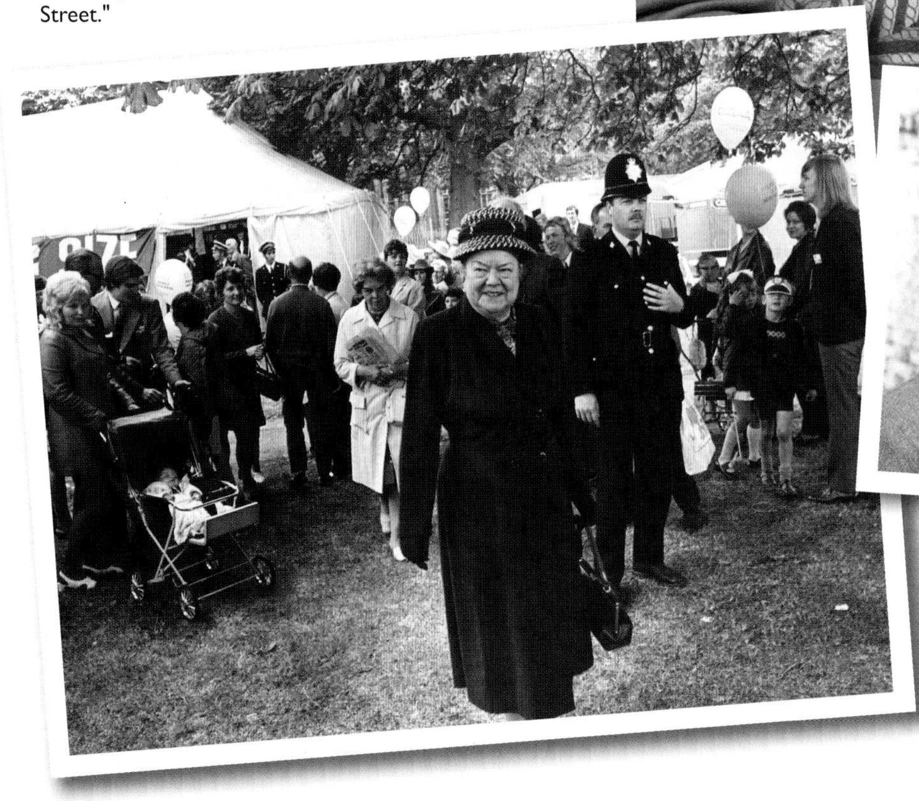

Clockwise from top: Violet Carson, pictured in 1974; the sweet smell of success as Violet has a rose named after her; "Once in every Preston Guild" – the Corrie cast on an outing to the famous showground in August 1972

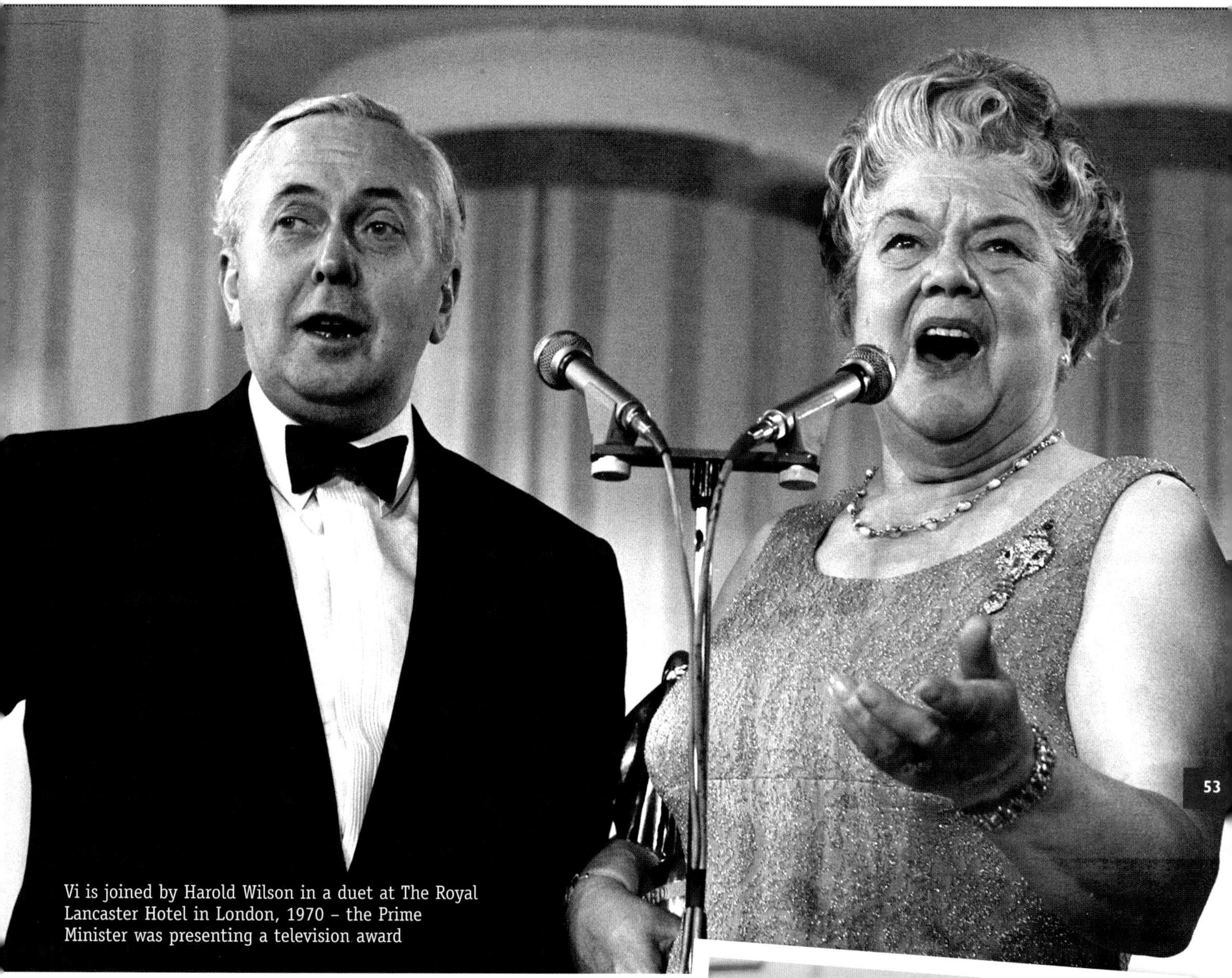

Vi is joined by Harold Wilson in a duet at The Royal Lancaster Hotel in London, 1970 – the Prime Minister was presenting a television award

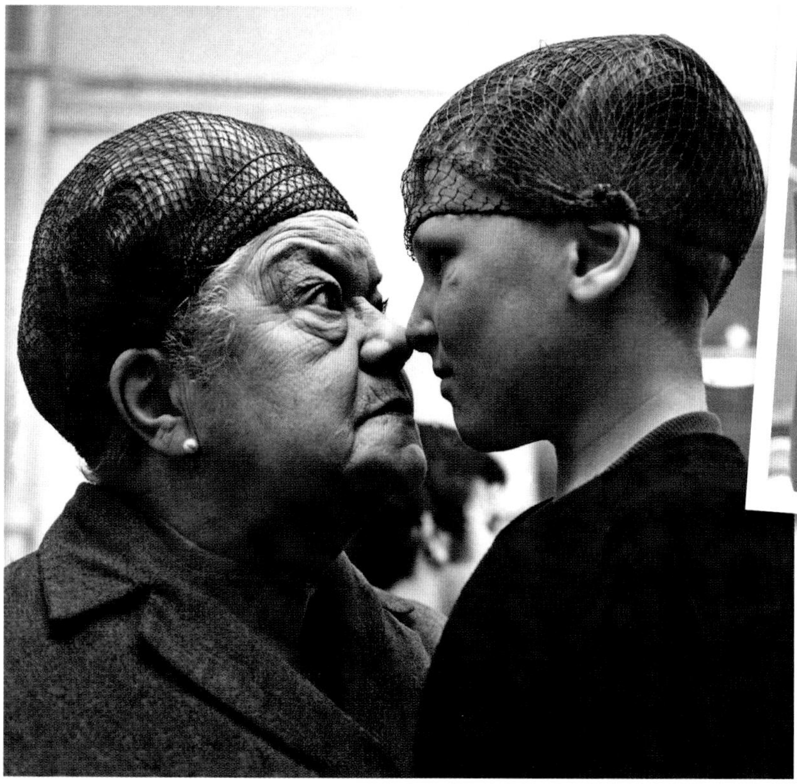

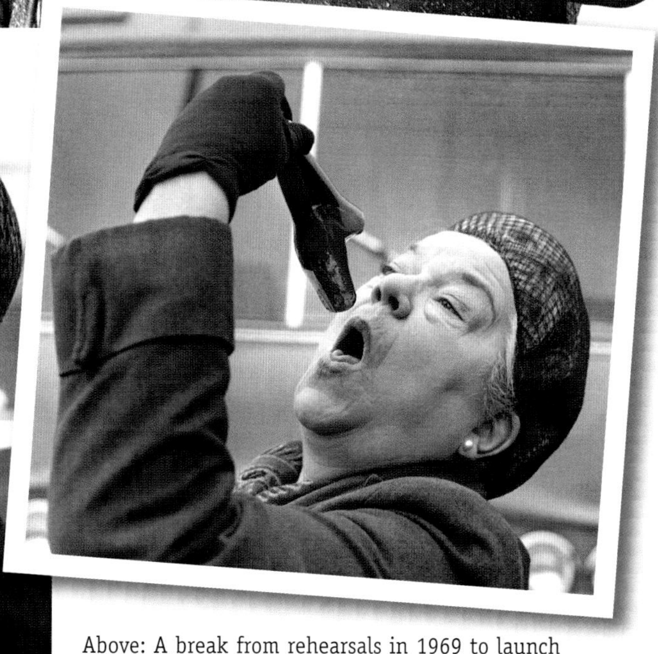

Above: A break from rehearsals in 1969 to launch Granada Television's colour TV scanner with a bottle of beer – Ena makes sure nothing is left in the bottle

Left: Ena Sharples comes face to face with eight-year-old Jimmy Jamieson, complete with hairnet, during a cast visit to the Remedial Teaching Centre at Clayton-le-Moors, Lancashire

Saturday, October 28, 2006

Julie Goodyear: The most explosive showbiz memoir of the year

EVEN the boldest soap scriptwriter wouldn't have inflicted a string of disastrous marriages, same-sex flings and mental meltdown on Coronation Street barmaid Bet Lynch.

But Julie Goodyear, the actress who played her for 25 years, has endured more secret tragedy and heartache than her Corrie character ever did.

Now, in the most explosive showbiz memoir of the year, Julie is finally lifting the lid on her extraordinary life.

In an exclusive interview with the Mirror, Julie, now a 64-year-old gran-of-three, says: "My life has run the gamut of human emotions, with as many heartbreaks and sorrows as joys and happiness."

Julie was encouraged to put pen to paper by her friend and chat-show host Paul O'Grady.

"I did find it very traumatic," she says. "It brought back a lot of painful memories, but I have kept my sense of humour."

By her own admission, Julie has had a disastrous love life. She was just 17 when she became pregnant with her son Gary, now 46. "I was a single mum and that was something to be ashamed of then."

Within a year of her shotgun wedding, her husband had left. Her second walked out before the reception, her third refused to live in the same country and her first same-sex partner left her on the eve of Julie's cancer op.

Cynics could have predicted a similarly bleak outlook 10 years ago, when a trucker half her age delivered cement to Julie's farm. But Julie says that her relationship with Scott Brand, 37, is her most successful yet. "It is the longest any has lasted," she says.

"Maybe it's because I'm not working full-time any more. I was a workaholic when I was on Corrie, but I was living my dream and wouldn't have it any other way."

She left Coronation Street in 1995, but was persuaded to return four years later to find it went out five times a week instead of three – and there was no longer time for rehearsals.

"I just couldn't keep up," she admits. "The schedule was relentless. I wouldn't go back full-time but I wouldn't have any hesitation in doing a guest appearance.

"During the recent domestic violence storyline, when Shelley was being beaten up, I received lots of letters from viewers begging me to go back to the Rovers and sort out Charlie.

"It is lovely to know that, after all these years, Bet is still held in great affection by the British public.

"The highlight of my career was receiving the MBE for services to television and drama from the Queen in 1996, because it is the highest accolade that can be given in my business.

"It was wonderful and I felt I had come a long way from the back streets of Heywood in Lancashire. I hope I can give hope to any kid born in a back street anywhere."

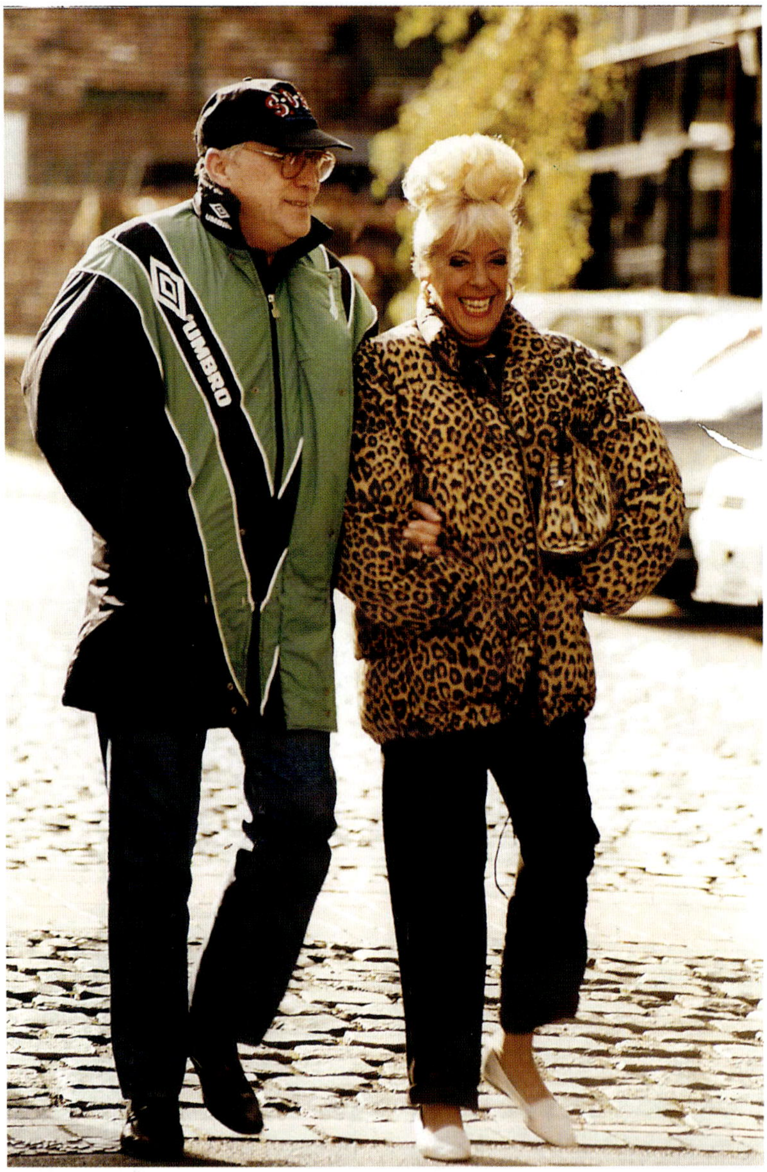

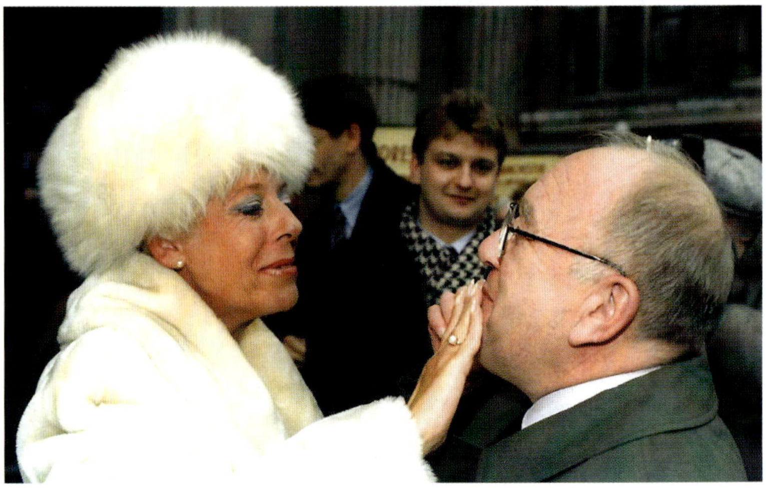

Above, right: Arm in arm with Bill Tarmey as they arrive for a day's filming in 1993

Right: Keeping actor Roy Barraclough quiet. Roy played Bet's husband Alec Gilroy

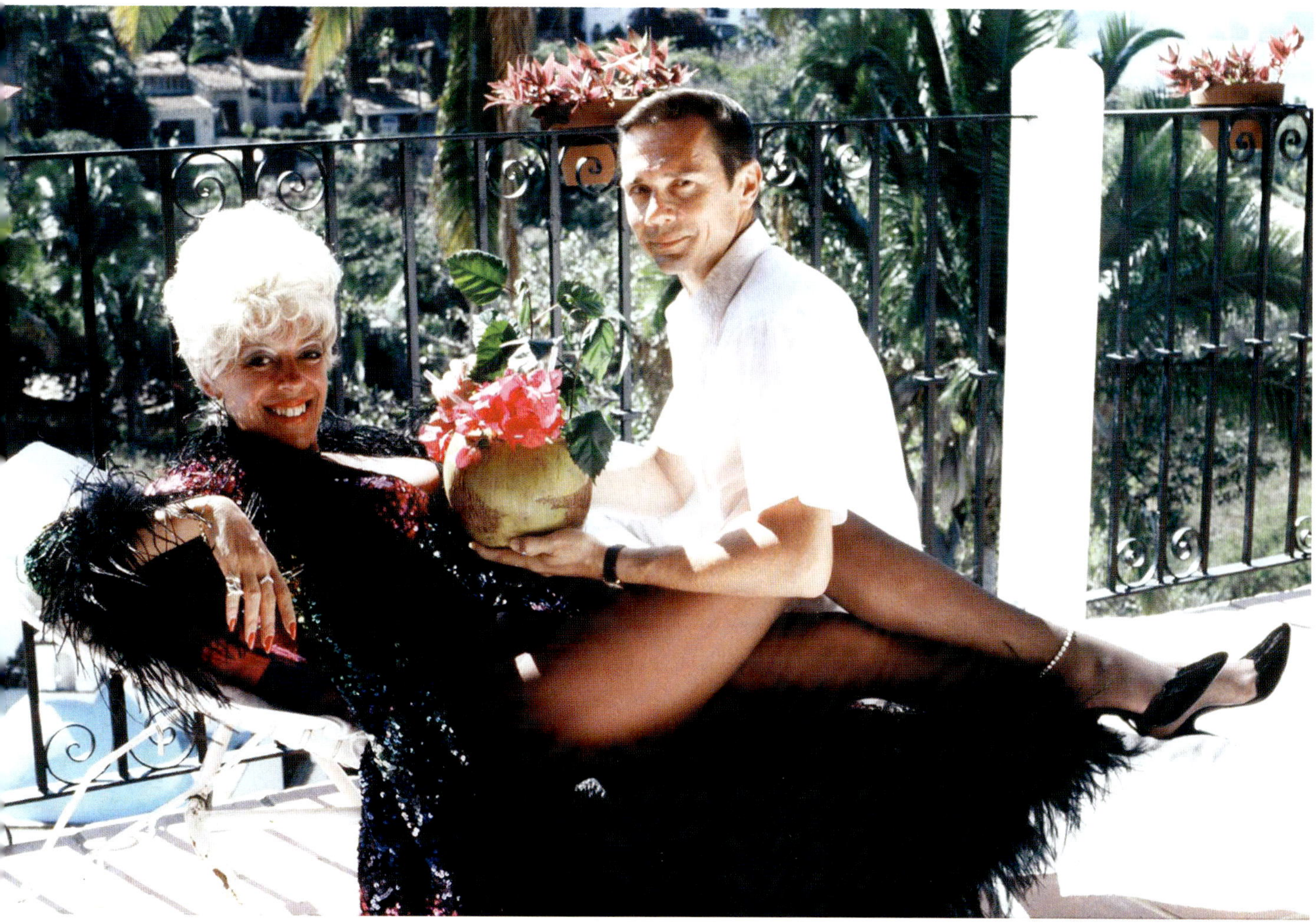

Above: Julie relaxes in 1985 after her third marriage, to Richard Skrob

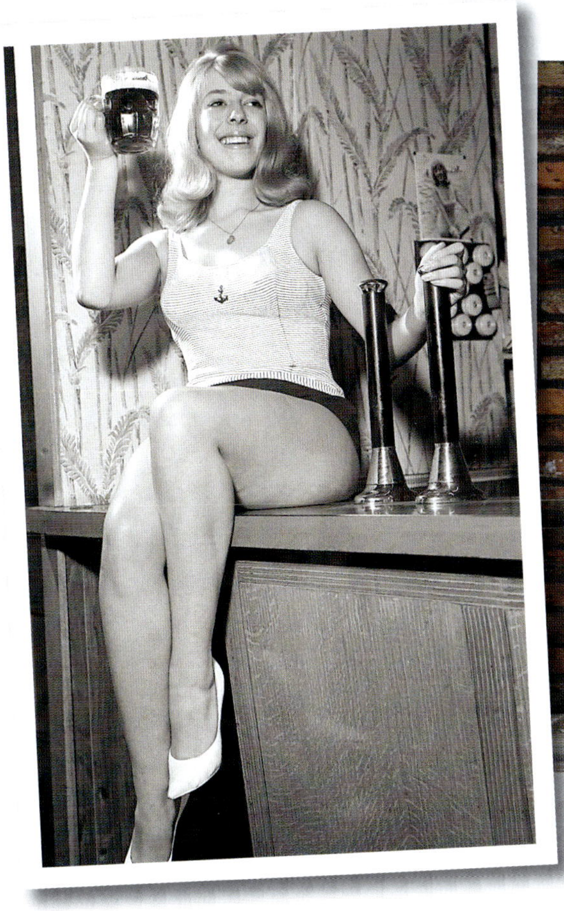

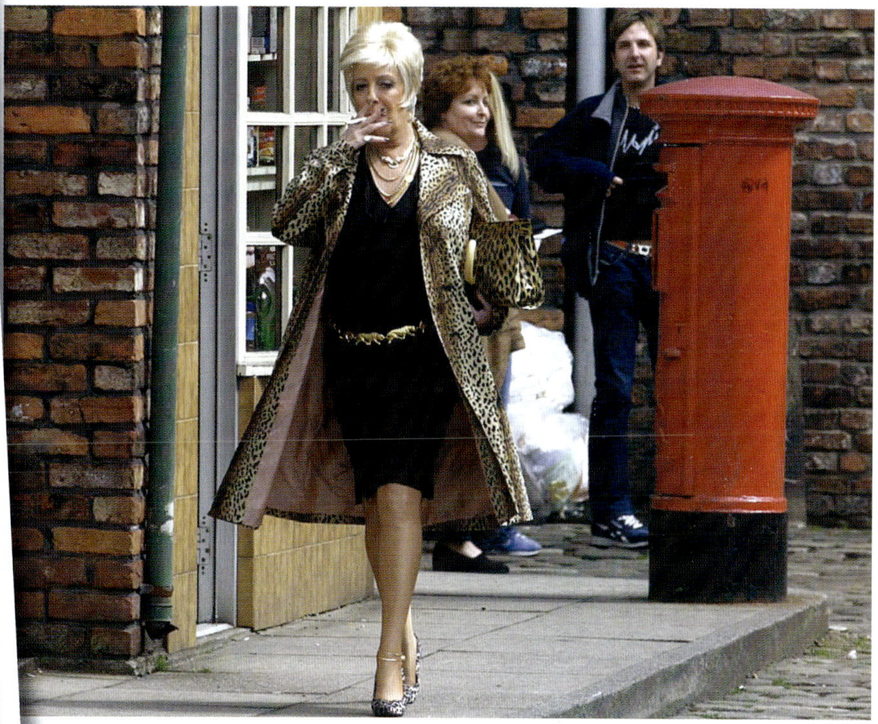

Above: A brief return to the Street in 2002. To the left, life anticipates art as aspiring actress Julie displays a pint in 1964, two years before her first appearance as Bet

Friday, 13 March, 2009

"I've got a bit of baggage..."

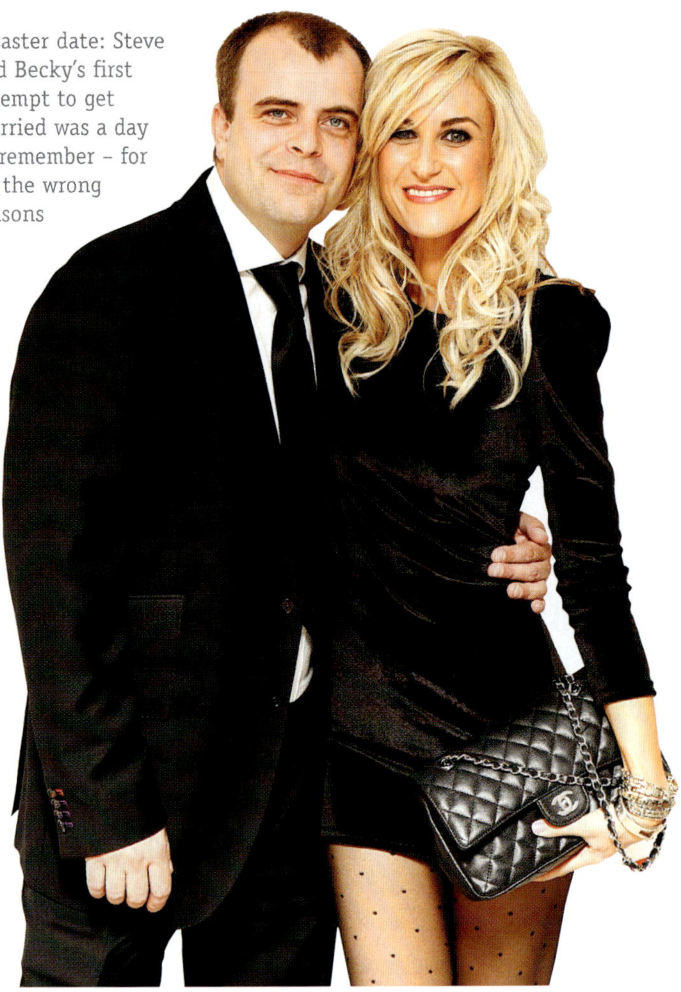

Disaster date: Steve and Becky's first attempt to get married was a day to remember – for all the wrong reasons

Steve McDonald on his frantic love life

NO fear of Corrie's Steve McDonald getting cold feet about becoming a married man tonight – it's not like it's his first time. If his wedding to madcap Becky Granger goes ahead, this will be Steve's FOURTH "I do" in 20 years on the soap.

Of course, this being Weatherfield, there is bound to be a hitch when it comes to getting hitched.

The bride rips her dress and turns up late and drunk, and the ceremony descends into chaos. Well, it is Friday 13th.

"I think Steve is relieved when Becky does actually make it to the church, even though she is steaming drunk," says Simon Gregson, 34, who has played Steve since he was 15 years old.

"He doesn't care that it's Friday the 13th either. Ultimately Steve is just glad Becky turns up. He wants to prove their doubters wrong."

Blushing bride Becky – played by Katherine Kelly – probably has a few doubts of her own. After all, Steve has been around the cobbles a few times.

Simon laughs: "The lad has had his fair share but there is nothing wrong with that.

"Would I call Steve a ladies' man? He used to be before he got fat and bald.

"Most of the women Steve has been out with are completely insane.

"Becky is mad but I don't think she has got as many issues as some of his previous loves – for one, she is not a murderer and she's not prone to beating him up."

Out of the many beauties he has locked lips with playing Steve, who was the best?

"Me! I have definitely been the best kisser," he jokes. "Although it took me a while to get the hang of it."

All Steve's weddings have also had an impact on Simon's own marriage plans with fiancee Emma Gleave, 26. Together since Christmas 2005, they have an 18-month-old son, Alfie.

He says: "After filming four weddings in cold and drizzly Manchester, ours would have to be somewhere hot.

"And I would have no excuse to forget my vows – imagine if I did!"

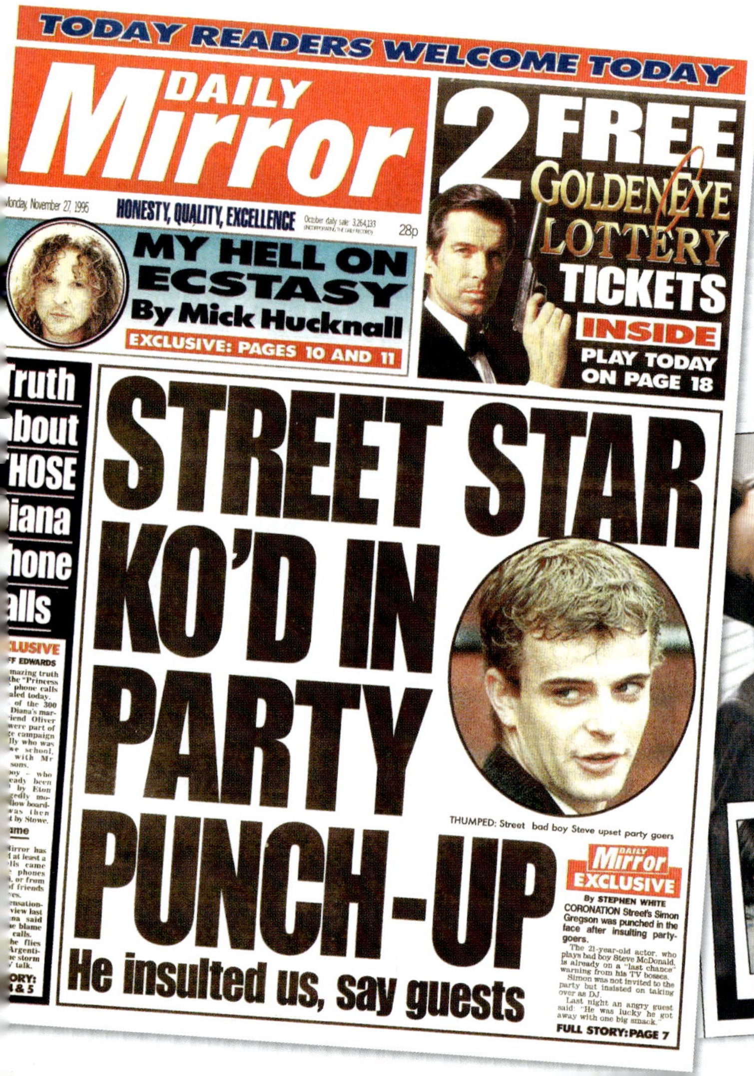

TODAY READERS WELCOME TODAY

DAILY Mirror

Monday, November 27, 1995 HONESTY, QUALITY, EXCELLENCE 28p

2 FREE GOLDENEYE LOTTERY TICKETS INSIDE
PLAY TODAY ON PAGE 18

MY HELL ON ECSTASY By Mick Hucknall
EXCLUSIVE: PAGES 10 AND 11

STREET STAR KO'D IN PARTY PUNCH-UP

He insulted us, say guests

THUMPED: Street bad boy Steve upset party goers

DAILY Mirror EXCLUSIVE

By STEPHEN WHITE

CORONATION Street's Simon Gregson was punched in the face after insulting party-goers.

The 21-year-old actor, who plays bad boy Steve McDonald, is already on a "last chance" warning from his TV bosses.

Simon was not invited to the party but insisted on taking over as DJ.

Last night an angry guest said: "He was lucky he got away with one big smack."

FULL STORY: PAGE 7

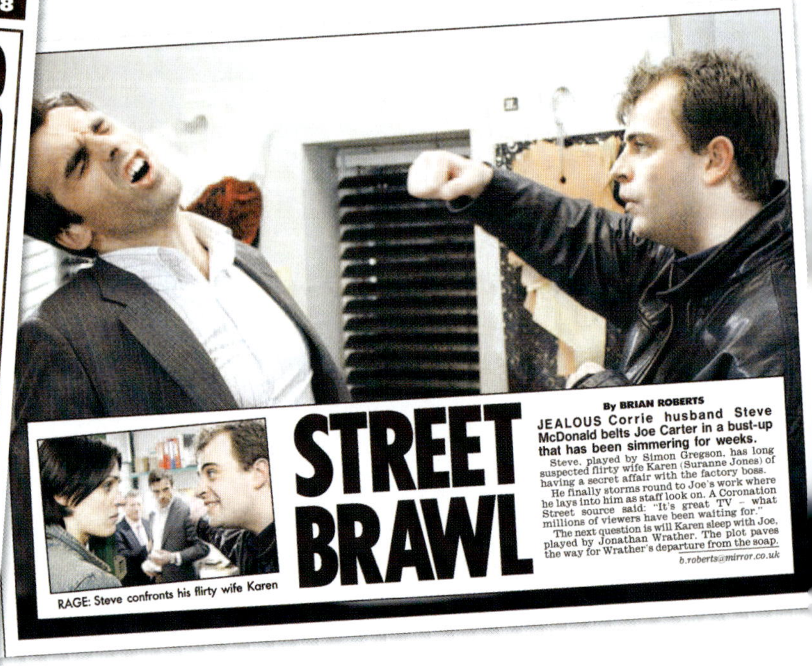

STREET BRAWL

By BRIAN ROBERTS

JEALOUS Corrie husband Steve McDonald belts Joe Carter in a bust-up that has been simmering for weeks.

Steve, played by Simon Gregson, has long suspected flirty wife Karen (Suranne Jones) of having a secret affair with the factory boss.

He finally storms round to Joe's work where he lays into him as staff look on. A Coronation Street source said: "It's great TV – what millions of viewers have been waiting for."

The next question is will Karen sleep with Joe, played by Jonathan Wrather. The plot paves the way for Wrather's departure from the soap.

b.roberts@mirror.co.uk

RAGE: Steve confronts his flirty wife Karen

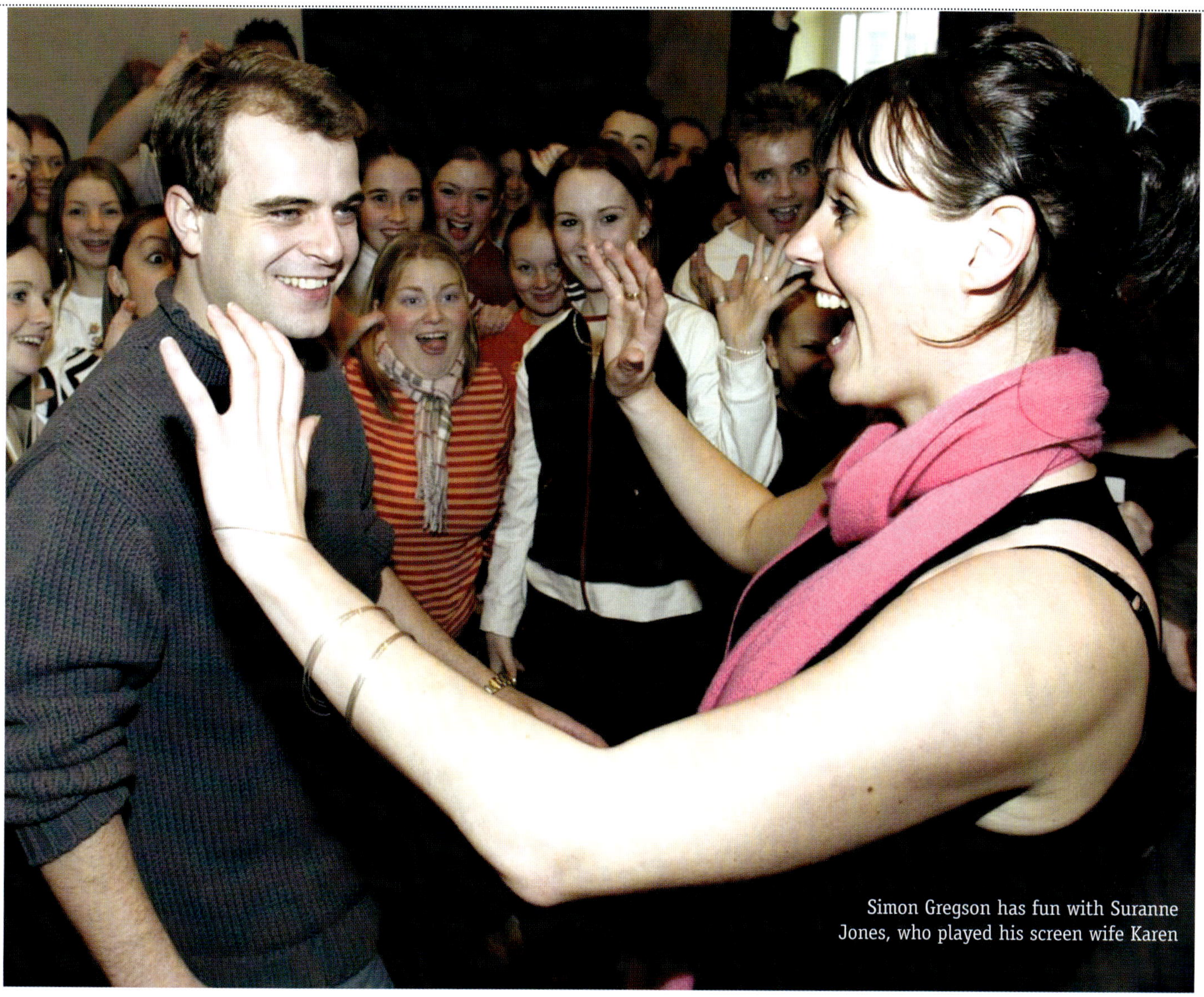

Simon Gregson has fun with Suranne Jones, who played his screen wife Karen

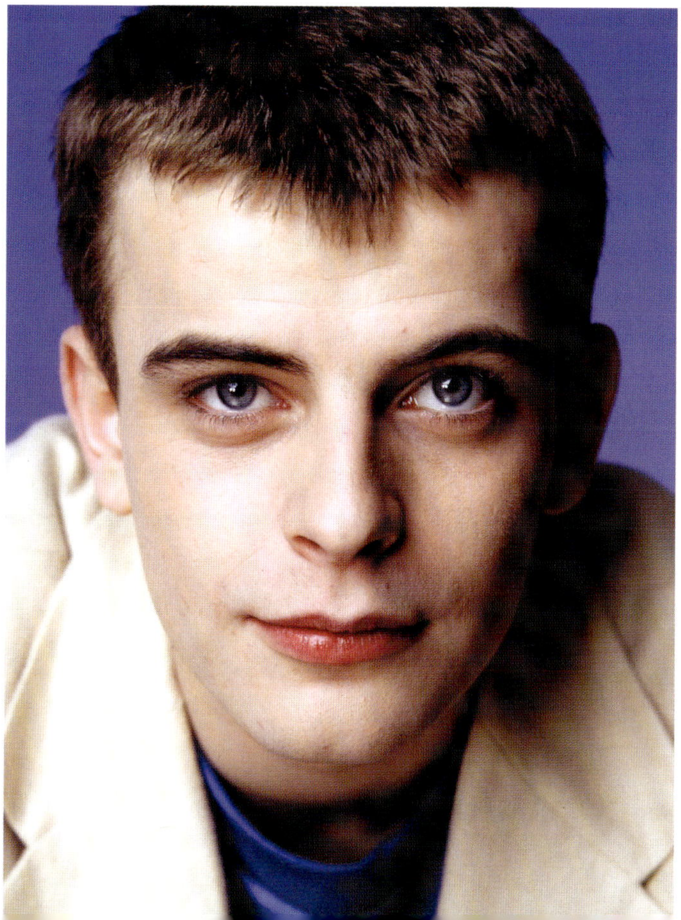

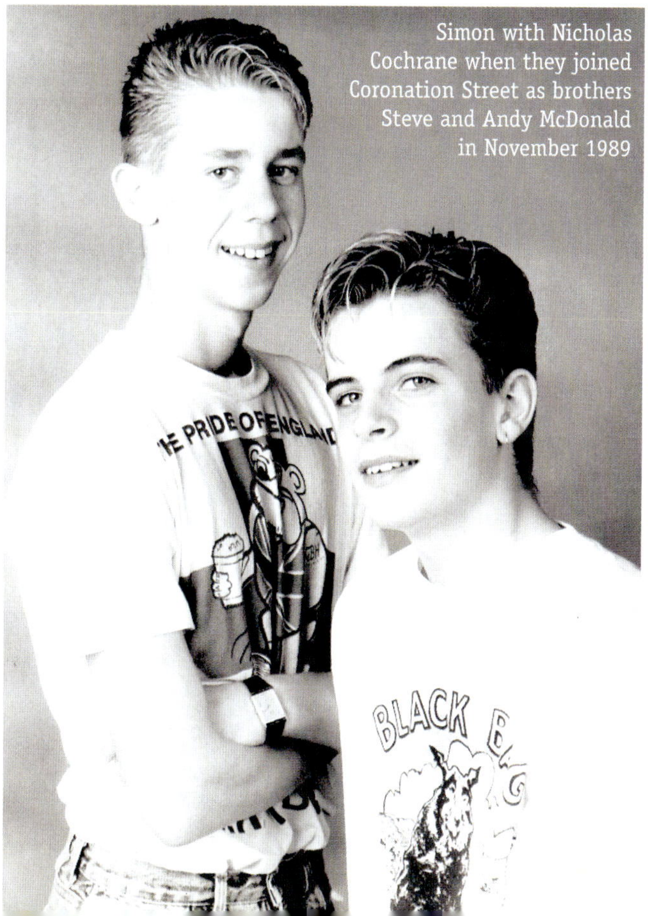

Simon with Nicholas Cochrane when they joined Coronation Street as brothers Steve and Andy McDonald in November 1989

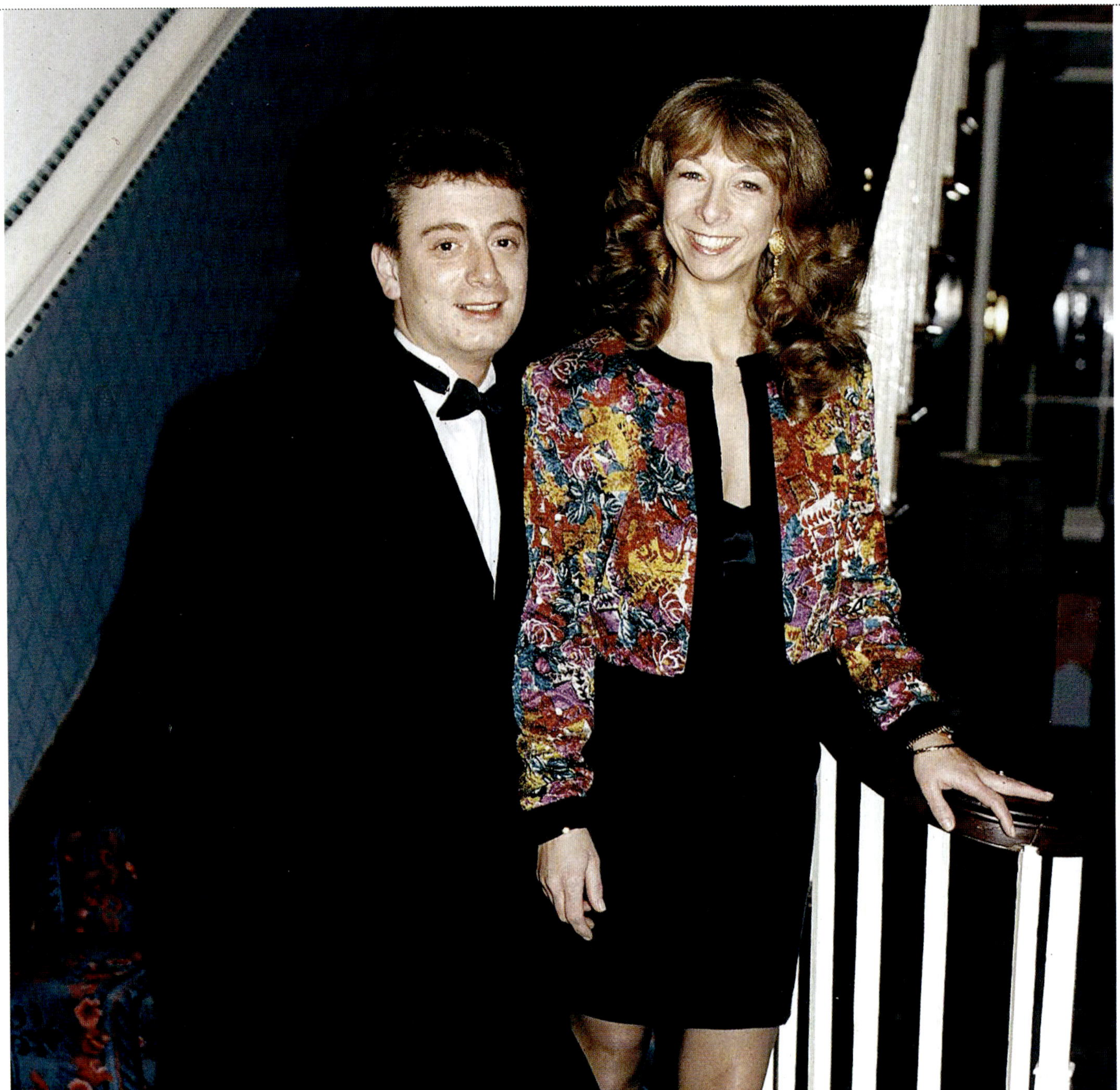

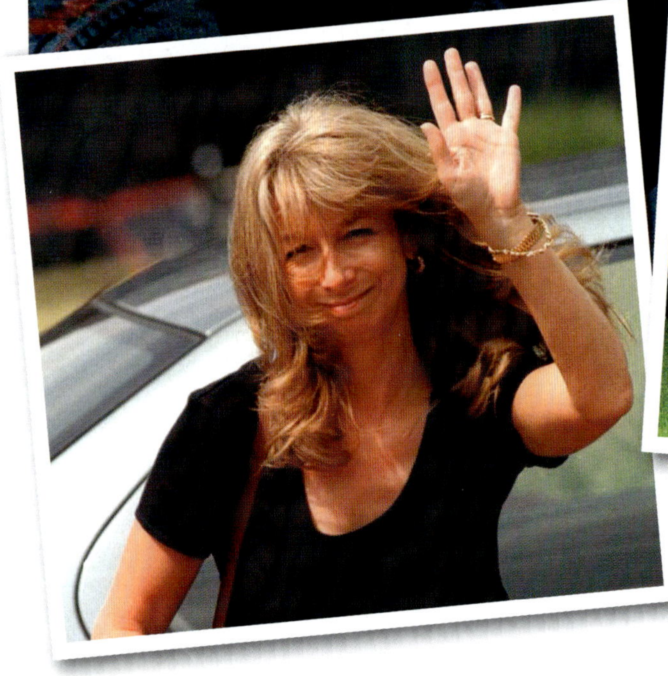

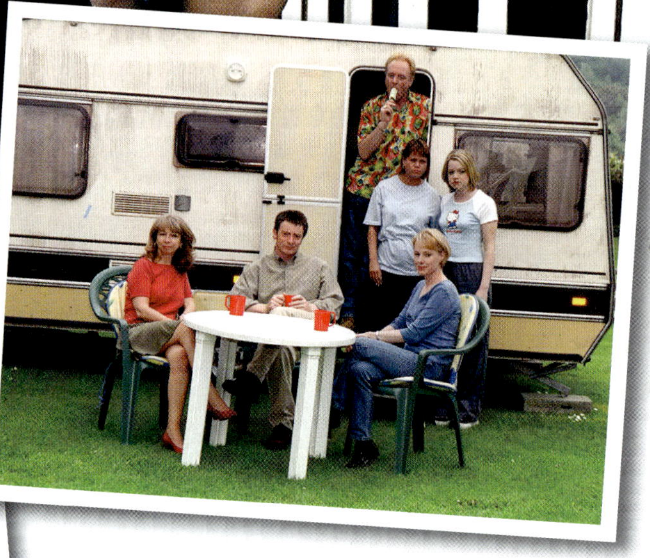

Above: Unhappy families as Gail and Martin Platt's caravan break is ruined by the arrival of the Battersbys. Main picture, with Sean Wilson who played Gail's second husband, Martin

Saturday, March 10, 2001

I'm 50, a survivor and not a bit like Gail

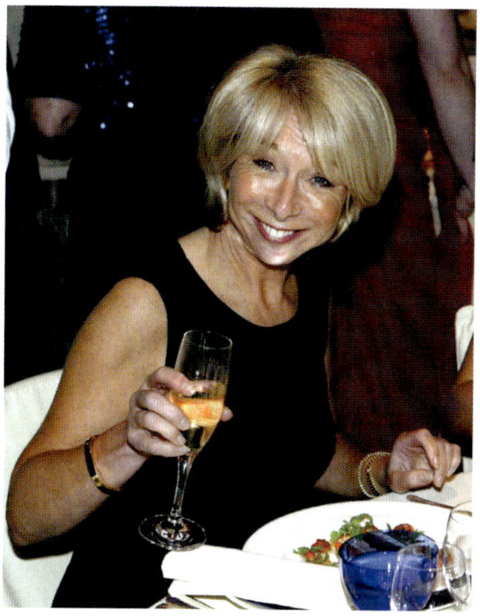

GAIL PLATT might be mumsy and much maligned – but Helen Worth is anything but.

A fitness addict with her own personal trainer, her wardrobe is bursting with Ralph Lauren and Gucci, her passion is theatre and her favourite restaurant is The Ivy, the smart London eaterie beloved by the stars.

When she talks, it is of architecture and world travel rather than the price of carrots in the corner shop.

"My world isn't exactly Weatherfield," she laughs. "I have to say that I do like the fine things in life, and I'm now at an age where I can finally enjoy them without feeling guilty about it."

Helen has had a life as full of drama as her on-screen existence.

There was the slow and painful collapse of her marriage to actor Michael Angelis, a union thought to be one of the strongest in showbiz.

There was the death of her mother, mown down by a car when Helen was just 20.

"Now that I have got to 50, and survived all the ups and downs on the way, I realise that I'm actually a survivor."

Groomed for the stage from the age of three, Helen admits that she had an unconventional childhood.

By the age of 12, she was living in London, 400 miles from her mum and dad, and supporting herself.

She was barely out of her teens when Helen lost the mother who had steered her path into the world of showbiz. Gladys Wigglesworth died just before her own 50th birthday when she was knocked down by a car while out walking the family dog. She never saw her daughter land the television role that would change her life.

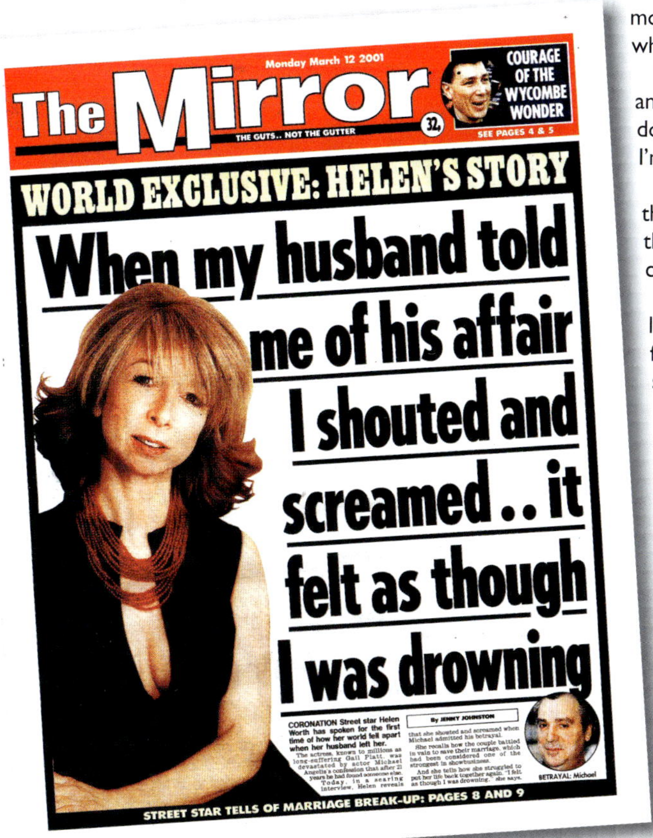

Monday March 12 2001

The Mirror

32p

THE GUTS.. NOT THE GUTTER

COURAGE OF THE WYCOMBE WONDER

SEE PAGES 4 & 5

WORLD EXCLUSIVE: HELEN'S STORY

When my husband told me of his affair I shouted and screamed.. it felt as though I was drowning

By JENNY JOHNSTON

CORONATION Street star Helen Worth has spoken for the first time of how her world fell apart when her husband left her.

The actress, known to millions as long-suffering Gail Platt, was devastated by actor Michael Angelis's confession that after 21 years he had found someone else.

Today, in a searing interview, Helen reveals that she shouted and screamed when Michael admitted his betrayal.

She recalls how the couple battled in vain to save their marriage, which had been considered one of the strongest in showbusiness.

And she tells how she struggled to put her life back together again. "I felt as though I was drowning," she says.

BETRAYAL: Michael

STREET STAR TELLS OF MARRIAGE BREAK-UP: PAGES 8 AND 9

Helen was 24 when she landed the role of Gail Potter. She was young and naive when legendary figures like Vi Carson, Doris Speed and Pat Phoenix came into her life, becoming like a second family to her.

Coronation Street has never been just a job to Helen Worth. It also filled a huge gap in more recent years when Helen's husband – and partner of 21 years – left her after a highly publicised affair.

It has taken three years for Helen to adjust to the reality of being a single woman again. She talks of those dark days with astonishing candour.

"So many women define themselves by their relationship with a man," she reveals.

"It took me a long time to realise that I could be happy on my own. A lot of women go through difficult times like this, and now I can understand why some of them go under. That period of my life was the most unhappy time I have known. At the time, I couldn't see any way out.

"I want to tell everyone that no matter what you go through, you can survive. You can even be happy again. I am 50, I am single and I have never been happier. And I want to shout it from the rooftops."

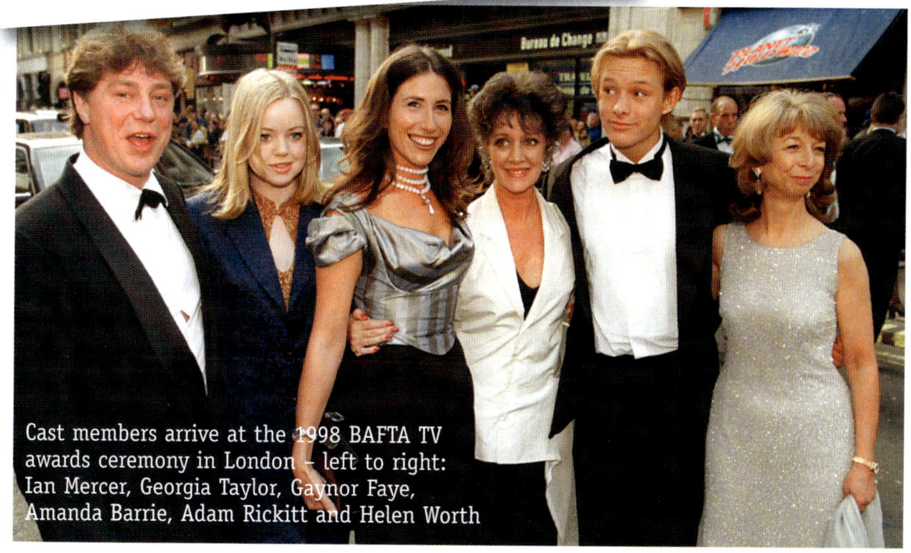

Cast members arrive at the 1998 BAFTA TV awards ceremony in London – left to right: Ian Mercer, Georgia Taylor, Gaynor Faye, Amanda Barrie, Adam Rickitt and Helen Worth

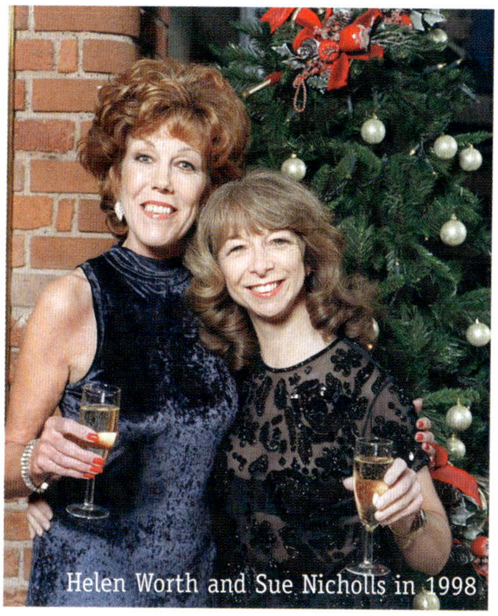

Helen Worth and Sue Nicholls in 1998

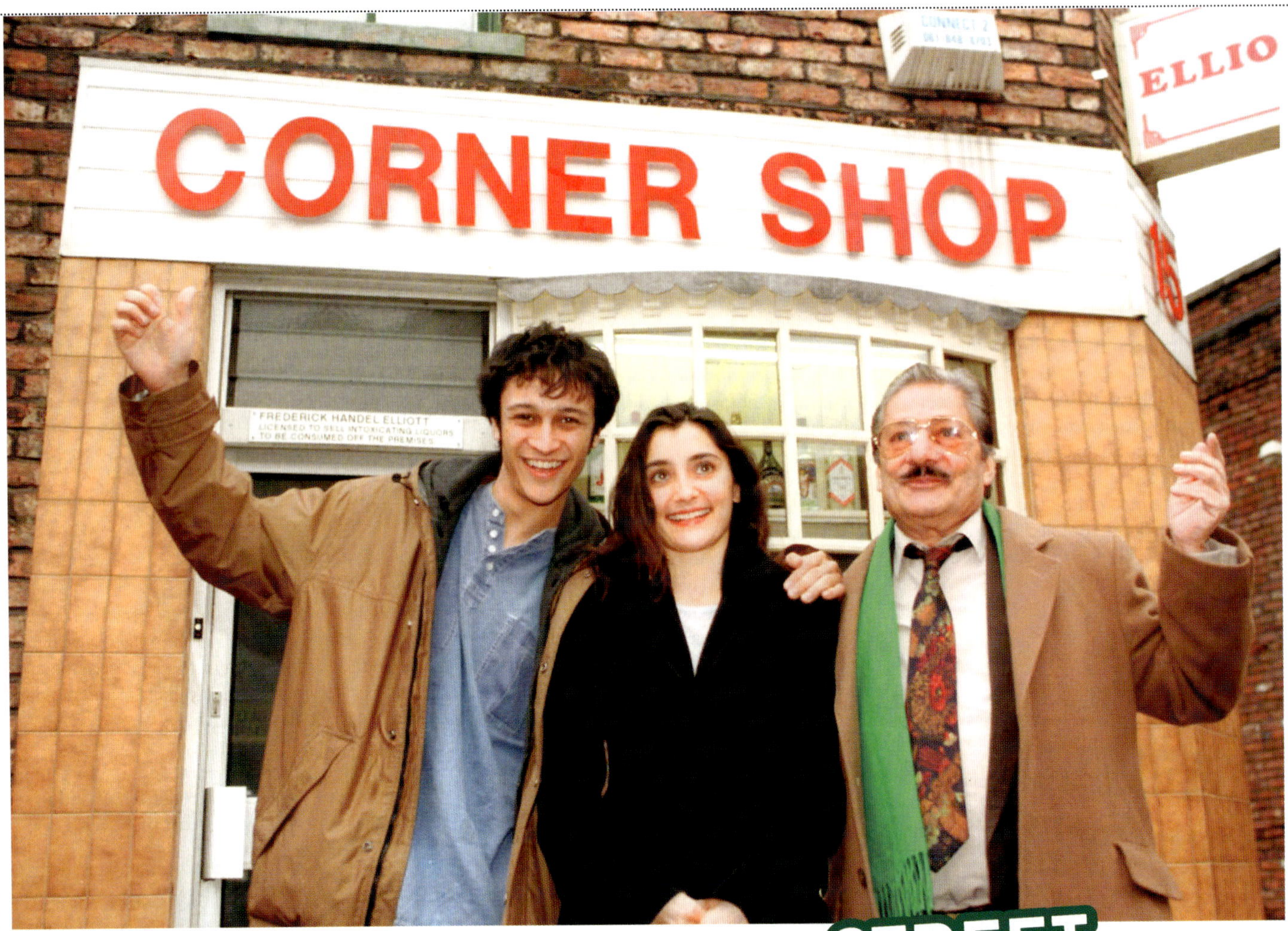

Thursday, November 19, 1998

CoronAsian Street

TV soap gets first Asian family after 38 years

THE first Asian family is to move into Coronation Street where they will run the corner shop.

Secret auditions have been held by the soap's top brass to find the ideal actors to play the roles.

It is the first time in the show's 38-year history that an Asian family will be part of the line-up.

But Granada bosses are determined they will be around for years to come by establishing them as leading characters.

And they have pledged not to turn the family – which will include three generations – into ethnic stereotypes.

The show's most famous names are among those who have run the comer shop in the past.

Final decisions on castings – most of the actors are likely to be unknowns – are expected by the end of the month. Filming will start in February.

A Street production source said last night: "Everyone's very excited. One thing is for sure, the new residents won't be mere tokens. There are big plans for them to make a huge impact in the programme.

"For starters, there will be a teenage son who turns out to be a tearaway. He'll quickly be established as a bit of a troublemaker.

"Scriptwriters are itching to get stuck into scenes for them. But cliched storylines, such as racist attacks, will be avoided.

"It's long overdue that we should have a solid ethnic family. There's always a buzz about the place when new characters come in."

The corner shop has always played a key role in the Street. And the flat upstairs, where the Asian family are to live, has seen a host of famous lodgers.

STREET LIFE

Corrie was first filmed in Archie Street, Salford. It became known as Coronarchie Street

The shop featured at the start of the first episode in 1960 when Elsie Lappin (Maud Edwards) sold the business to Florrie Lindley (Betty Alberge).

Other well-known owners include Elsie Howard (Pat Phoenix); Renee Bradshaw (Madge Hindle); Alf Roberts (Bryan Mosley); Reg and Maureen Holdsworth (Ken Morley and Sherrie Hewson); Maggie Clegg (Irene Sutcliffe); Idris and Vera Hopkins (Richard Davies and Kathy Staff); and Irma Barlow (Sandra Gough).

The arrival of an Asian family is the final legacy of former Street producer Brian Park. He became known as the axeman for sacking several stars. But he was also determined to make the show more multi-racial. Before he quit, he asked his successor, David Hanson, to see the plan through.

When the Asian family settle into the flat above the corner shop, they will follow a long line of lodgers.

Among the famous characters who have lived there are: Jerry Booth, Emily Nugent, Cyril and Betty Turpin, Bet Lynch, Gail Potter, Deirdre Langton, Kevin and Sally Webster, Curly Watts and Shirley Armitage, Ken Barlow, Bill Webster, Chris Collins and Greg Kelly.

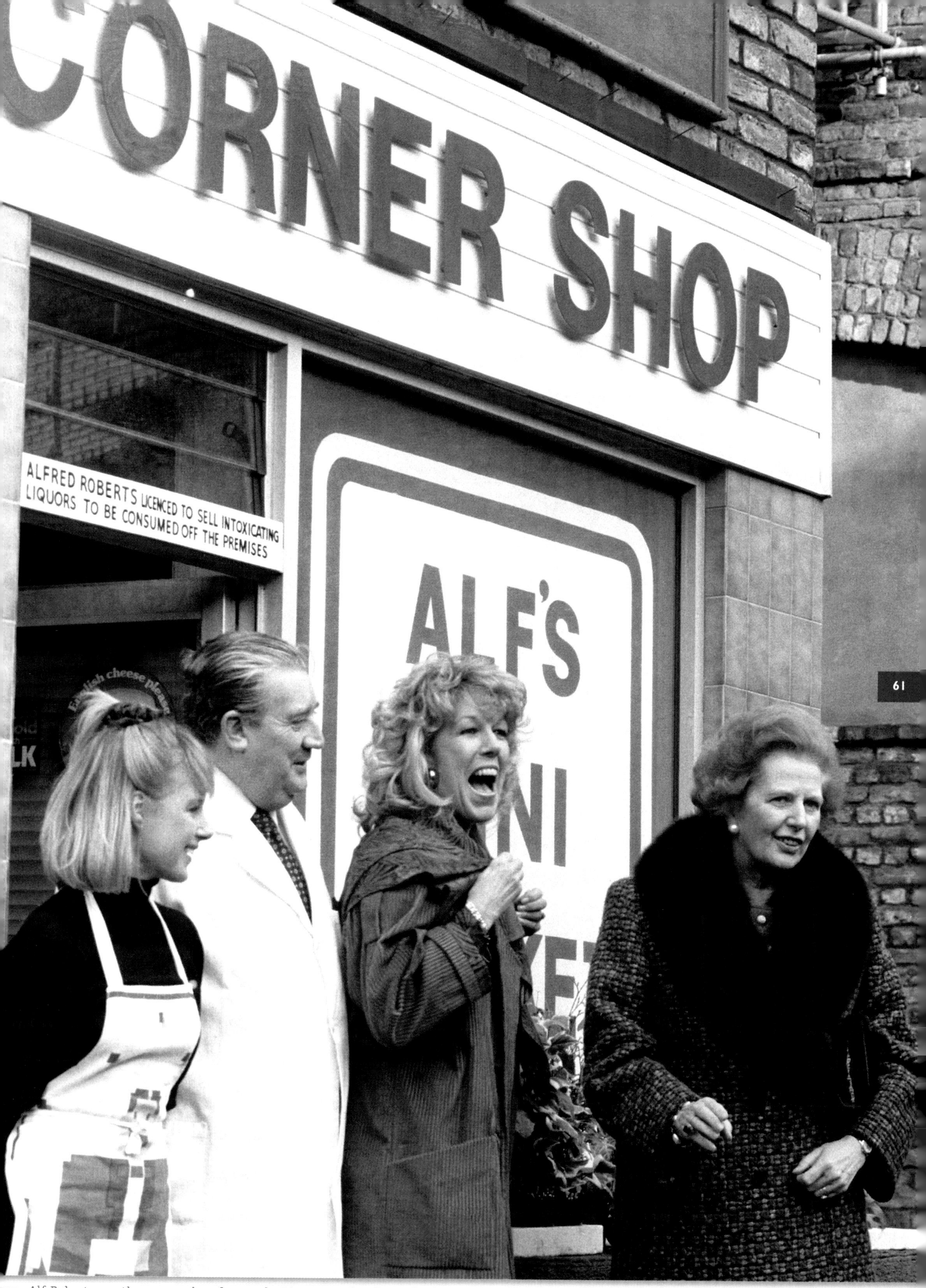

ove: Alf Roberts ran the corner shop for nearly 20 years and welcomed a famous visitor in 1990 – then Prime Minister Margaret Thatcher

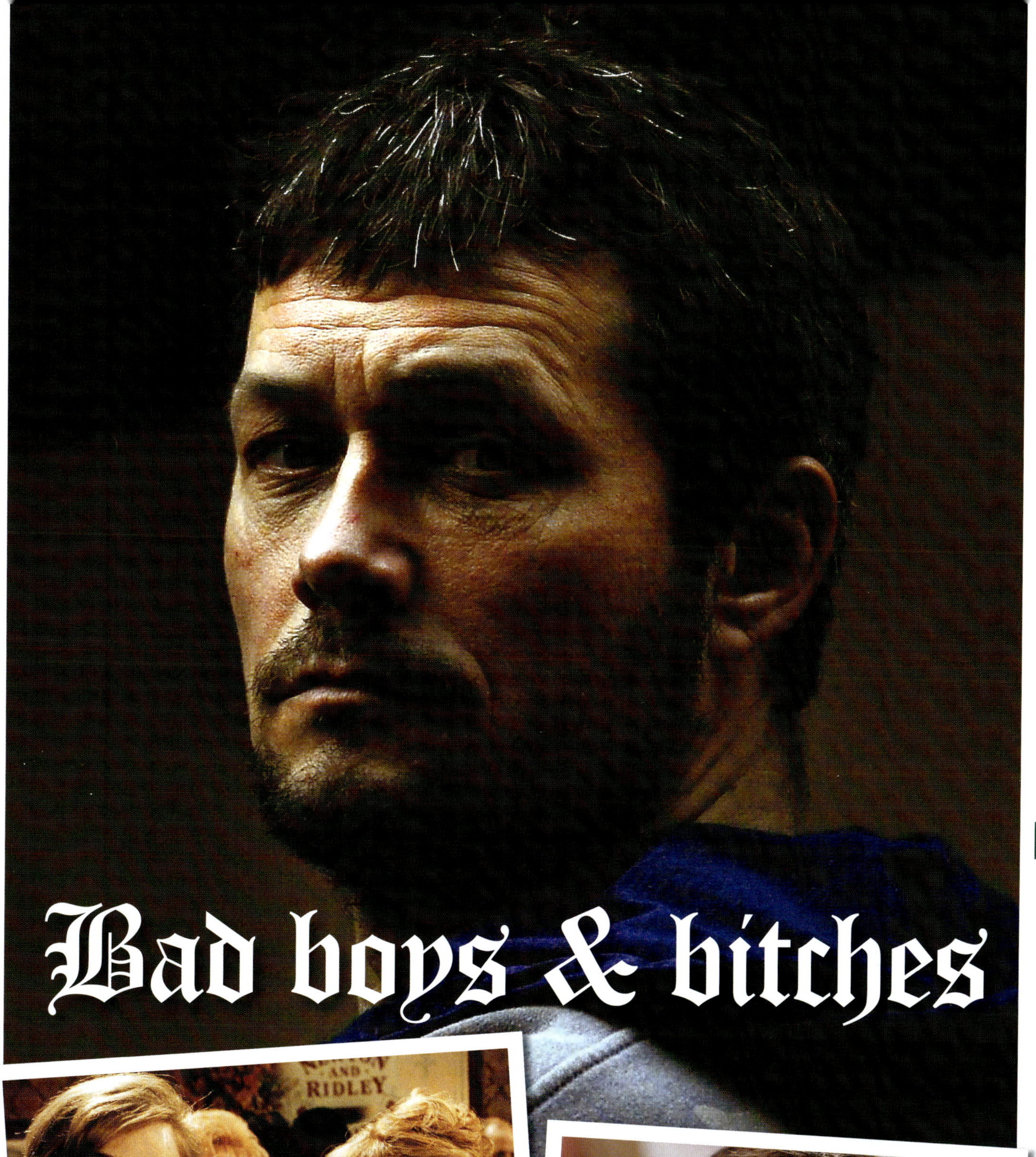

Bad boys & bitches

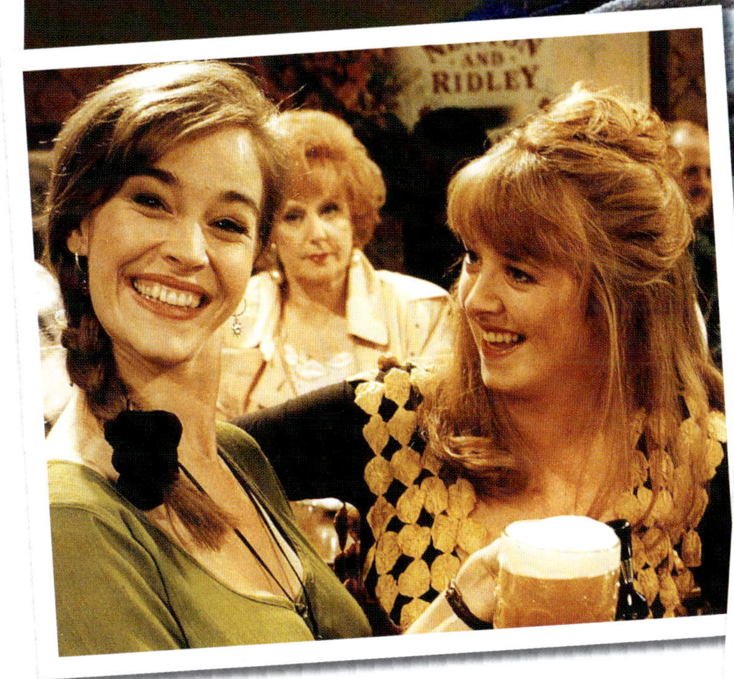

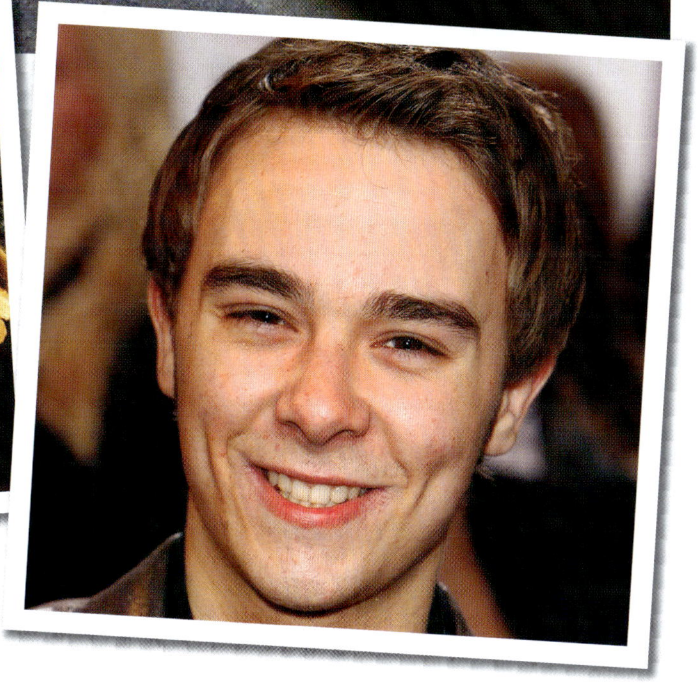

Main picture: A mean glare from Bill Ward, who played Charlie Stubbs. Above left, Rovers superbitch Tanya Pooley (Eva Pope) and right, David Platt, who has caused his niece to take ecstasy, been banged up and tried to murder his mum

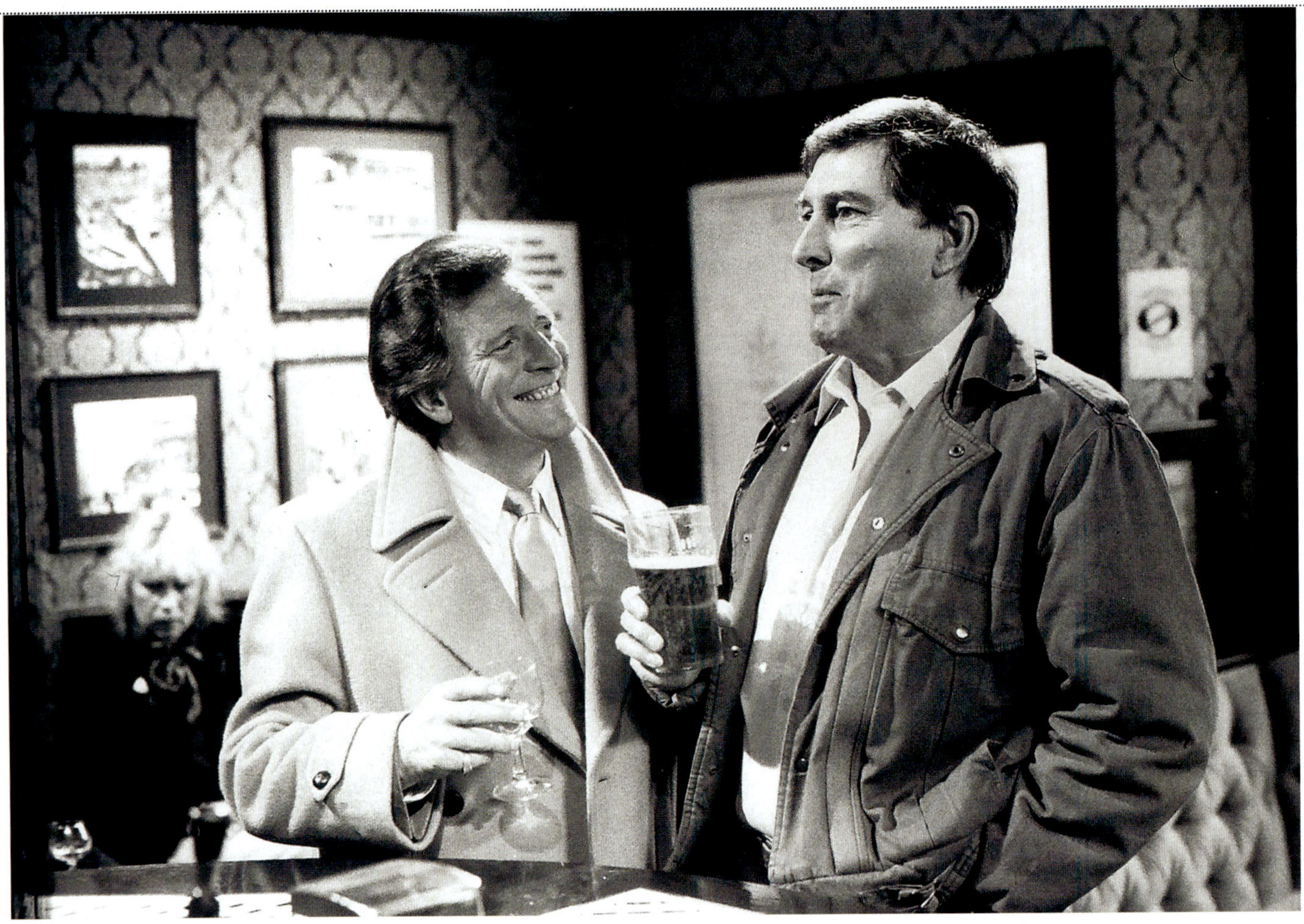

Above: Alan Bradley chats with Mike Baldwin in the Rovers in 1989. Bradley came to a sticky end underneath a Blackpool tram

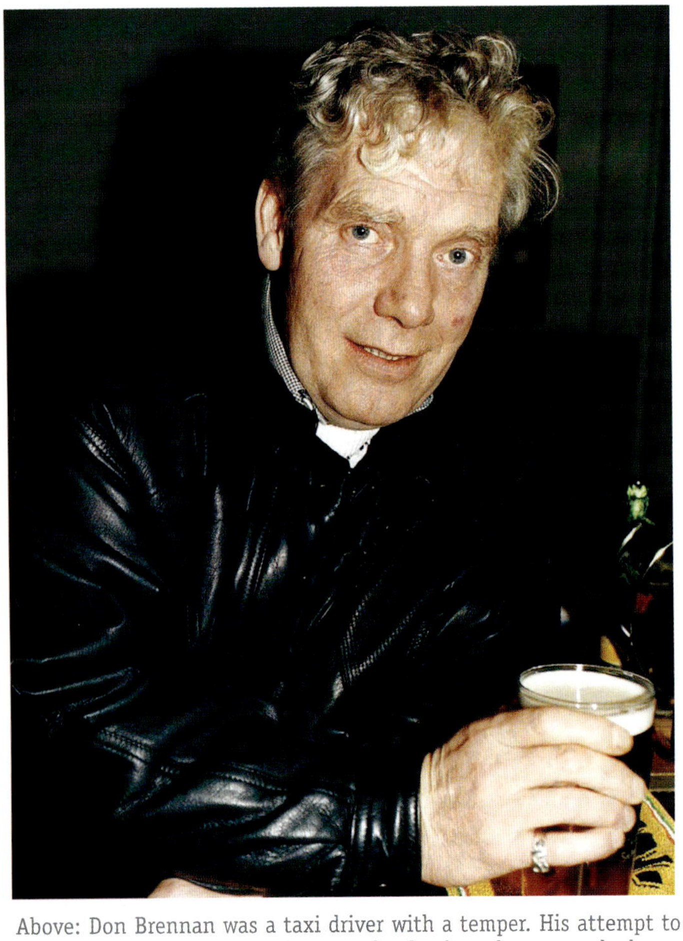

Above: Don Brennan was a taxi driver with a temper. His attempt to run over Mike Baldwin saw his own death when the car crashed

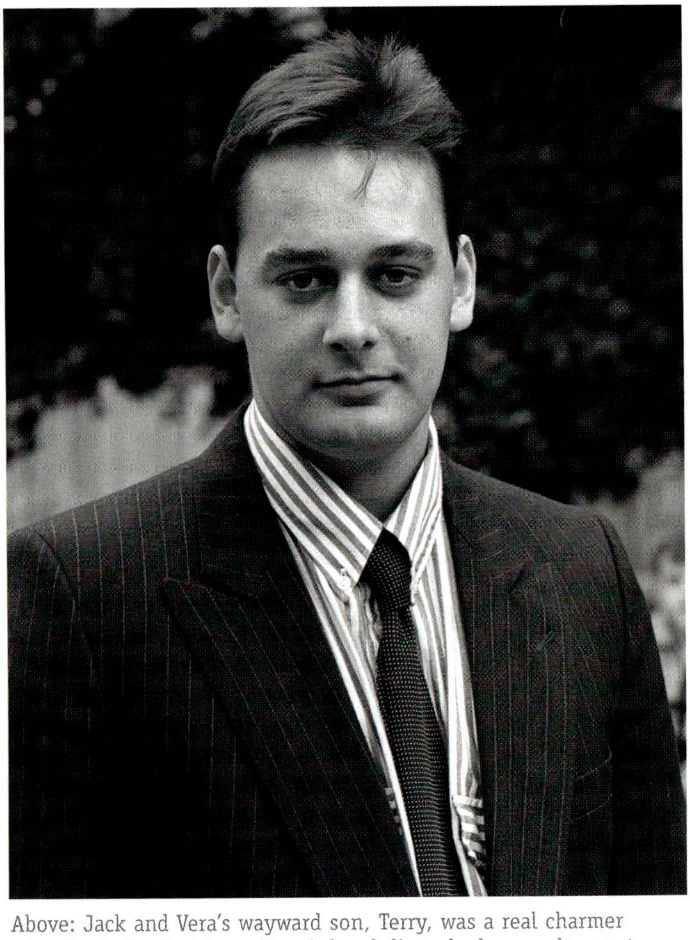

Above: Jack and Vera's wayward son, Terry, was a real charmer with the ladies but brought grief and discord wherever he went

DAILY MIRROR, Wednesday, March 10, 2004 PAGE 3

BAPTISM OF IRE

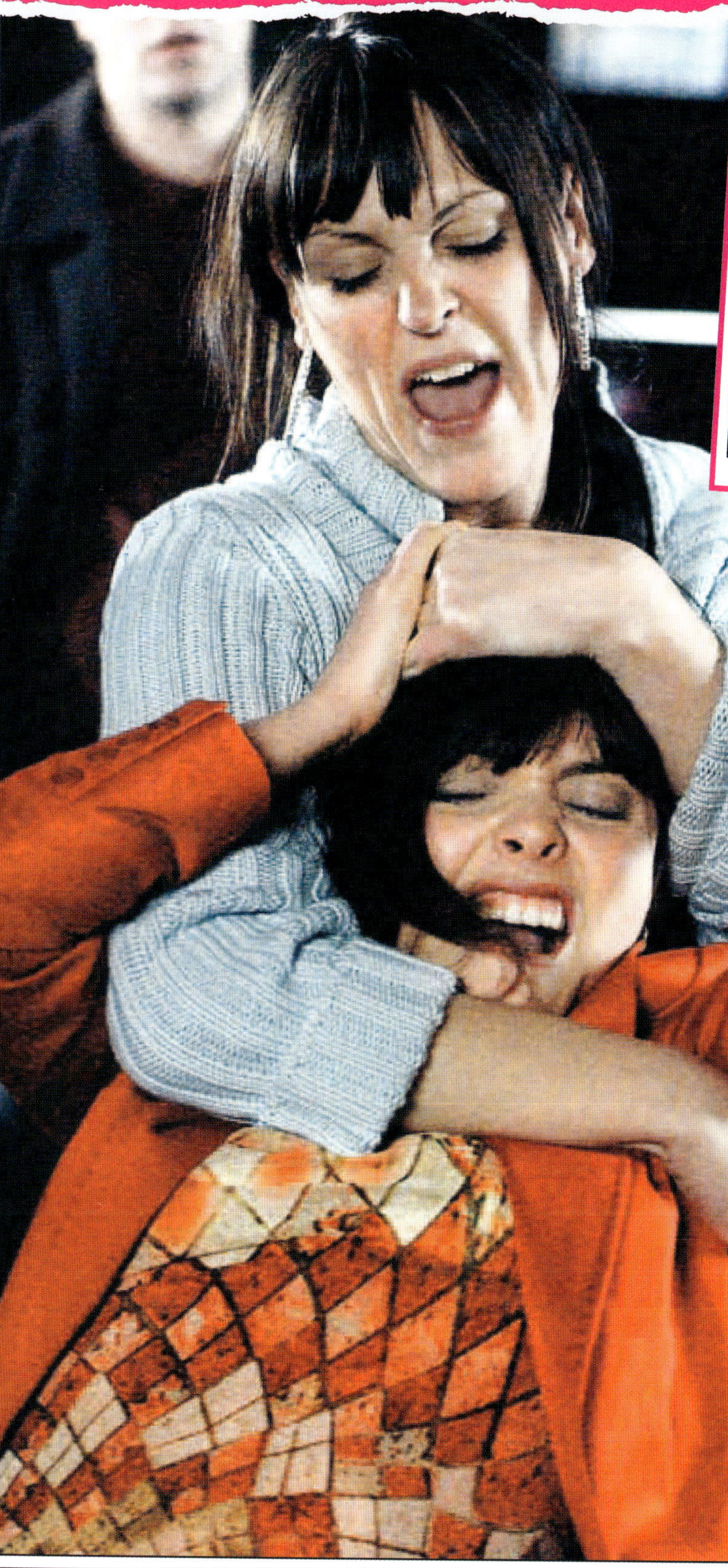

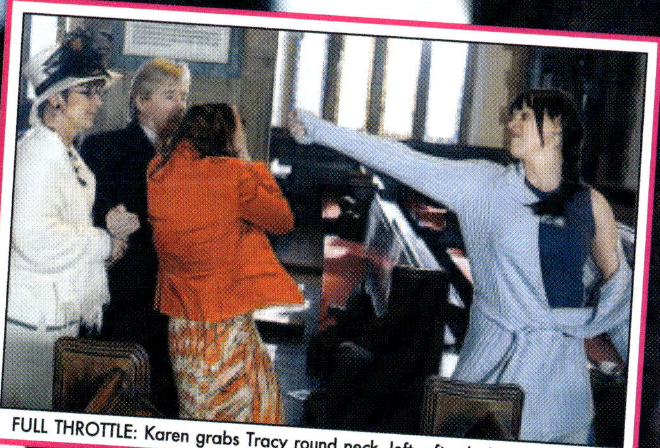

FULL THROTTLE: Karen grabs Tracy round neck, left, after lashing out, above

Corrie Karen wallops Tracy

By BRIAN ROBERTS

THIS is the moment Coronation Street's Karen McDonald gets spectacular revenge on Tracy Barlow for wrecking her wedding.

Karen (Suranne Jones) storms into the church where Tracy (Kate Ford) is having her baby Amy christened – and grabs Tracy, half-throttling her.

She yells: "Do unto others like you did to my wedding. I really owe you. This is pay back. Big time."

The rip-roaring catfight comes barely a month after Tracy burst in on Karen's big day to reveal that her groom Steve was Amy's dad.

This time the pair got so carried away there were real bruises and real hair was yanked out. Suranne said: "We were going for it and Anne Kirkbride (Deirdre Rachid) got knocked over.

"It was only when the director yelled 'cut' that I realised I had really been gripping Kate round the neck.

"She was making these strange noises but didn't say stop filming because she was sure it looked good! I had bruises where she clutched my arm."

Last time the pair battled it out in church, 16 million tuned in.

b.roberts@mirror.co.uk

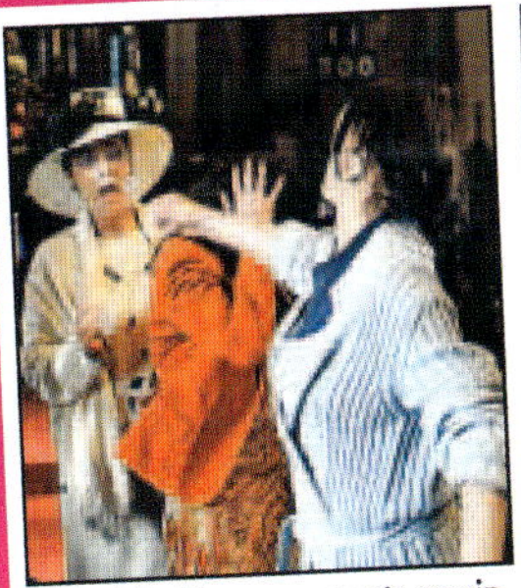

WHAM: Karen connects again

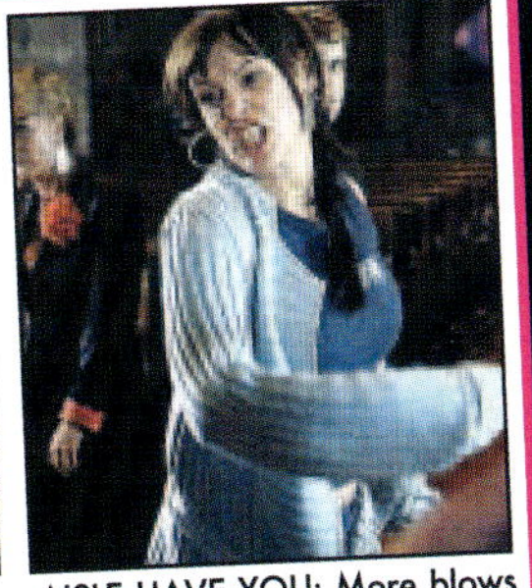

AISLE HAVE YOU: More blows

Monday, September 26, 2005

Mr Nasty loves Superbitch

CORONATION STREET bosses have lined up a relationship so nasty it threatens to blow Weatherfield apart.

Evil builder Charlie Stubbs is set to bed bitchy Tracy Barlow and spark a rollercoaster romance.

A Corrie insider said: "It's a piece of genius by the writers pairing the show's biggest bitch with the vilest villain.

"The antics they will get up to will obviously cause misery and heartache for many people."

Bill Ward, who plays Charlie, has made a huge impression on Corrie chiefs while portraying the twisted womaniser. Ratings soared last week for the climax to his dramatic wedding day to Rovers landlady Shelley Unwin (Sally Lindsay).

For months he had controlled Shelley with his evil mind games, reducing her to an emotional wreck.

But to the delight of millions of TV viewers Shelley eventually dumped him at the altar.

This time it was the builder who was humiliated and embarrassed...but in true Charlie fashion he'll be back to his old nasty self. He makes a move for Tracy Barlow, played by Kate Ford, when she is dumped by her mechanic boyfriend Nathan Harding (Ray Fearon).

They begin a steamy relationship which is only revealed to Tracy's mum and dad Deirdre and Ken, actors Anne Kirkbride and Bill Roache, on Christmas Day.

The Corrie insider said: "To Ken and Deirdre's horror, Tracy brings Charlie home for Christmas Day dinner.

"Her parents are appalled that Tracy has started a sexual relationship with Charlie and know that he will bring out the evil worst in their daughter.

"But despite their attempts to persuade Tracy she has made a bad choice of partner, she will revel in the drama and turmoil that her relationship with Charlie has created."

In a secret three-day storyline conference this month, Corrie's top brass discussed several possible storylines that will see the couple embark on a life of crime together. They believe the romance between Charlie and Tracy will make compulsive viewing.

Producer-to-be Steve Frost met the writers, who told him they have some dynamic storylines planned for the lovers.

The insider said: "It was decided that the two characters of Charlie and Tracy were very much part of the programme's long-term future.

"It therefore made sense to cement them together as a couple and to give them storylines guaranteed to make them two of Weatherfield's most hated."

Tracy has secured her superbitch status with storylines including bedding Deirdre's ex-flame Dev Alahan (Jimmi Harkishin), then cutting up all his clothes when he wouldn't marry her.

But her nastiest trick was drugging Roy Cropper (David Neilson) and pretending he had made her pregnant, when in fact Steve McDonald (Simon Gregson) was the father.

Charlie has done himself no favours either, seducing a string of women including barmaid Violet (Jenny Platt) and even Shelley's mum Bev (Susie Blake).

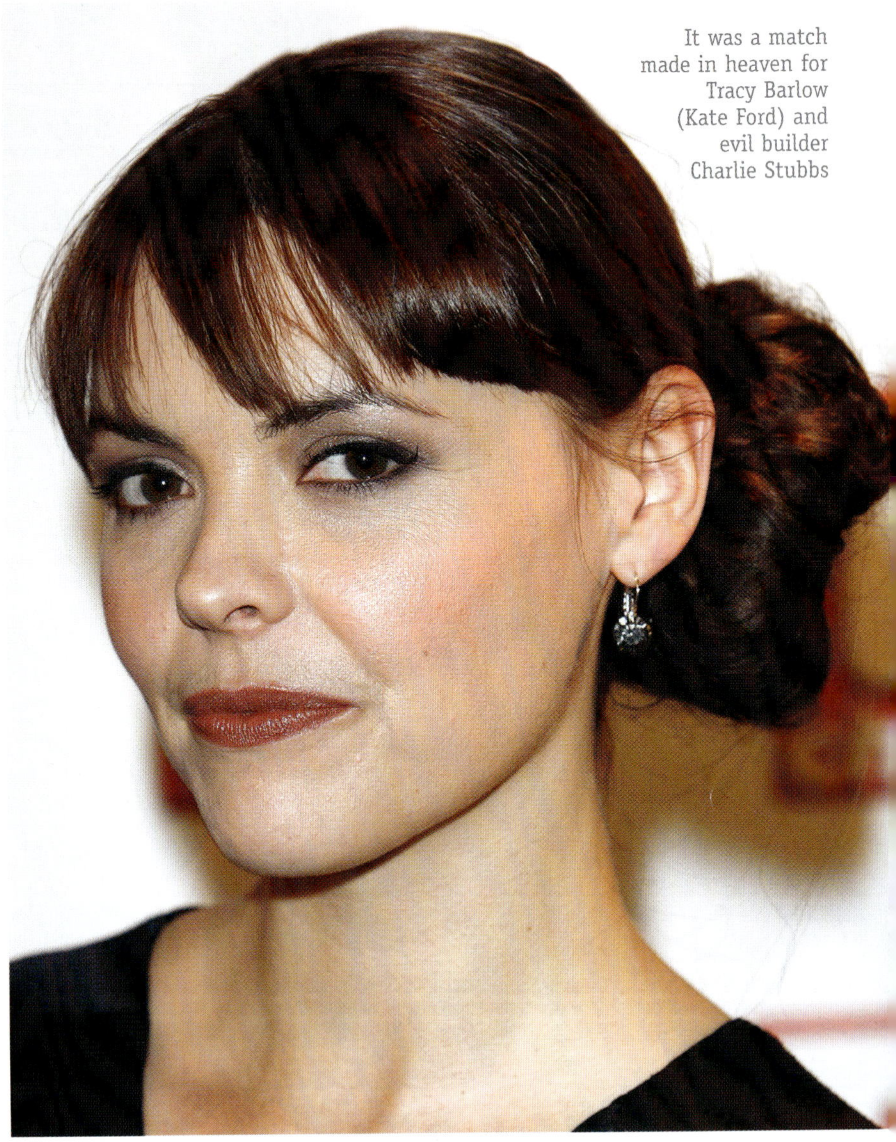

It was a match made in heaven for Tracy Barlow (Kate Ford) and evil builder Charlie Stubbs

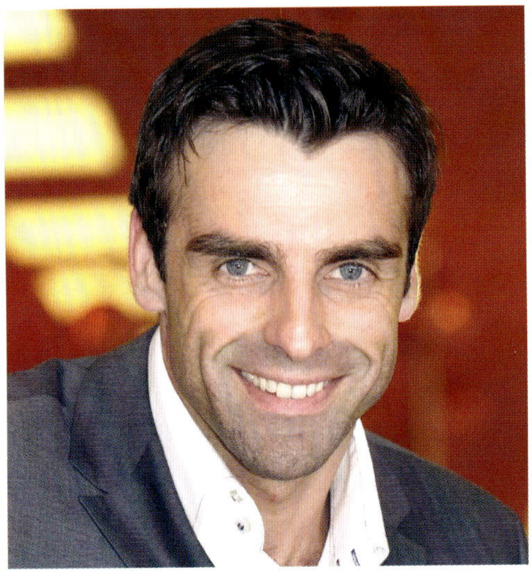

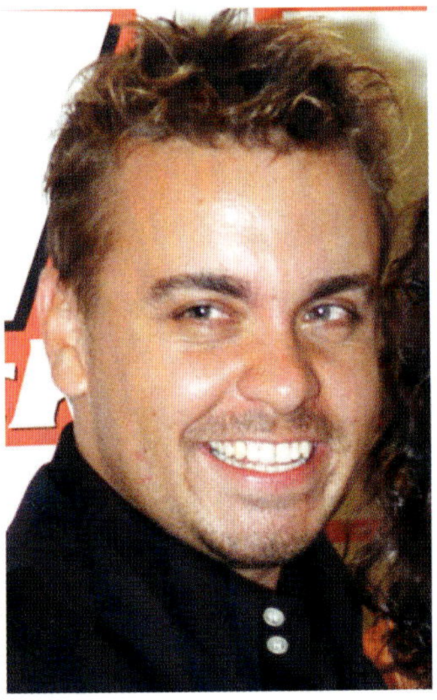

Above left: Jonathon Wrather as Joe Carter, Underworld manager and ladies' man of the factory. Right: Lee Boardman, who played drug dealer and gangster Jez Quigley

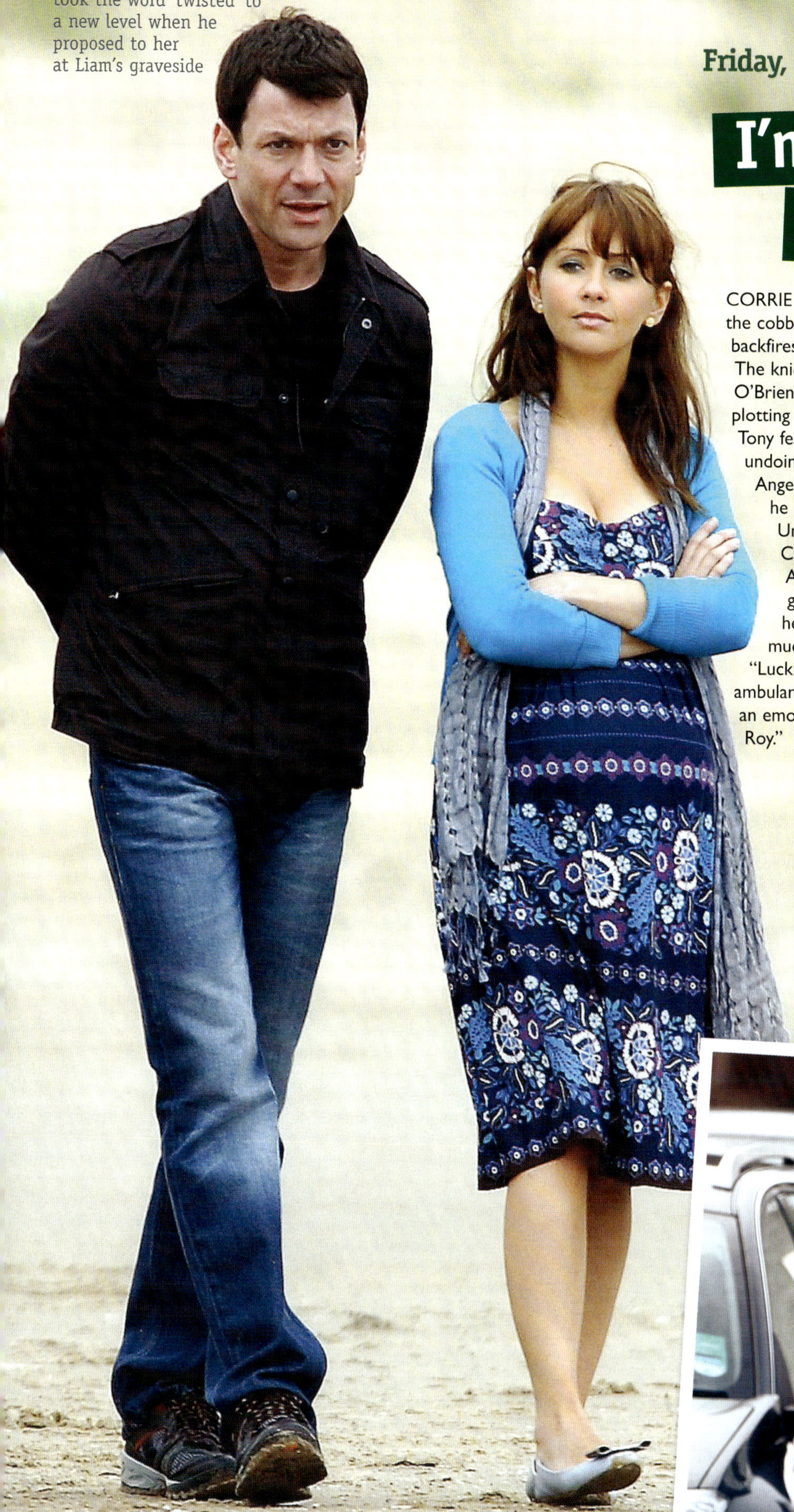

Not content with murdering Maria's husband, Tony Gordon took the word 'twisted' to a new level when he proposed to her at Liam's graveside

Friday, October 16, 2009

I'm having a Corrienary!

CORRIE killer Tony Gordon slumps on the cobbles after his evil scheming backfires – and nearly costs him his life.

The knicker factory boss, played by Gray O'Brien, keels over from a heart attack while plotting to bump off his ex-wife, Carla.

Tony fears his murderous past will be his undoing following Carla's shock return from Los Angeles on Monday. She threatens to reveal that he murdered Liam unless he hands over his Underworld shares. So Tony decides to silence Carla – for good.

An insider on the ITV1 soap said: "Tony does get Carla out of his life, but not in the way he intended. Then the stress proves too much.

"Luckily, Roy Cropper is passing and calls an ambulance. Thinking he's about to die, Tony makes an emotional confession about Liam's murder to Roy."

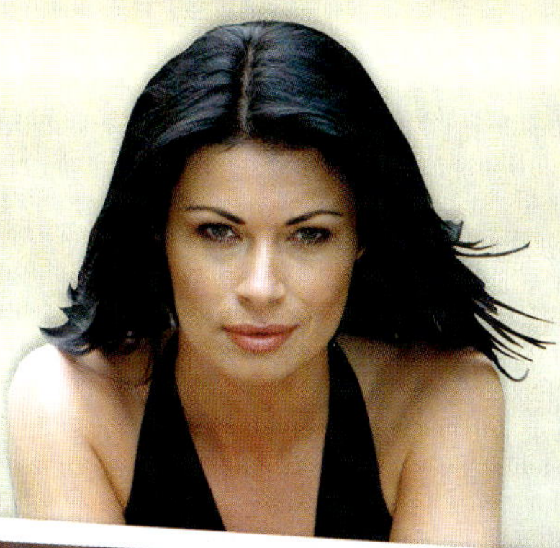

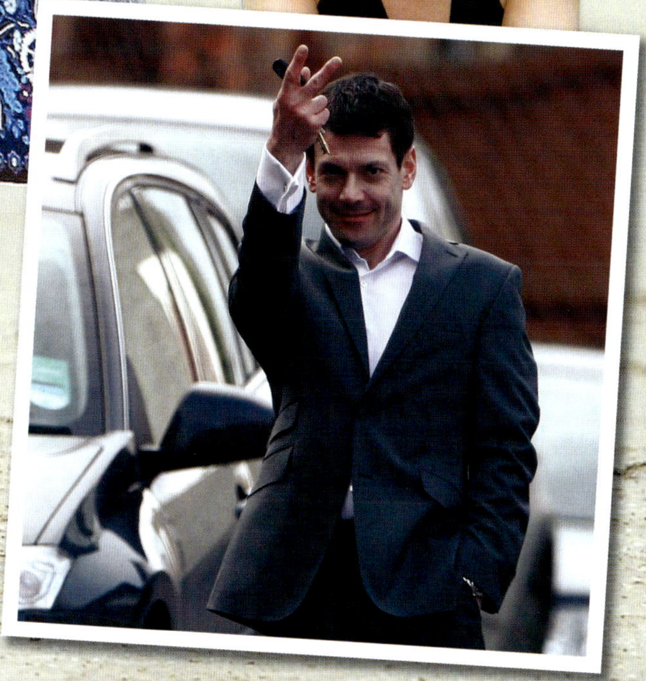

Rest in peace...

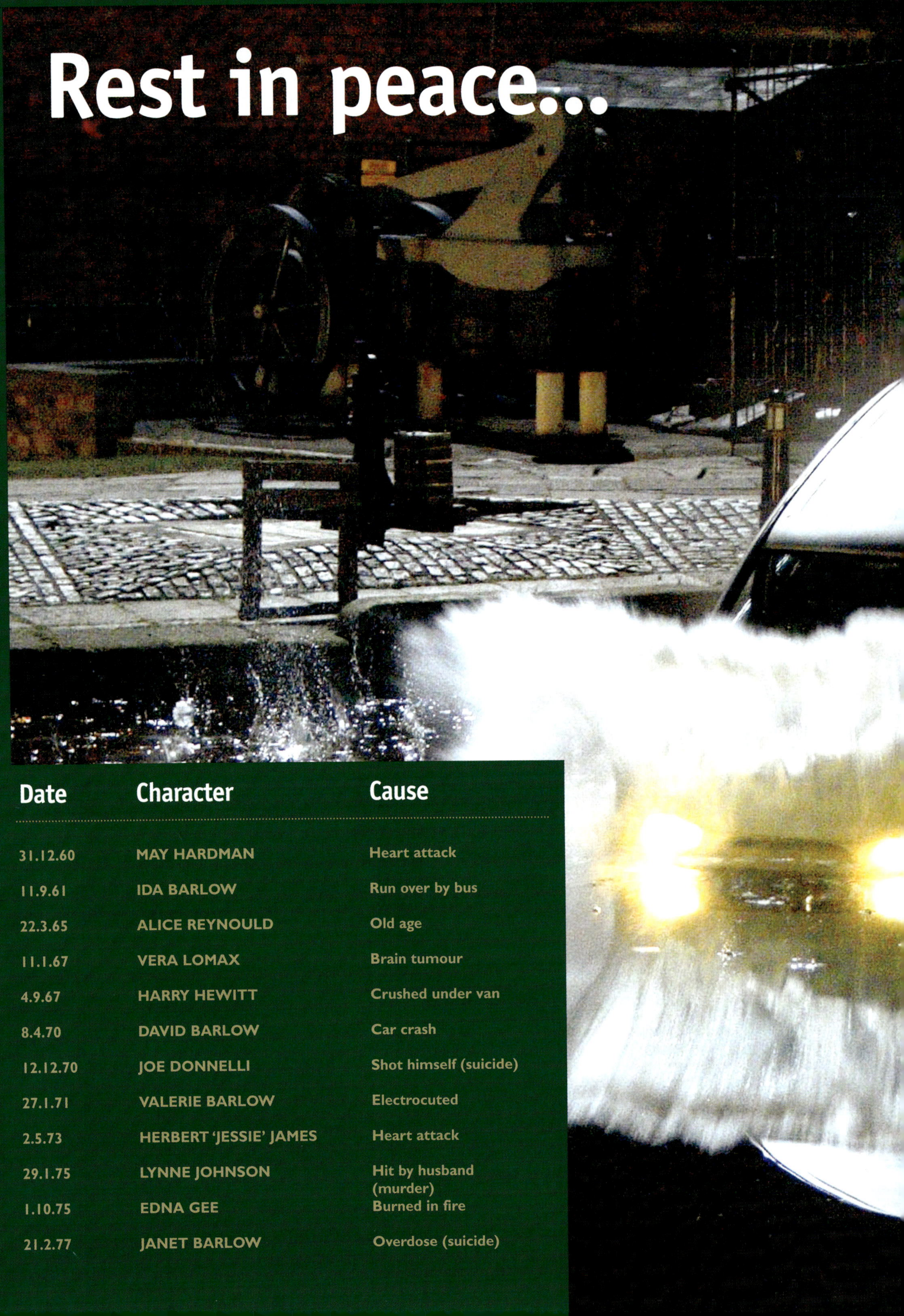

Date	Character	Cause
31.12.60	MAY HARDMAN	Heart attack
11.9.61	IDA BARLOW	Run over by bus
22.3.65	ALICE REYNOULD	Old age
11.1.67	VERA LOMAX	Brain tumour
4.9.67	HARRY HEWITT	Crushed under van
8.4.70	DAVID BARLOW	Car crash
12.12.70	JOE DONNELLI	Shot himself (suicide)
27.1.71	VALERIE BARLOW	Electrocuted
2.5.73	HERBERT 'JESSIE' JAMES	Heart attack
29.1.75	LYNNE JOHNSON	Hit by husband (murder)
1.10.75	EDNA GEE	Burned in fire
21.2.77	JANET BARLOW	Overdose (suicide)

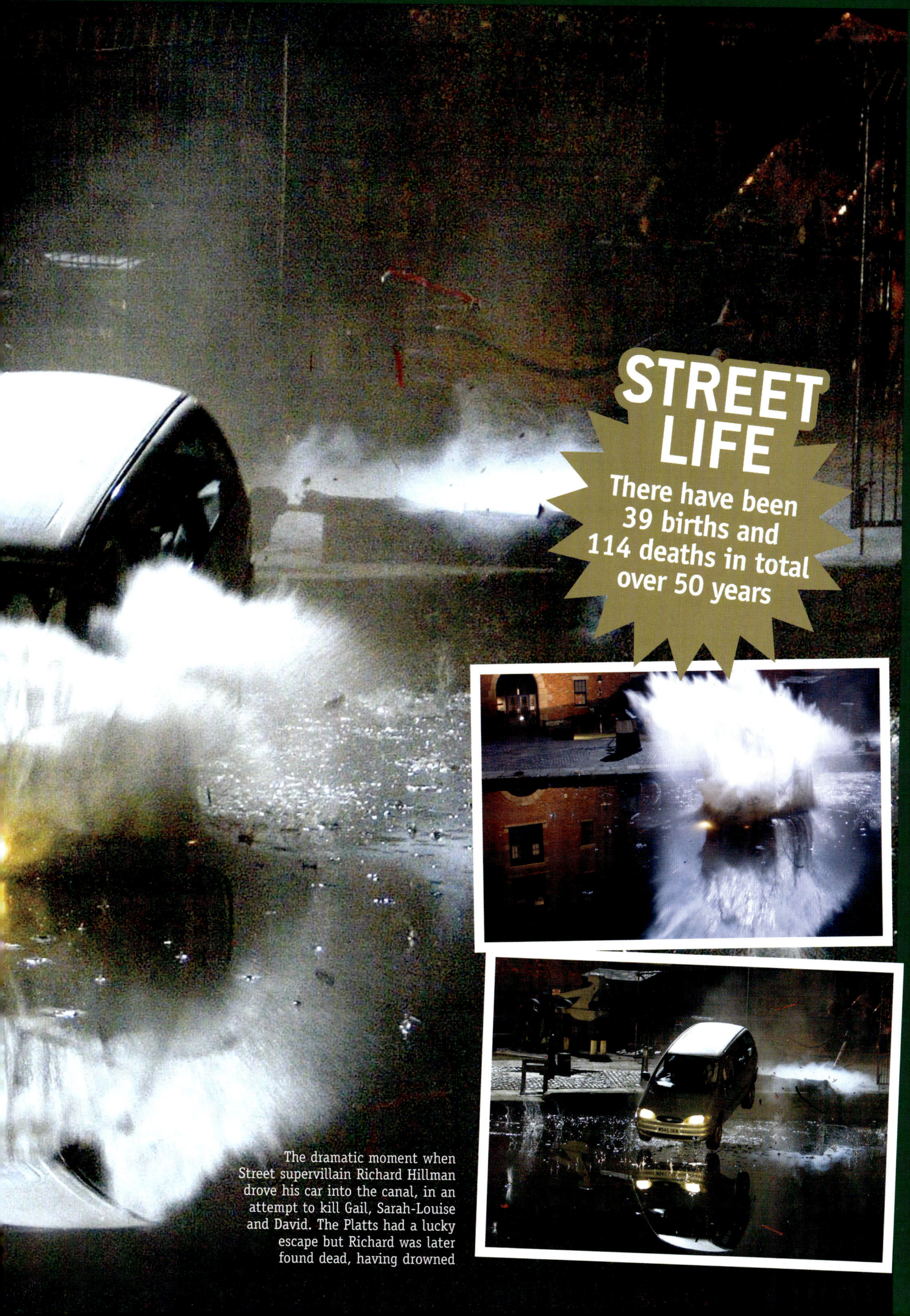

STREET LIFE

There have been 39 births and 114 deaths in total over 50 years

The dramatic moment when Street supervillain Richard Hillman drove his car into the canal, in an attempt to kill Gail, Sarah-Louise and David. The Platts had a lucky escape but Richard was later found dead, having drowned

DEATHS

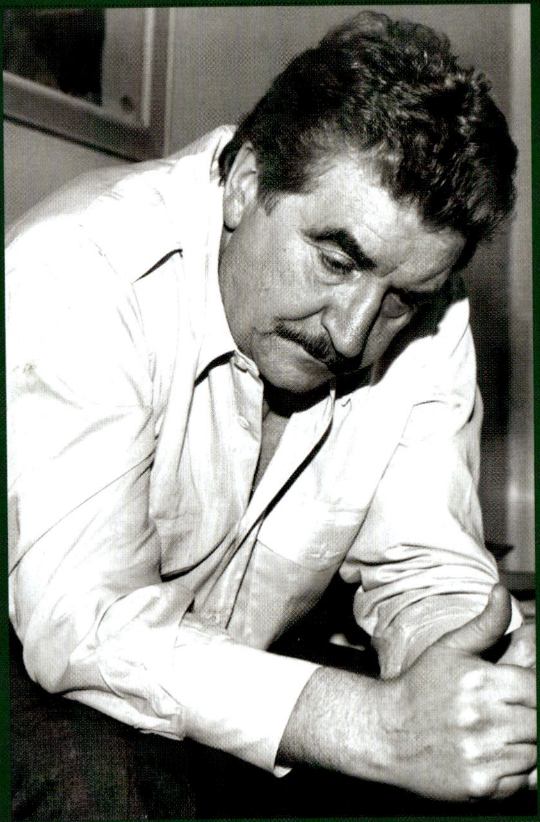

17.8.77	EDIE RILEY	Old age
11.1.78	ERNEST BISHOP	Shot (murder)
30.7.80	RENEE ROBERTS	Car crash
7.12.83	LEN FAIRCLOUGH	Car crash
14.5.84	ALBERT TATLOCK	Old age
21.11.84	STAN OGDEN	Old age
3.6.85	DON ASHTON	Drowned
23.11.87	JOAN LOWTHER	Heart attack
15.2.89	BRIAN TILSLEY	Stabbed (murder)
8.12.89	ALAN BRADLEY	Run over by a tram
17.8.90	PETER INGRAM	Heart attack
18.2.91	AMY BURTON	Heart attack
19.7.91	SANDRA ARDEN	Car crash

19.7.91	TIM ARDEN	Car crash
9.9.92	TED SULLIVAN	Brain Tumour
12.2.93	LISA DUCKWORTH	Brain damage
5.5.93	LES CURRY	Heart attack
20.8.93	BRENDAN SCOTT	Heart attack
25.3.94	MANDY BAKER	Cardiac arrest
2.6.95	SAMIR RACHID	Fractured skull (murder)
21.6.95	CLIFF DUCKWORTH	Car crash
21.6.95	ELSIE DUCKWORTH	Car crash

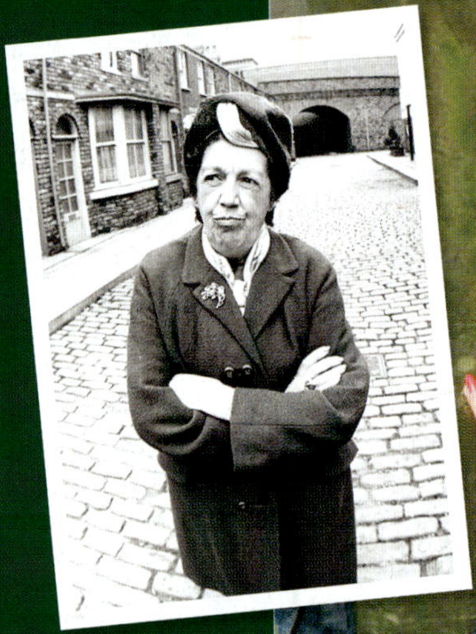

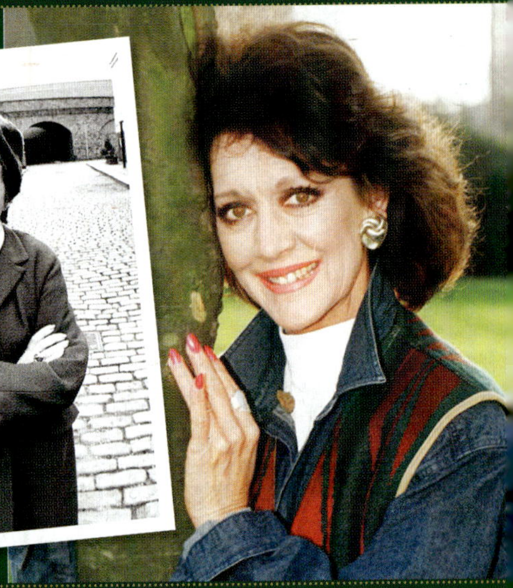

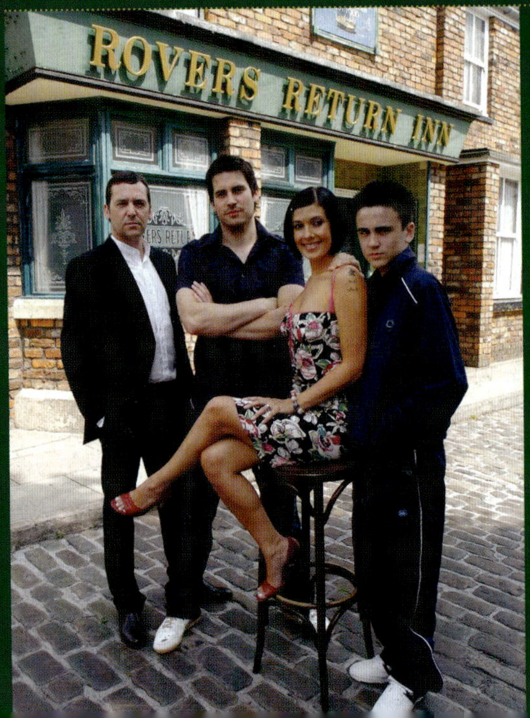

23.8.95	IVY BRENNAN	Stroke
21.2.97	JOYCE SMEDLEY	Broken neck
7.4.97	DEREK WILTON	Heart attack
8.10.97	DON BRENNAN	Car crash
3.11.97	BILLY WILLIAMS	Heart attack
18.3.98	BABS FANSHAWE	Heart attack
17.4.98	SHANNON TATTERSALL	Meningitis
25.5.98	ELSIE SEDDON	Stroke
9.10.98	ANNE MALONE	Frozen to death
18.11.98	DES BARNES	Heart attack (murder)
1.1.99	ALF ROBERTS	Heart attack
7.2.99	WALTER BYFORD	Heart attack

6.8.99	SIDNEY TEMPLETON	Heart attack
24.9.99	JUDY MALLETT	Embolism
7.6.00	ALISON WEBSTER	Hit by lorry (suicide)
15.9.00	JEZ QUIGLEY	Internal injuries after fight
12.10.00	DEAN SYKES	Shot
11.2.01	SUSAN BARLOW	Car crash
17.6.01	ALMA HALLIWELL	Cervical cancer
19.9.01	EDNA MILLER	Heart attack
2.1.02	DENNIS STRINGER	Car crash
4.2.02	DUGGIE FERGUSON	Fell through banister
20.5.02	PATRICIA HILLMAN	Hit with a shovel (murder)
13.1.03	MAXINE PEACOCK	Hit with a crowbar (murder)

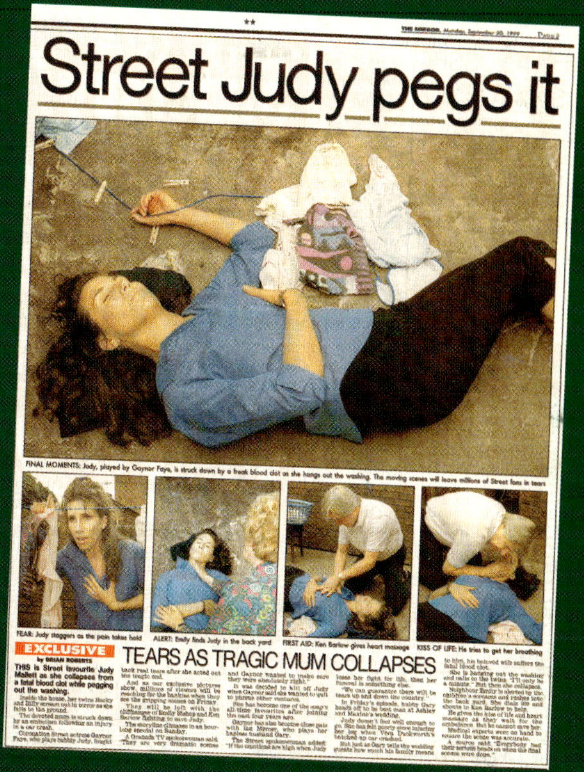
Street Judy pegs it
EXCLUSIVE
TEARS AS TRAGIC MUM COLLAPSES

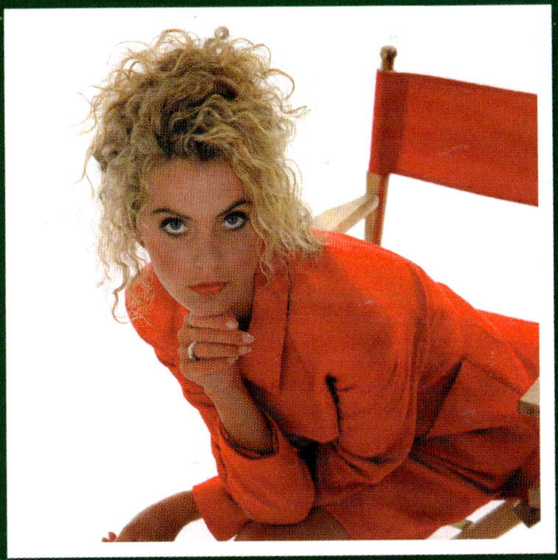

11.3.03	RICHARD HILLMAN	Drowned (suicide)
28.11.03	CECIL NEWTON	Heart attack
2.6.04	BILLY PLATT	Premature birth
2.3.05	TOMMY HARRIS	Hit with a wrench (murder)
10.4.05	RAY LANGTON	Stomach cancer
20.4.05	KATY HARRIS	Cerebral Oedema (suicide)
7.4.06	MIKE BALDWIN	Alzheimer's & heart attack

9.10.06	FRED ELLIOTT	Stroke
15.1.07	CHARLIE STUBBS	Hit with ornament (murder)
16.4.07	KASIA BAROWICZ	Broken neck
6.6.07	PAUL CONNOR	Car crash
3.10.07	FRANK NICHOLS	Old age
18.1.08	VERA DUCKWORTH	Heart attack
30.4.08	PAUL CONNOR	Still birth
16.10.08	LIAM CONNOR	Run over by a car (murder)
30.1.09	MIKE SCOTT	Clot on lung
18.5.09	COLIN GRIMSHAW	Heart attack
8.2.10	JOE MCINTYRE	Drowned
1.6.10	ROBBIE SLOANE	Shot (murder)
1.6.10	TONY GORDON	Burned in fire (suicide)
30.7.10	COLIN FISHWICK	Haemorrhage after fight

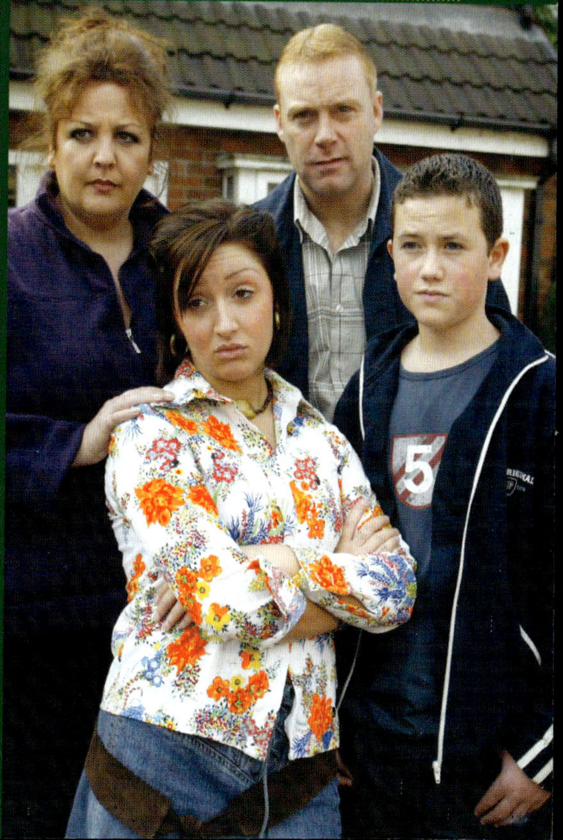

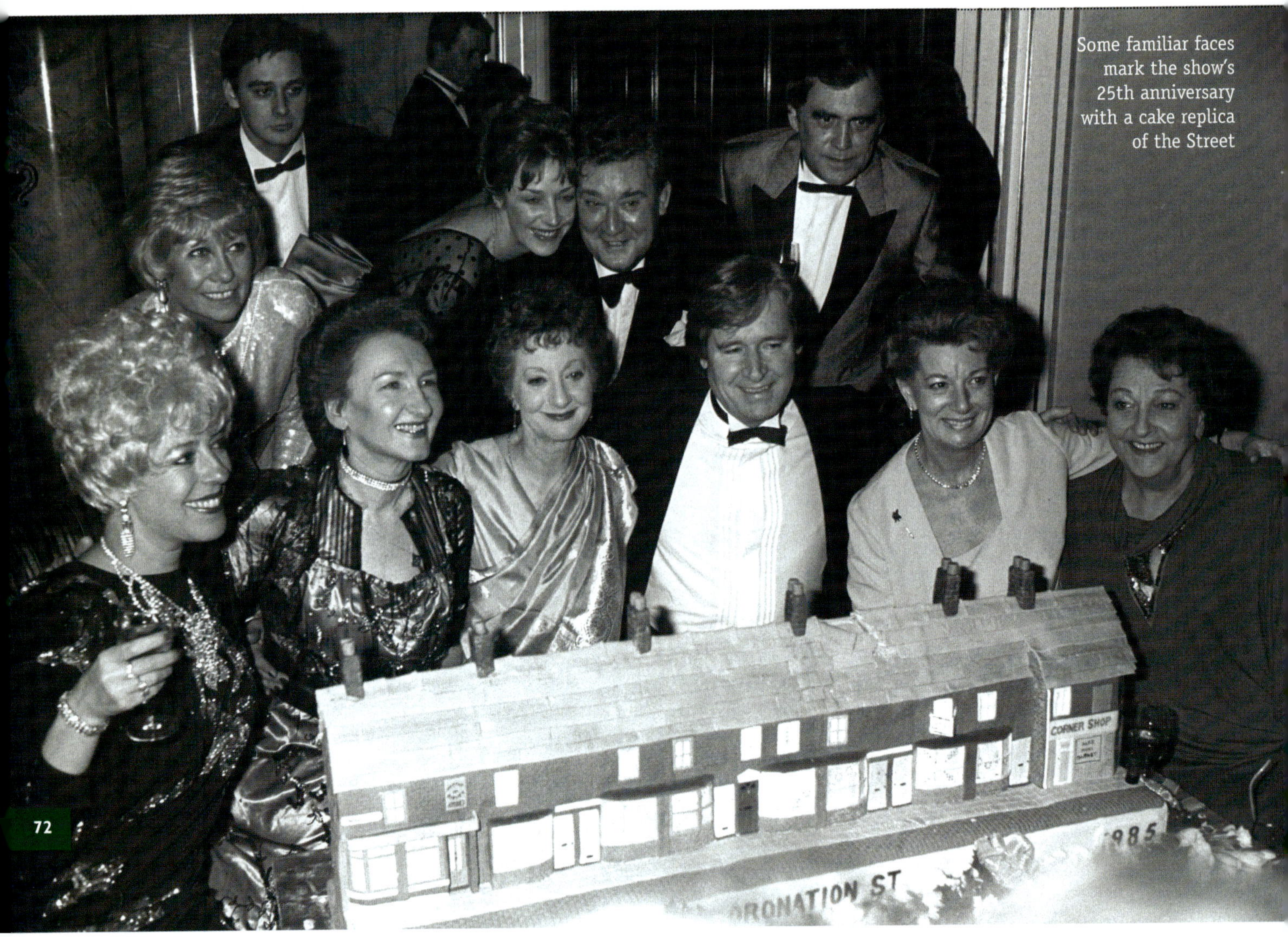

Some familiar faces mark the show's 25th anniversary with a cake replica of the Street

Faces we'll remember

Over the past 50 years, countless characters have made their home on Coronation Street. Here's a small selection of some of our favourites who are no longer in the show . . .

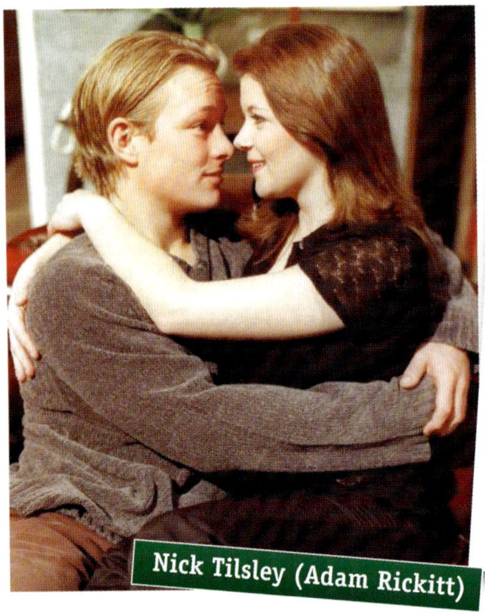

Nick Tilsley (Adam Rickitt)

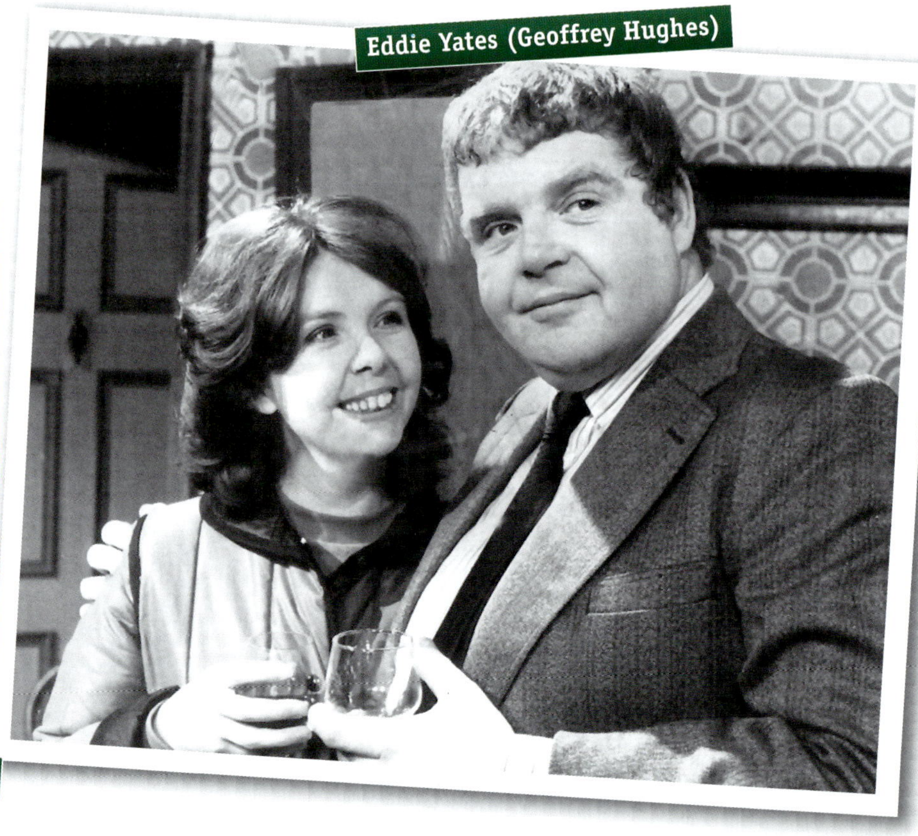

Eddie Yates (Geoffrey Hughes)

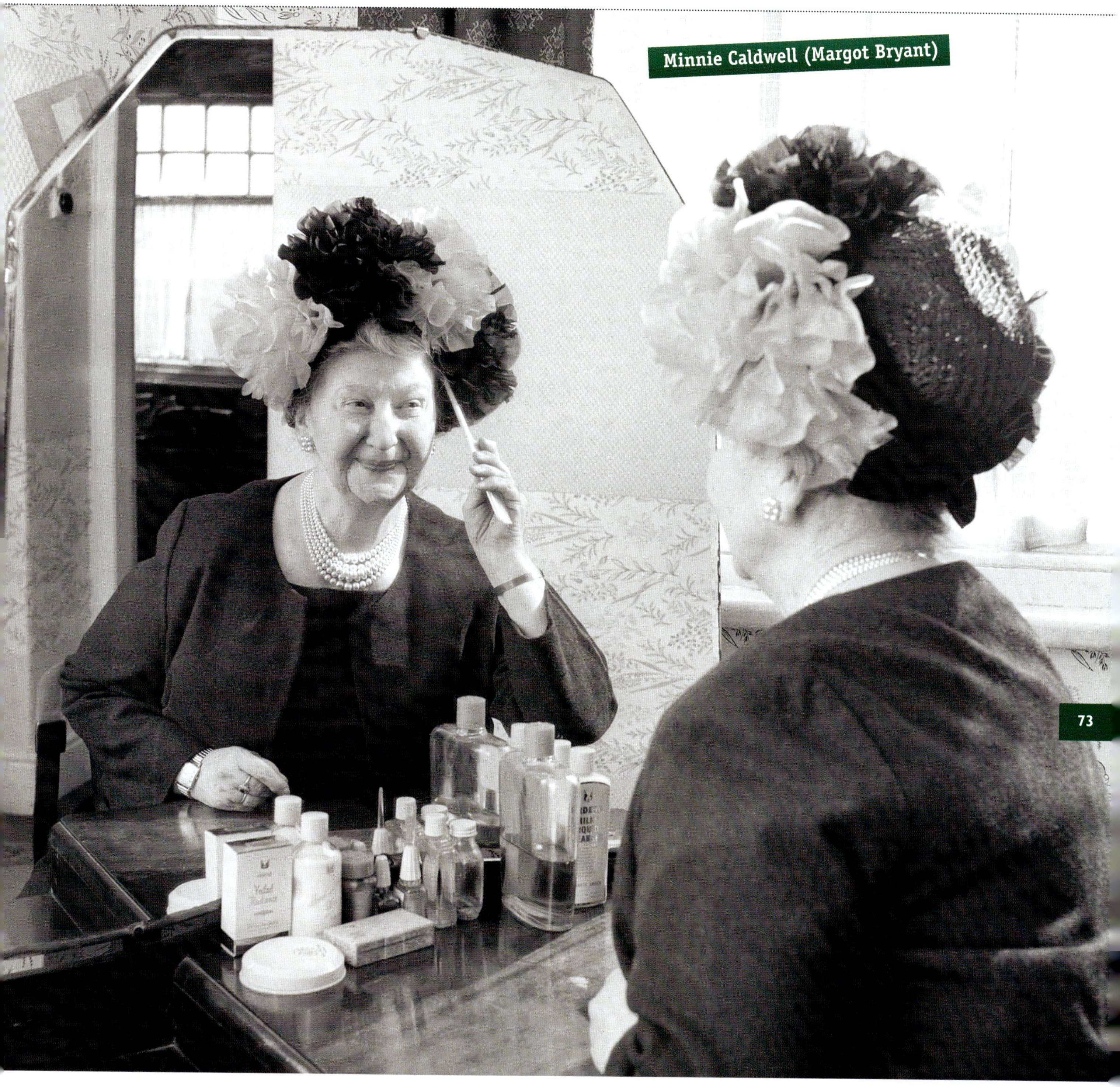

Minnie Caldwell (Margot Bryant)

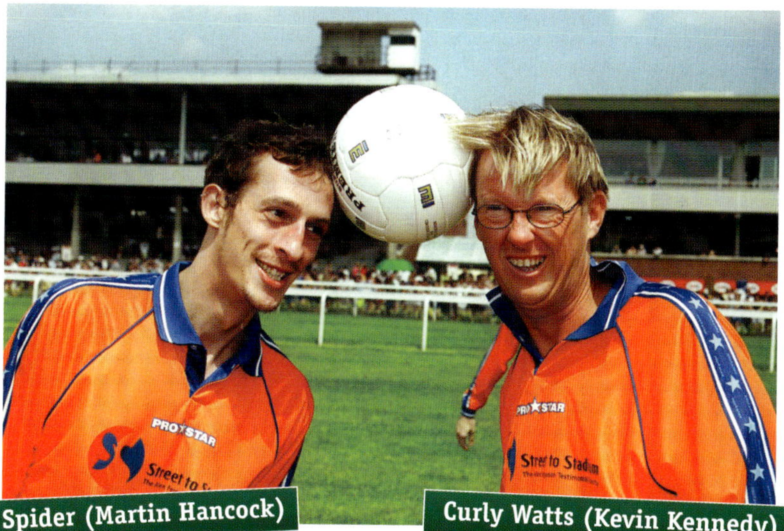

Spider (Martin Hancock)

Curly Watts (Kevin Kennedy)

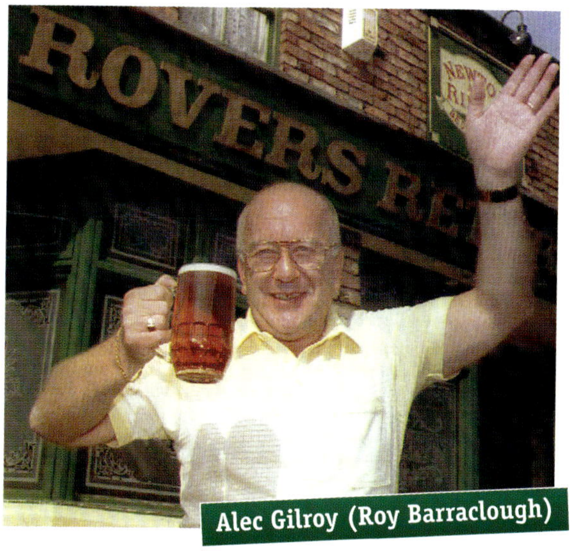

Alec Gilroy (Roy Barraclough)

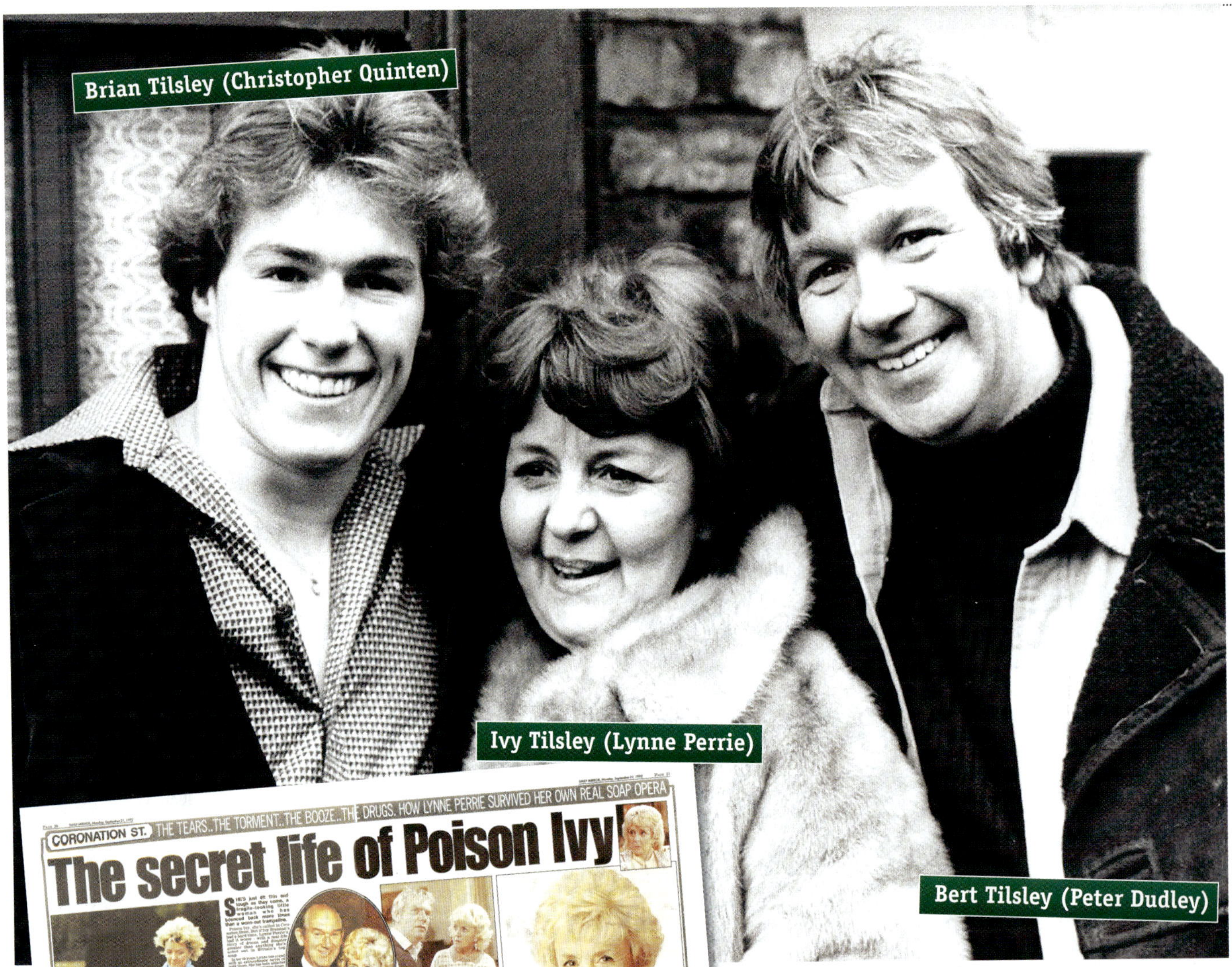

Brian Tilsley (Christopher Quinten)

Ivy Tilsley (Lynne Perrie)

Bert Tilsley (Peter Dudley)

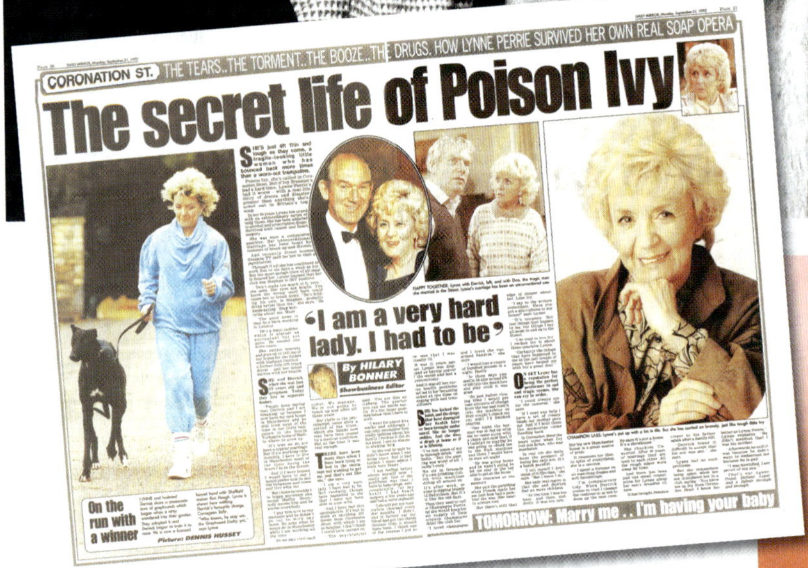

CORONATION ST. THE TEARS..THE TORMENT..THE BOOZE..THE DRUGS. HOW LYNNE PERRIE SURVIVED HER OWN REAL SOAP OPERA

The secret life of Poison Ivy

SHE'S just 4ft 11in and tough as they come, a fragile-looking little woman who has bounced back more times than a worn-out trampoline.

'I am a very hard lady. I had to be'

By HILARY BONNER
Showbusiness Editor

On the run with a winner

Picture: DENNIS HUSSEY

TOMORROW: Marry me . . I'm having your baby

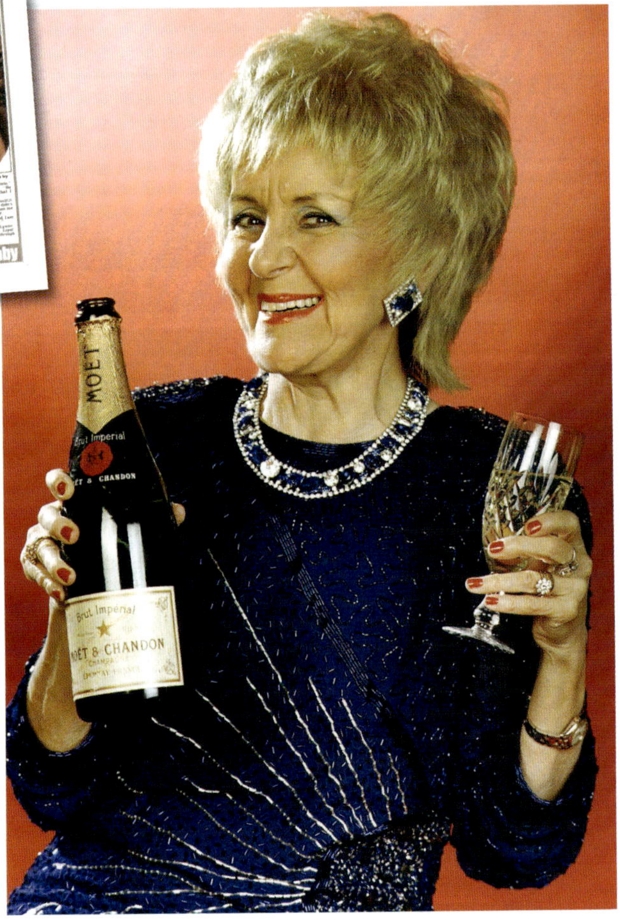

Alf Roberts (Bryan Mosley)

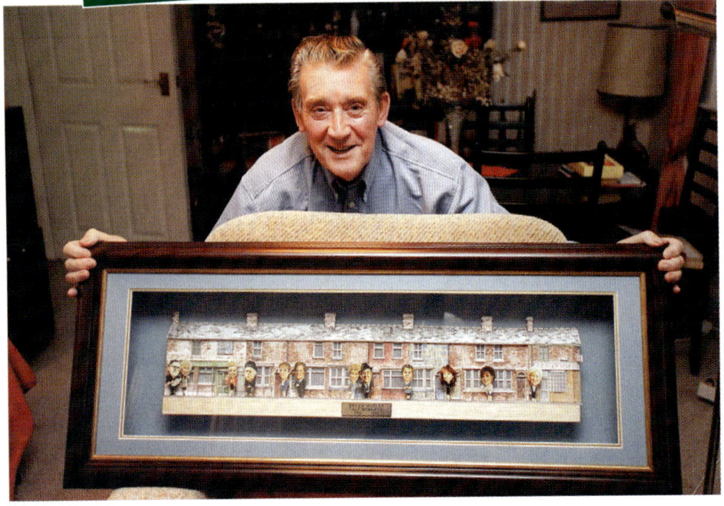

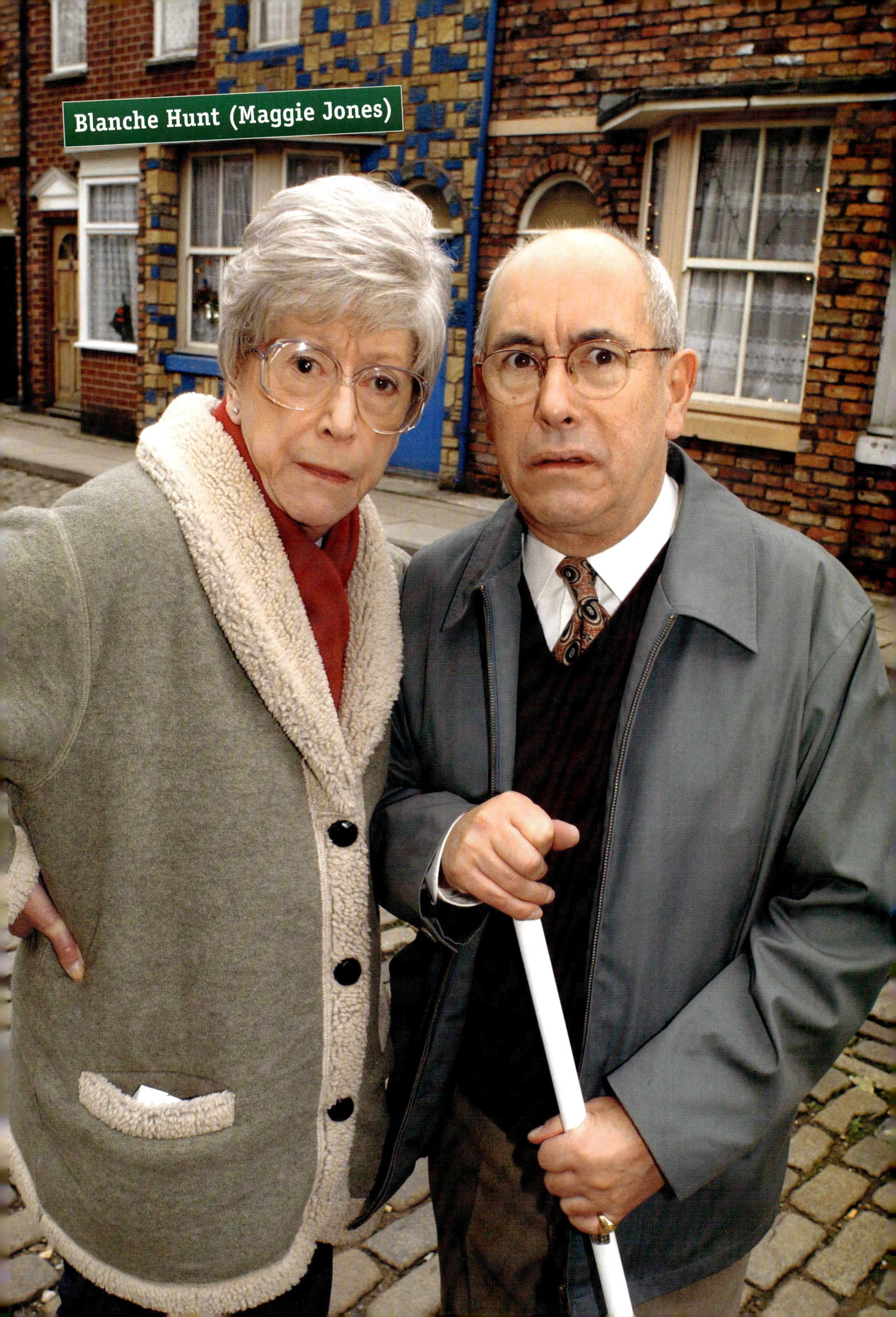

Blanche Hunt (Maggie Jones)

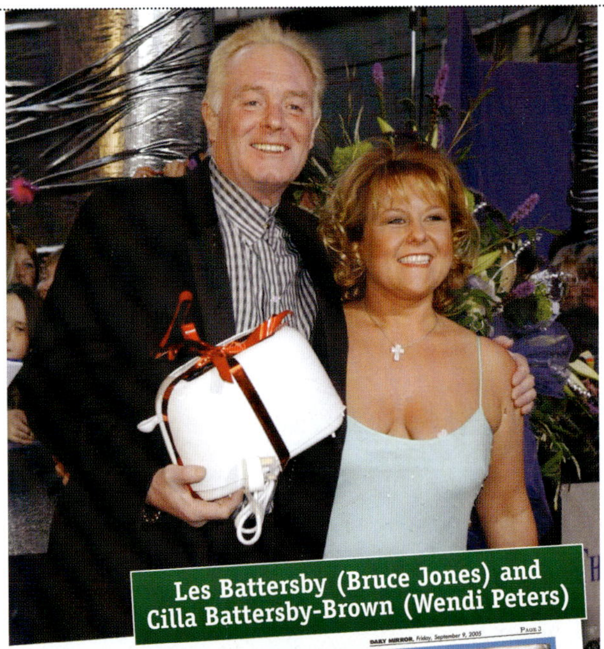

Les Battersby (Bruce Jones) and
Cilla Battersby-Brown (Wendi Peters)

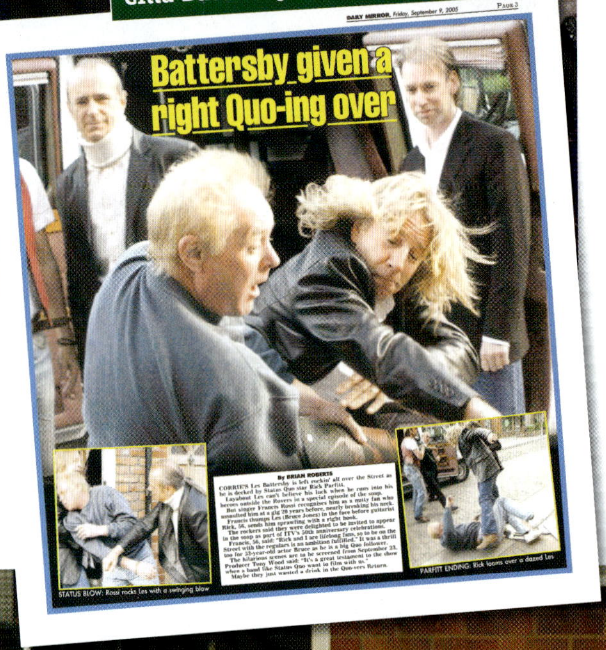

DAILY MIRROR, Friday, September 9, 2005 PAGE 3

Battersby given a right Quo-ing over

By BRIAN ROBERTS

CORRIE'S Les Battersby is left rockin' all over the Street as he is decked by Status Quo star Rick Parfitt.

Layabout Les can't believe his luck when he runs into his heroes outside the Rovers in a special episode of the soap.

But singer Francis Rossi recognises him as a nutty fan who assaulted him at a gig 20 years before, nearly breaking his neck.

Francis thumps Les (Bruce Jones) in the face before guitarist Rick, 56, sends him sprawling with a right hook.

The rockers said they were delighted to be invited to appear in the soap as part of ITV's 50th anniversary celebrations.

Francis, 56, said: "Rick and I are lifelong fans, so to be on the Street with the regulars is an ambition fulfilled." It was a thrill too for 52-year-old actor Bruce as he is a big Quo follower.

The hilarious scenes are to be screened from September 23.

Producer Tony Wood said: "It's a great testament to the show when a band like Status Quo want to film with us."

Maybe they just wanted a drink in the Quo-vers Return.

STATUS BLOW: Rossi rocks Les with a swinging blow

PARFITT ENDING: Rick looms over a dazed Les

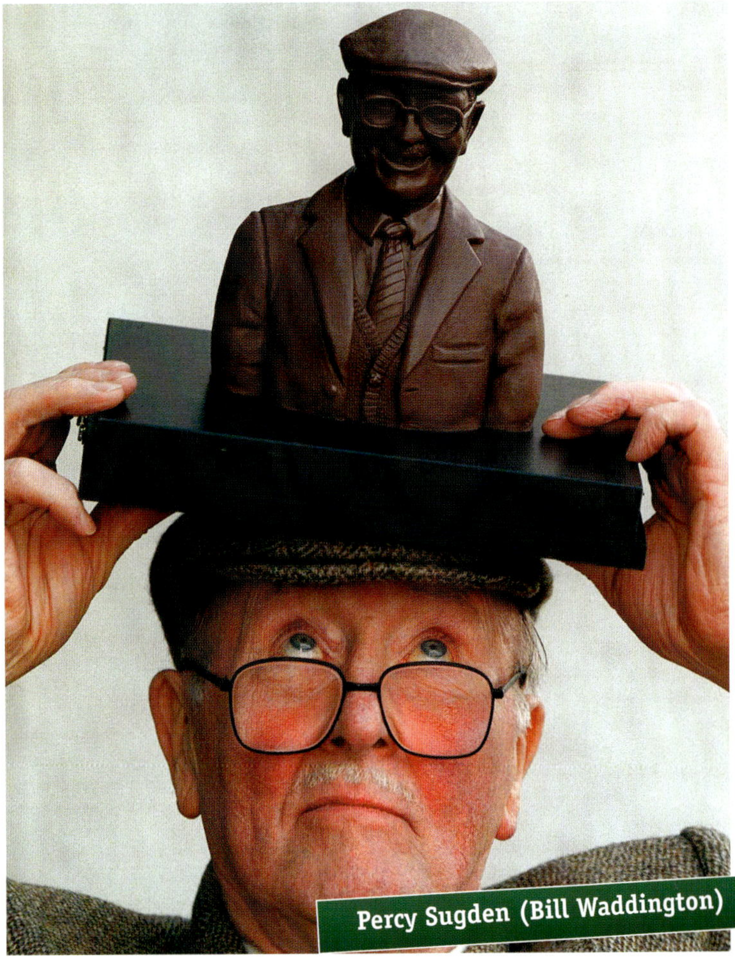

Percy Sugden (Bill Waddington)

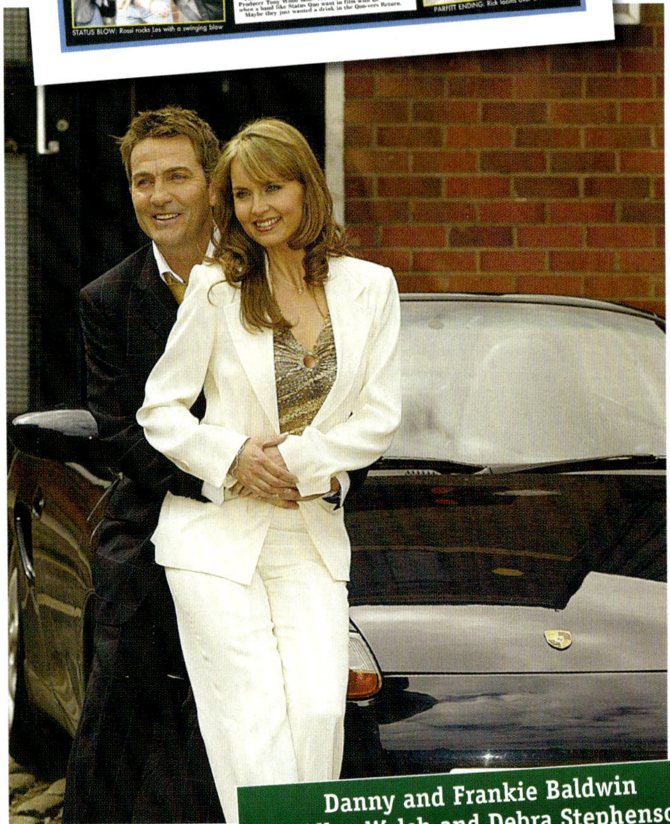

Danny and Frankie Baldwin
(Bradley Walsh and Debra Stephenson)

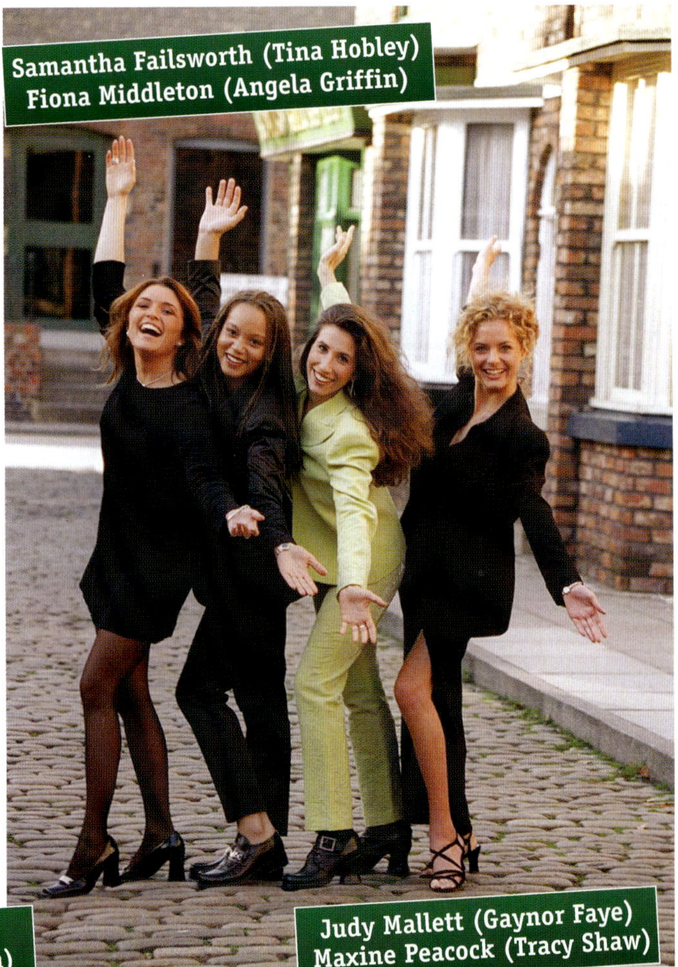

Samantha Failsworth (Tina Hobley)
Fiona Middleton (Angela Griffin)
Judy Mallett (Gaynor Faye)
Maxine Peacock (Tracy Shaw)

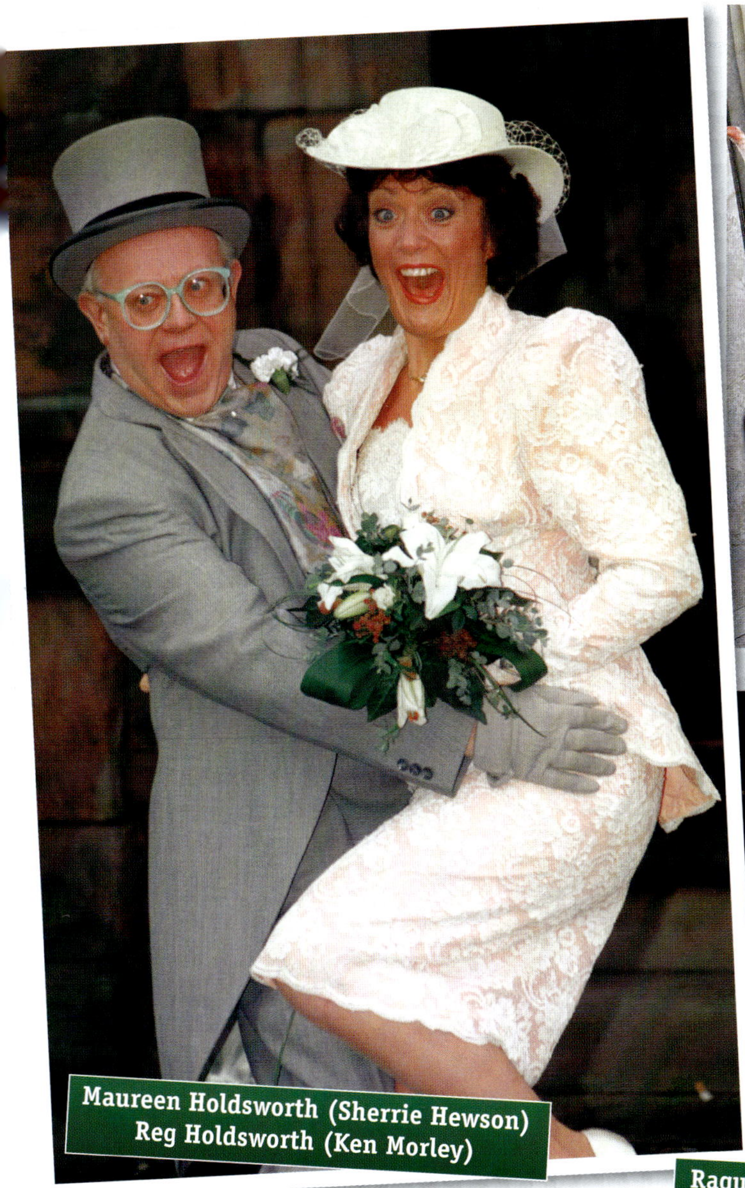

Maureen Holdsworth (Sherrie Hewson)
Reg Holdsworth (Ken Morley)

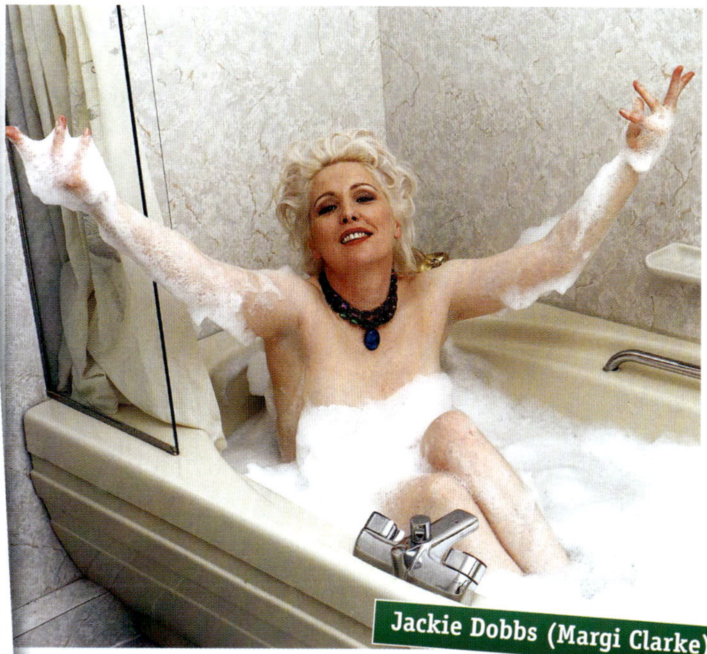

Jackie Dobbs (Margi Clarke)

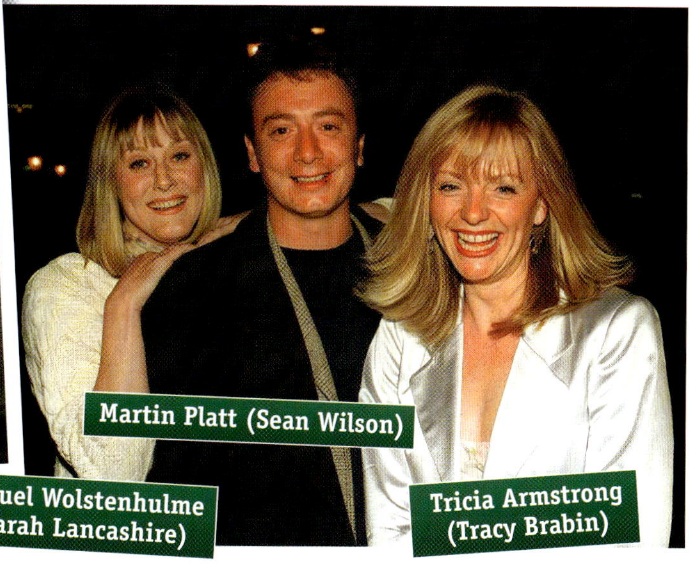

Martin Platt (Sean Wilson)

Raquel Wolstenhulme (Sarah Lancashire)

Tricia Armstrong (Tracy Brabin)

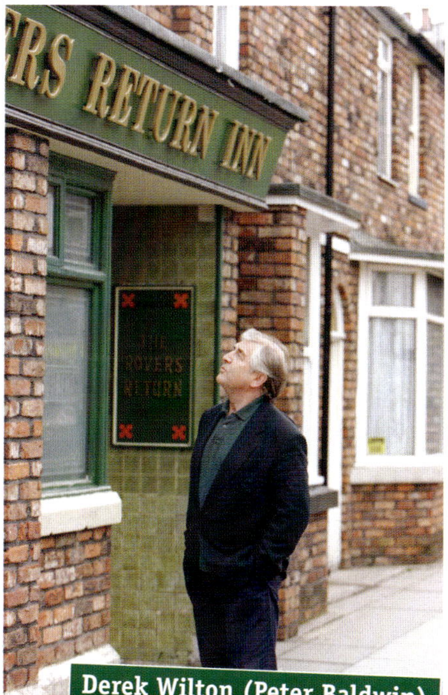

Derek Wilton (Peter Baldwin)

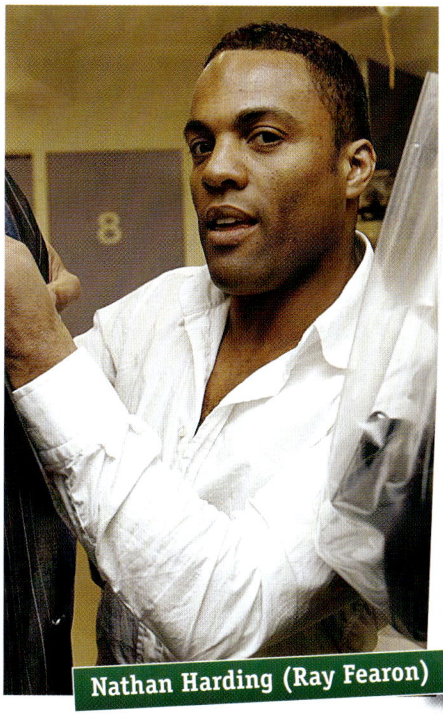

Nathan Harding (Ray Fearon)

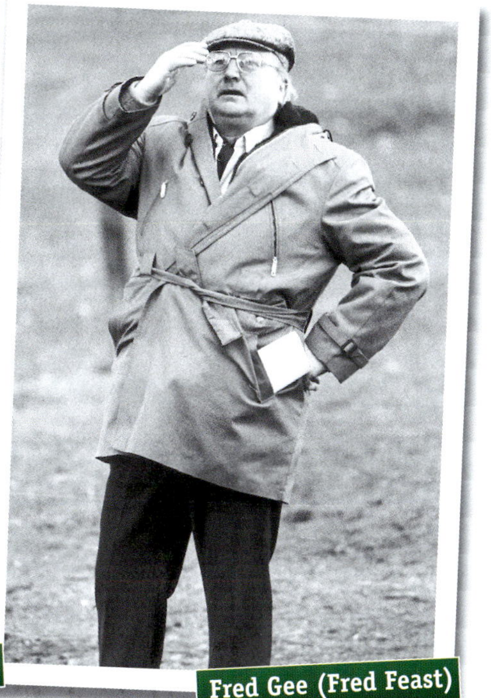

Fred Gee (Fred Feast)

Screen favourites

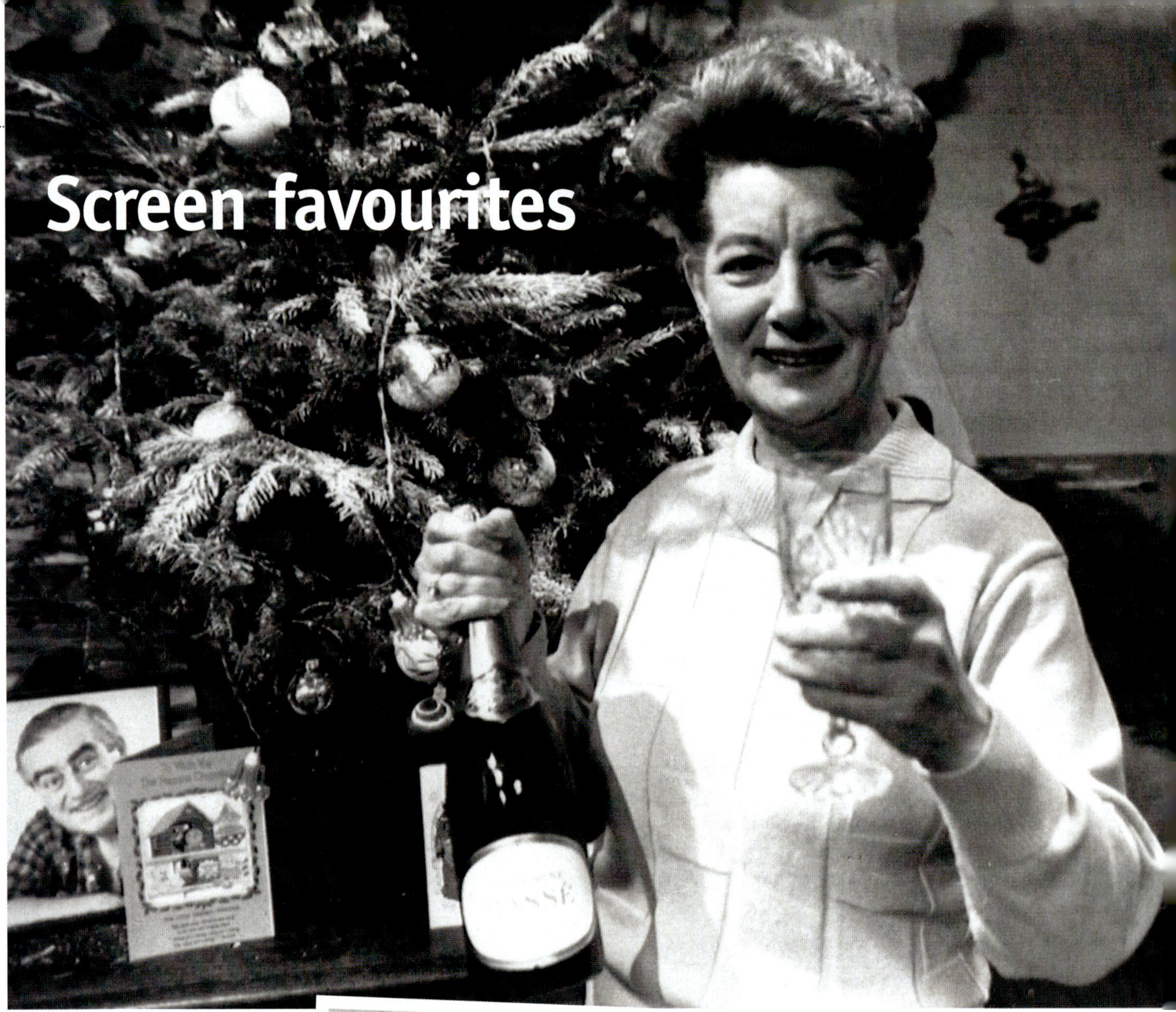

- **Hilda's farewell – 26.6 million (1987)**
- **Deirdre/Mike/Ken love triangle – 20 million (1983)**
- **Richard Hillman's confession – 19.4 million (2003)**
- **Alan Bradley under tram – 19 million (1989)**
- **Deirdre sent to prison – 18.9 million (1998)**
- **Don dies on screen – 17.3 million (1997)**

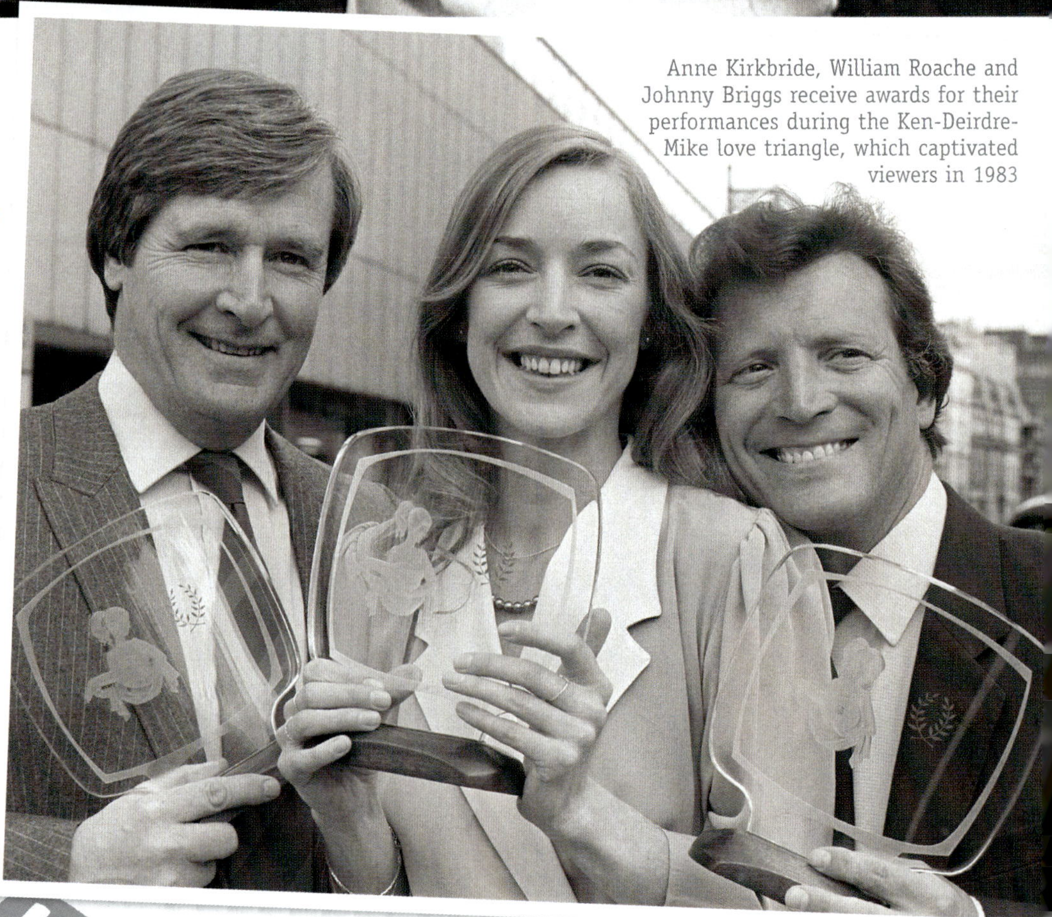

Anne Kirkbride, William Roache and Johnny Briggs receive awards for their performances during the Ken-Deirdre-Mike love triangle, which captivated viewers in 1983

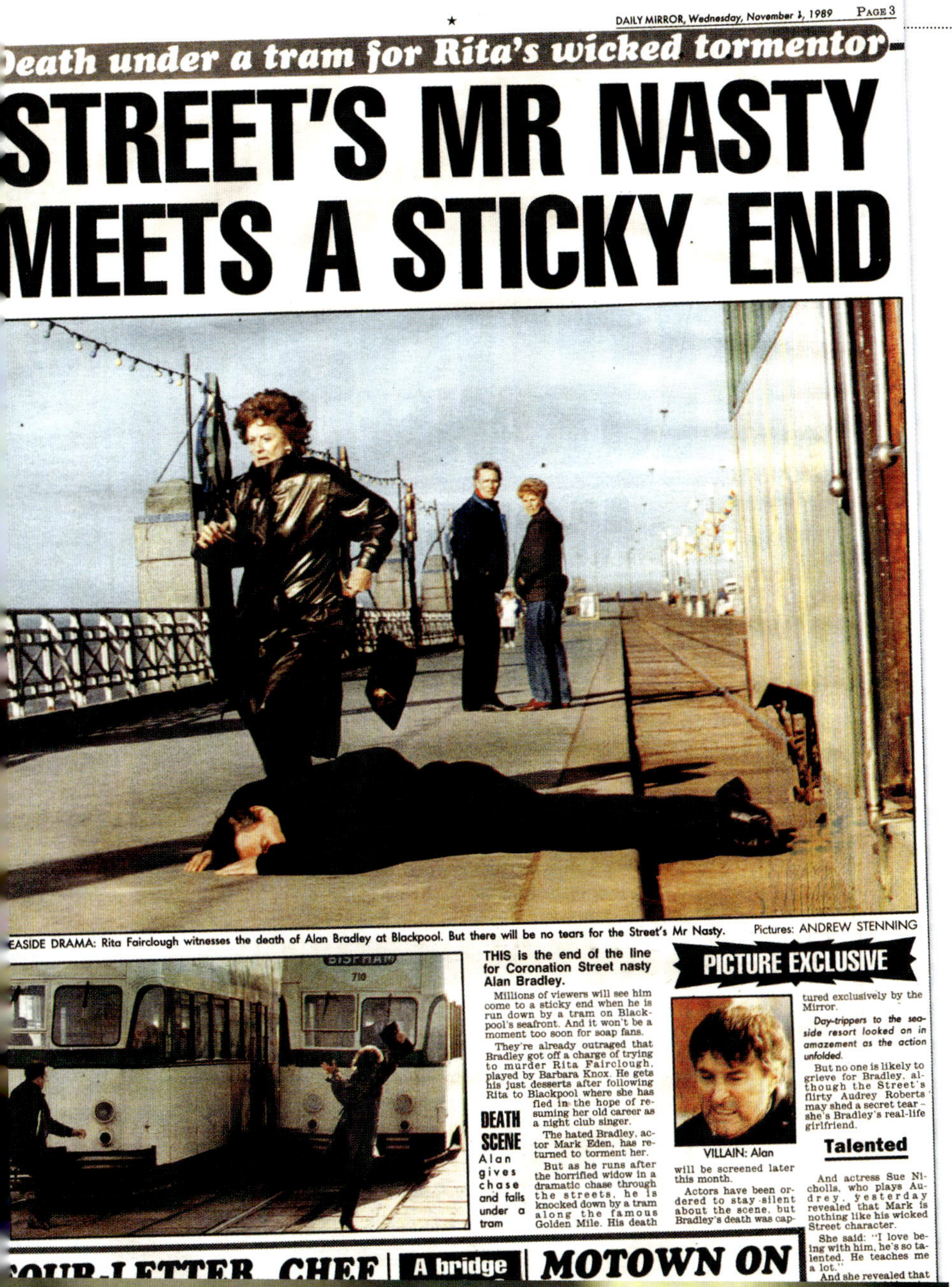
DAILY MIRROR, Wednesday, November 1, 1989 PAGE 3

Death under a tram for Rita's wicked tormentor

STREET'S MR NASTY MEETS A STICKY END

EASIDE DRAMA: Rita Fairclough witnesses the death of Alan Bradley at Blackpool. But there will be no tears for the Street's Mr Nasty. Pictures: ANDREW STENNING

THIS is the end of the line for Coronation Street nasty Alan Bradley.

Millions of viewers will see him come to a sticky end when he is run down by a tram on Blackpool's seafront. And it won't be a moment too soon for soap fans.

They're already outraged that Bradley got off a charge of trying to murder Rita Fairclough, played by Barbara Knox. He gets his just desserts after following Rita to Blackpool where she has fled in the hope of resuming her old career as a night club singer.

DEATH SCENE Alan gives chase and falls under a tram

The hated Bradley, actor Mark Eden, has returned to torment her.

But as he runs after the horrified widow in a dramatic chase through the streets, he is knocked down by a tram along the famous Golden Mile. His death will be screened later this month.

PICTURE EXCLUSIVE

VILLAIN: Alan

Actors have been ordered to stay silent about the scene, but Bradley's death was captured exclusively by the Mirror.

Day-trippers to the seaside resort looked on in amazement as the action unfolded.

But no one is likely to grieve for Bradley, although the Street's flirty Audrey Roberts may shed a secret tear – she's Bradley's real-life girlfriend.

Talented

And actress Sue Nicholls, who plays Audrey, yesterday revealed that Mark is nothing like his wicked Street character.

She said: "I love being with him, he's so talented. He teaches me a lot."

And she revealed that

FOUR-LETTER CHEF | A bridge | MOTOWN ON

- Fiona left at the aisle – 17.5 million (1997)
- Mike and Linda's wedding – 15.8 million (2000)
- Sarah-Lou teen pregnancy – 15 million (2000)
- Steve and Karen wedding – 15 million (2004)

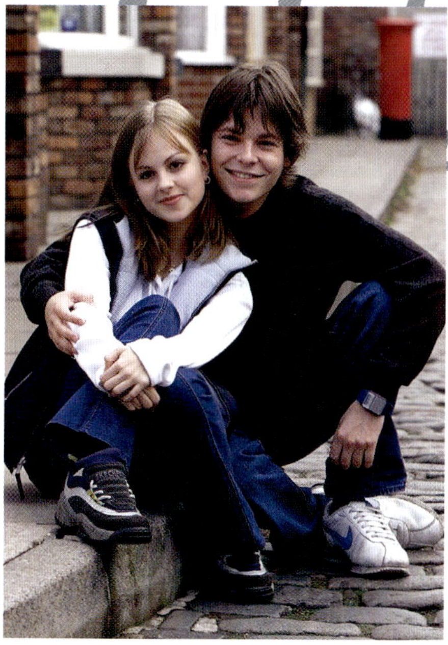

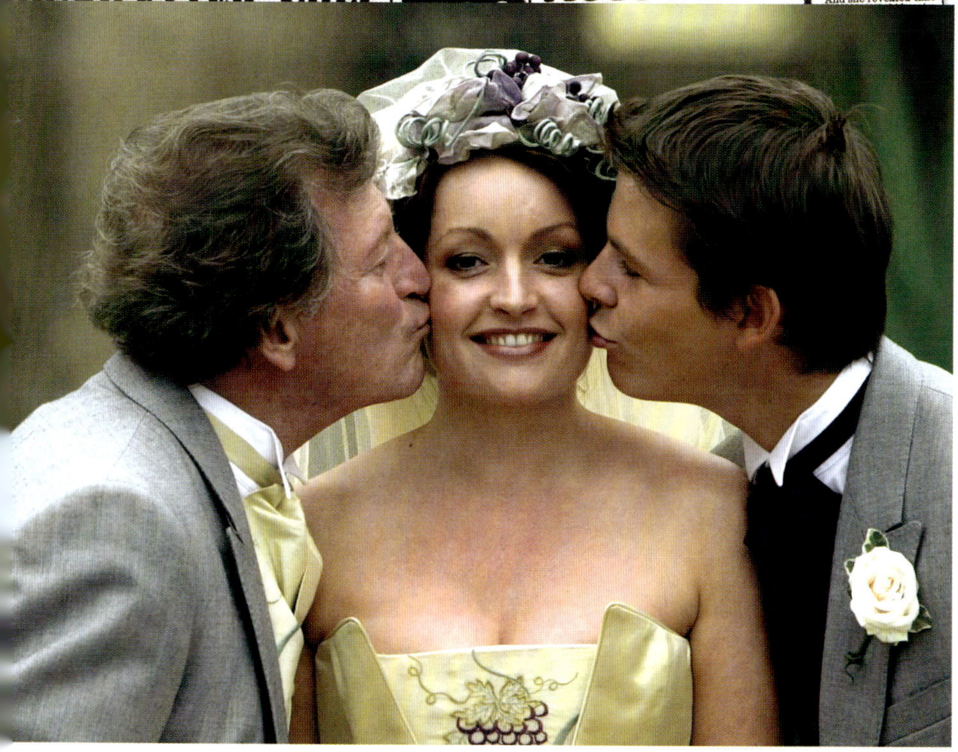

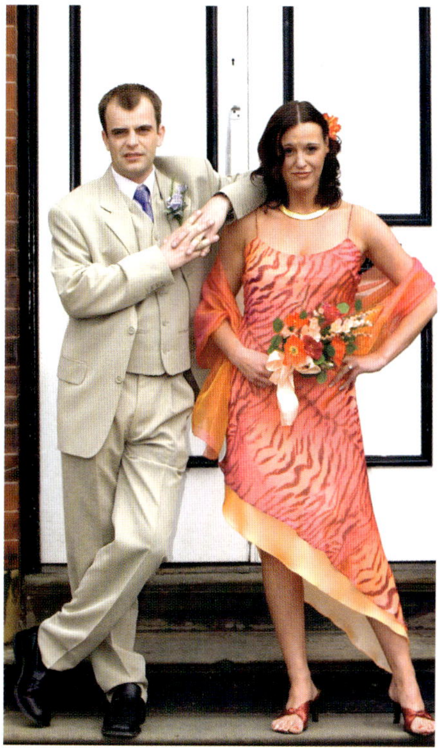

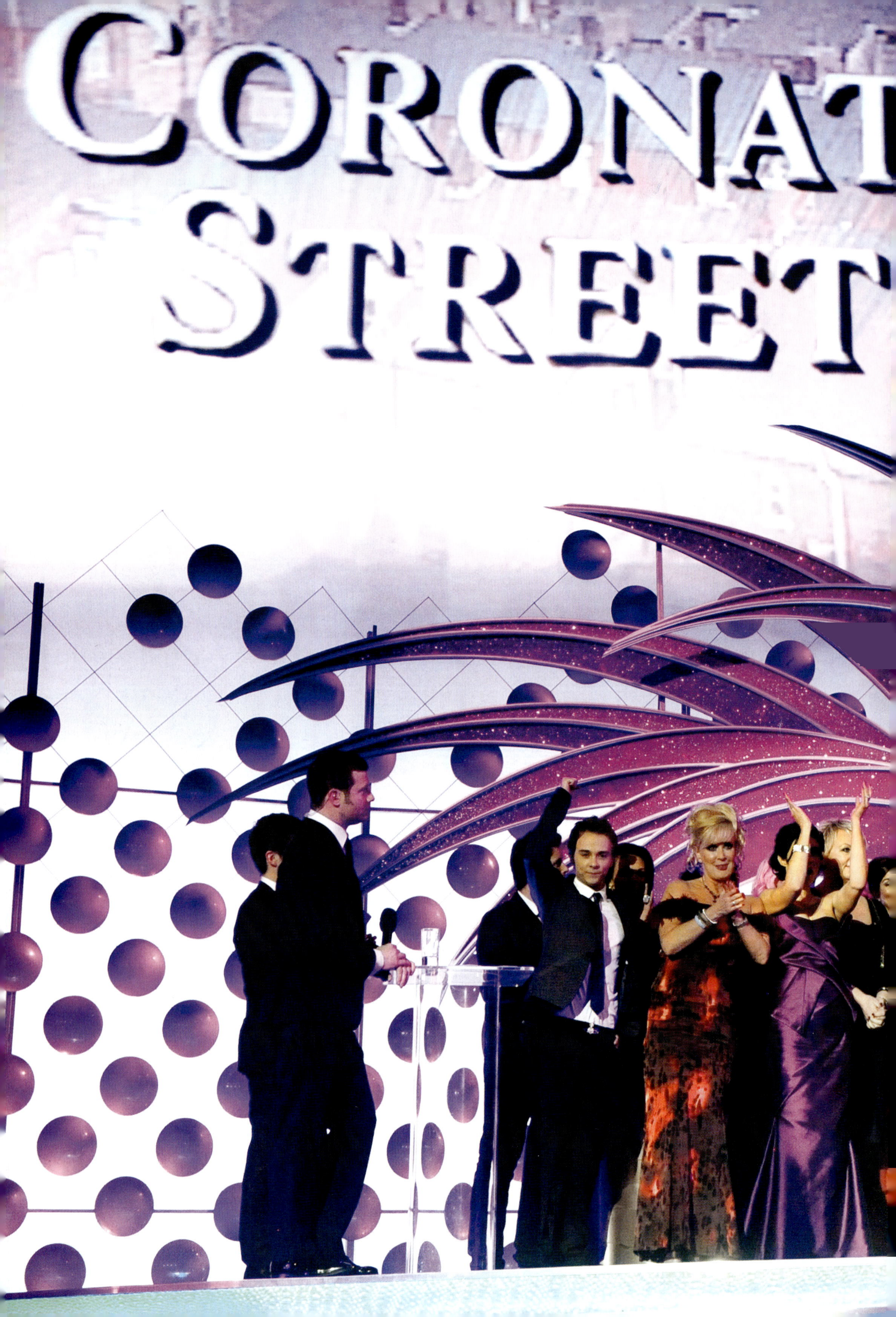
CORONAT
STREET

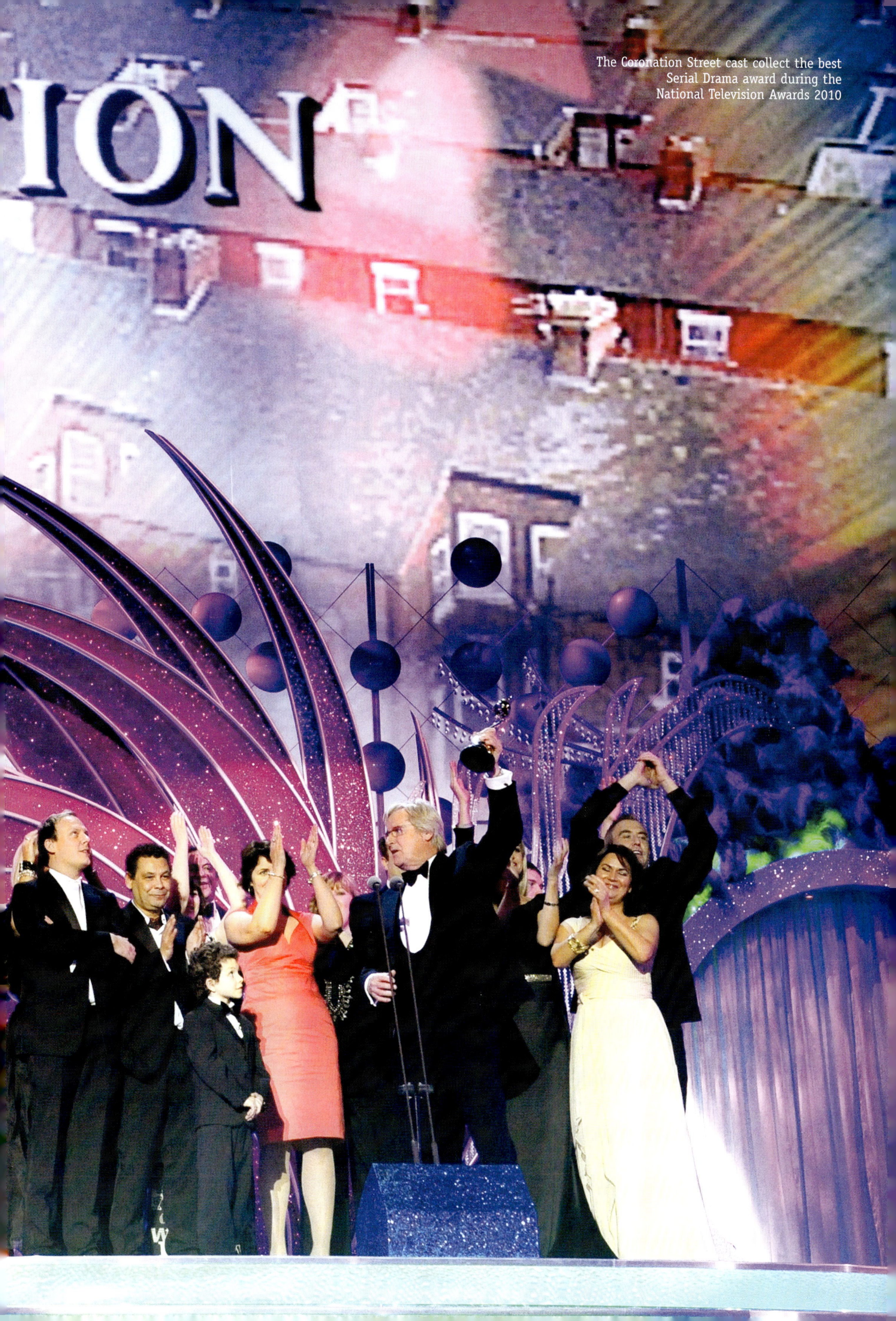

The Coronation Street cast collect the best Serial Drama award during the National Television Awards 2010

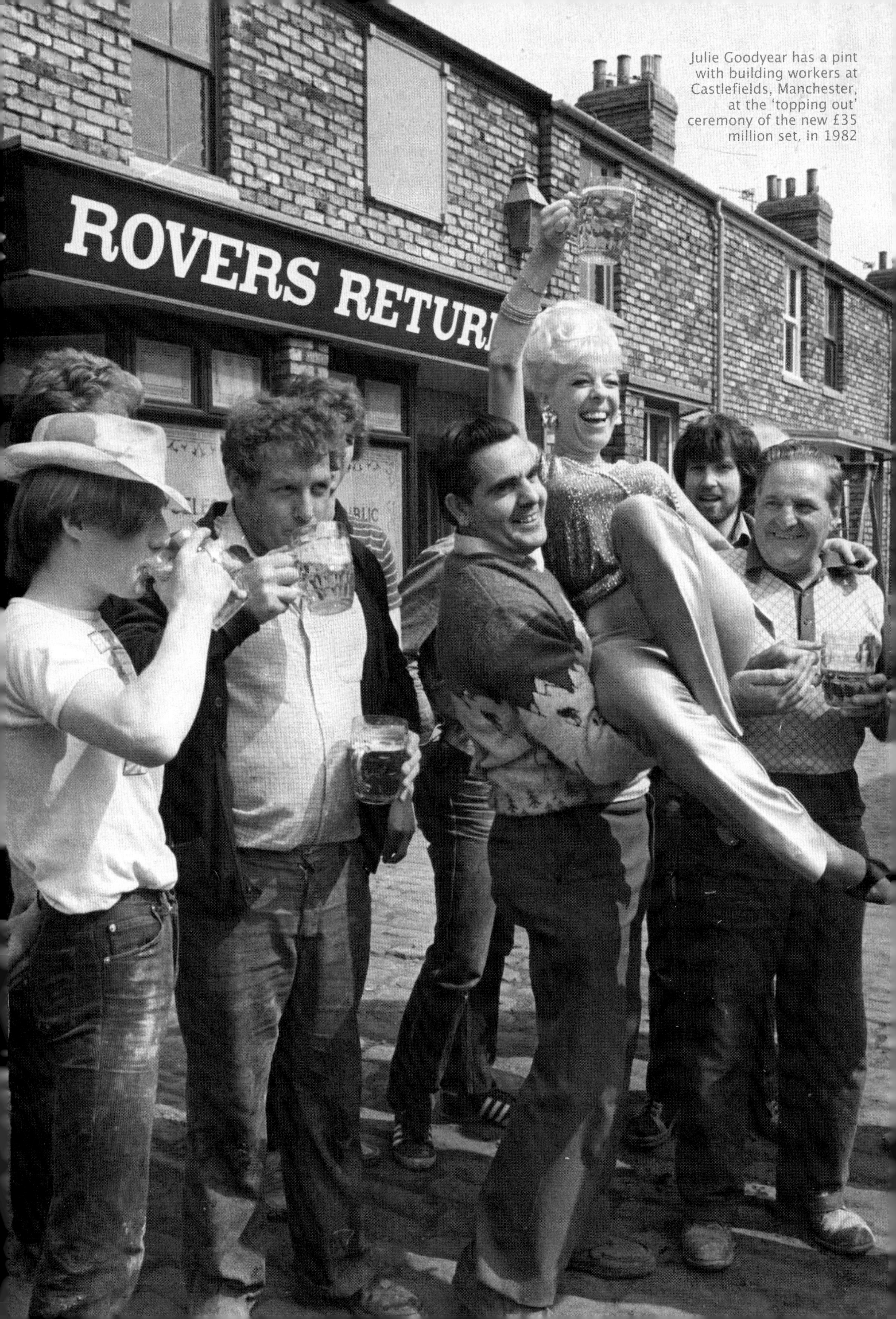

Julie Goodyear has a pint with building workers at Castlefields, Manchester, at the 'topping out' ceremony of the new £35 million set, in 1982